A Necessary Balance

A Necessary Balance

GENDER AND POWER AMONG INDIANS OF THE COLUMBIA PLATEAU

LILLIAN A. ACKERMAN

UNIVERSITY OF OKLAHOMA PRESS : NORMAN

Also by Lillian A. Ackerman

(with Laura F. Klein) *Women and Power in Native North America* (Norman, 1995)

Ethnographic Overview and Assessment of Federal and Tribal Lands in the Lake Roosevelt Area Concerning the Confederated Tribes of the Colville Indian Reservation (Pullman, Wash., 1996)

A Song to the Creator: Traditional Arts of Native American Women of the Plateau (Norman, 1996)

Library of Congress Cataloging-in-Publication Data

Ackerman, Lillian A. (Lillian Alice)
    A necessary balance : gender and power among Indians of the Columbia Plateau / Lillian A. Ackerman.
        p.   cm. — (The civilization of the American Indian series; v. 246)
    Includes bibliographical references and index.
    ISBN 0-8061-3485-2 (cloth: alk. paper)
    1. Colville Indians—Social life and customs.   2. Colville women—History.   3. Indians of North America—Columbia Plateau—Social life and customs.   4. Equality—Washington (State)—Colville Indian Reservation—History.   5. Sex role—Washington (State)—Colville Indian Reservation—History.   6. Colville Indian Reservation (Wash.)—History.   I. Title.   II. Series.

E99.C844 A25 2003
305.48'8979—dc21

                                                            20022075018

A Necessary Balance: Gender and Power among Indians of the Columbia Plateau is Volume 246 in The Civilization of the American Indian Series.

1   2   3   4   5   6   7   8   9   10

For Bob
and
the People of the Colville Confederated Tribes

Contents

Illustrations

PHOTOGRAPHS

All photographs are used by permission of Washington State University, Manuscripts, Archives, and Special Collections, Pullman, Washington.

MAPS

Tables

Acknowledgments

This work was made possible because of the many kindnesses extended to me by members of the Colville Confederated Tribes during my visits among them. I am grateful for their welcome, tolerance, and patience, which continue to this day. They are all good teachers. I thank the members of the Colville Business Council for their permission to conduct this research. The friendship of former council members who were particularly supportive of this work is appreciated: Shirley M. Palmer and Lucy Covington (both now deceased) and Andy Joseph. T. B. Charley, formerly of the Cultural Heritage Board, Adeline Fredin of the Tribal History Office, and Andy Joseph kindly read an earlier version of this manuscript and made valuable comments, for which I am grateful. Many consultants were extremely supportive, some of whom became my good friends. My special thanks to Isabel Arcasa, Nancy Judge, and Julian Timentwa (all now deceased). They readily shared their lives with me and were particularly concerned that I understood Plateau culture.

Thanks also to Richard D. Daugherty, the chairman of my dissertation committee, and Robert E. Ackerman, who read various drafts of the dissertation on which this work is based (Ackerman 1982). The present version, however, contains additional data and is more than twice as long. I am especially grateful to Laura F. Klein for her careful reading of the manuscript and numerous thoughtful suggestions on how to improve it and to Patricia Albers and an anonymous reviewer, who also reviewed the work and recommended excellent additions.

The dissertation research was supported by fellowships from the Woodrow Wilson National Fellowship Foundation and the American Association of University Women Educational Foundation and by grants from the Phillips Fund of the American Philosophical Society and Sigma Xi. I am grateful for their support. My thanks also to the staff of the Oregon Province Archives, Gonzaga University, Spokane, Washington, for allowing me access to early missionary records. The staff members of the Manuscripts, Archives, and Special Collections division at the Washington State University Libraries were extremely helpful and my thanks to them as well. My special appreciation extends to Trevor James Bond, the Special Collections librarian, who provided the photographs for this book.

I am particularly grateful to Robert E. Ackerman, my husband, for his support, encouragement, and objectivity through the years of this research. His role of sounding board for my ideas was invaluable. He also prepared maps 1, 2, 3, and 4, which is deeply appreciated. Map 3 is an adaptation of a map from a book by Verne F. Ray (1939:11), and map 4 is based on a map prepared by Jerry Scott. Their permission to use the maps is gratefully acknowledged.

I also thank the Nez Perce people who first introduced me to Plateau culture in 1965. The warm friendship extended to me in particular by Ida Blackeagle and Josephine Blackeagle Grant (both now deceased) is remembered with gratitude and affection.

A Necessary Balance

Introduction

This study describes the roles of women and men in a group of societies that practices gender equality with equal access to power, authority, and autonomy. These societies exist today on Indian reservations on the Columbia Plateau, referred to as the Plateau Culture Area of the Pacific Northwest. Gender equality on these reservations and reserves is not a recent cultural practice. It appears to predate the advent of Europeans in the area. Indeed, gender equality, as the narrative below demonstrates, is a *necessary* component of Plateau culture, without which the Plateau societies would be considerably different.

The subject of this narrative is primarily the peoples who make up the Colville Indian Reservation, part of the Plateau Culture Area. The gender equality that exists in their culture is described here in detail in the traditional fishing-gathering-hunting culture of the past, during the reservation period (when the Colville Reservation people were farming), and finally in contemporary times. Most of my fieldwork was carried out between 1979 and 1986, with additional observations made throughout the 1990s.

Gender studies pose a problem when examining the roles of Native North American women. Stereotypes have so clouded reality in the popular literature that until recently Indian women have been seen as only a reflection of Euro-American women (Klein and Ackerman 1995:3). Recent research has shown that women have a great deal of power in most Indian cultures and cannot be dismissed casually by terming them "squaws" or "Indian princesses" (Albers 1989:132; Klein and Ackerman 1995:5). The legend of Pocahontas, according to Europeans, was that she was a princess, submissive to men, and a helpmate to her European husband: in other words, a worthy European woman of her time. The story of her life has become a comfortable myth, which does not relate to the reality of her political role, her reasoned approach in marrying a European, and her death in England from disease (Green 1992:35, 36; Klein and Ackerman 1995:6). This narrative regarding gender equality on the Colville Indian Reservation may serve as a corrective to some of these misconceptions of Indian women, who should be viewed as complex, vital human beings, neither put on a pedestal nor dismissed as irrelevant to history.

The Colville Indian Reservation is located in north-central Washington State. The data on gender equality describe a larger universe than the one reservation, however. It is apparent to me after more than two decades of field research and contact with Plateau peoples from seven reservations and two Canadian reserves that the Plateau people practice gender equality—thus the inclusive title of this work. The Plateau is one cultural system. The concept of culture area may be suspect (though still used by many, including Eleanor Leacock [1971:10]); but in the case of the Plateau, where cultures strongly resemble each other because of extensive historic and prehistoric intermarriage and trade (Ackerman 1994), it is still valid. The societies, of course, are separate, just as the United States and Canada are separate societies whose cultures are nonetheless greatly alike. Similarly, though the societies in the Plateau were separate in the past, the cultures appeared to be fairly uniform, differing mainly in details of religion and politics, while domestic life and economics appeared to be largely uniform across the area. Specifically, however, the descriptions of sexual or gender equality that follow apply to the people of the Colville Indian Reservation, unless otherwise noted.

An investigation of gender status, equal or unequal, requires not just a description of the lives of women and men but an evaluation of the relationship of each gender to the other in as many social contexts as possible and the relationship of both genders to their society. No new theories of gender analysis are offered in this work, except for the methodology of evaluating gender status (chapter 2). Nor are the origins of gender equality in the Plateau area addressed in this work in any extensive manner. Instead, the emphasis is on the condition and descriptions of gender itself in the traditional, farming, and contemporary phases of the culture. Some issues relating to gender status that have been debated in the anthropological literature are explored in the Colville Reservation gender system, but this is an ethnography, not a theoretical work. Neither is it a historical work, though some history is included to put the data on gender status in context.

In the Plateau Culture Area of the Columbia Plateau, gender equality, which was implicit in early missionary records (Joset n.d.), was explicitly reported later by anthropologists (Ray 1939:24; Walters 1938:96); and autonomy, an aspect of gender equality, persists into the present (Ackerman 1971). Ray (1939:24) recorded the existence of female chieftainship among some groups in the Plateau and said that it was "a simple outgrowth of the principle of political and sexual equality" in the area. He noted that Sanpoil and Nespelem women, living on the Colville Reservation, controlled the use of the products of their labor (Ray 1932:26), a condition said to be the basis for high female status (Friedl 1975:6–7; Sanday 1974:191). Other observations suggesting gender equality in the Plateau include female participation in religious life and in the political process and the autonomy of men and women in matters of marriage and divorce. Such data gleaned from the ethnographic record suggest that Plateau women had at least high social status in the past, though not necessarily equality with men.

A mere tally of female rights, however, is insufficient to establish that gender equality existed in the Plateau. Many of the cultural variables pertaining to gender status were not noted by early investigators, leading to skepticism as to the validity of their judgment that gender equality was present. I undertook this study specifically to fill in the lacunae on gender roles and to determine the relative status of men and women in the Plateau Culture Area, as represented by the groups living on the Colville Indian Reservation today.

Observations regarding gender status gathered from historical sources are covered in chapter 1, along with a brief history of European and Euro-American contact in the Plateau. The methodology used for analysis during fieldwork is described next (chapter 2), followed by a general description of traditional Plateau culture (chapter 3). This narrative is derived from previously published sources, supplemented by information gathered during my fieldwork. It provides a background for gender status so that the results of the fieldwork may be better understood. For instance, when the data show that women were active in trade or in some other social arena, the reader may assess the importance of that arena as well as women's roles in it.

The following three chapters (4, 5, and 6) are the core of the work, presenting the results of my field investigations on gender on the Colville Indian Reservation. All ethnographic data in these three chapters, unless otherwise noted, are the findings of my fieldwork (1979–86) and my observations in the 1990s. The objectives of the fieldwork were to determine if gender equality did indeed exist in the traditional culture as reported (chapter 4), to discover what changes took place in gender status after people were restricted to reservations and persuaded to farm (chapter 5), and to learn whether gender equality survived in any form in contemporary times (chapter 6). The final chapter presents my conclusions regarding gender status on the Colville Reservation and some comparisons with the Euro-American gender system.

CHAPTER 1

Strangers Enter the Plateau

When Euro-Americans and Europeans first came to the Plateau, they found a series of elevated plains formed by extensive lava flows and cut by two great river systems, the Columbia and the Fraser. These rivers and their numerous tributaries provided the most abundant salmon (*Oncorhynchus* sp.) runs on the continent south of Alaska (Kroeber 1947:188, 55). The salmon constituted a key resource around which Plateau subsistence and religion revolved. It was this resource that helped form and define the Plateau culture of the great Columbia Plain of Northwest America.

Geographically, the Plateau Culture Area consists of the territory between the Rocky Mountains to the east and the Cascade Mountains to the west and from the Great Bend of the Fraser River to the north and, roughly, the Blue Mountains to the south (Ray 1939:1) (see map 1). The area includes eastern Washington, northern Idaho, a portion of Montana, southern British Columbia in Canada, and parts of eastern Oregon and northern California. Much of the country is semiarid, mountainous in parts, with pine forests in the higher elevations. Bunch-grass steppes abound (Kroeber 1947:56), which in proto-historic times provided the means for supporting large herds of horses. Ecological zones vary within this large area, and the variations were skillfully exploited by the indigenous peoples.

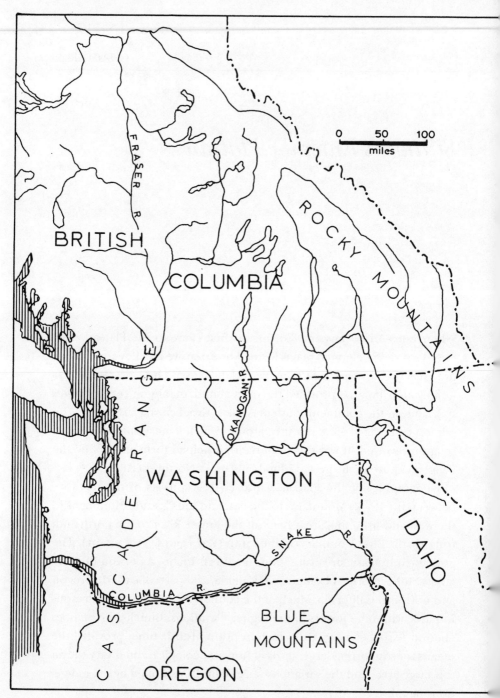

1. Geographic Features of the Plateau Culture Area. Map by R. E. Ackerman.

Most of the languages spoken in the Plateau belong to the Salish and Sahaptian linguistic stocks. The Sahaptian languages form a southern band across the Plateau and include the Kittitas, Yakama, Palus, Nez Perce, and other groups farther south. The Salishan-speaking groups form a northern band across the Plateau and include the Wenatchi, Columbia, Spokan, Coeur d'Alene, Flathead, and other groups farther north. These are the major linguistic groups. The Kutenai, though culturally Plateau, speak a language unique in the area. Three groups—the Carrier, Sekani, and Chilcotin—speak Athapascan languages (Ray 1939:2). Chinook is spoken by the Wishram and Wasco, and the Cayuse once had a language unique to the area (Anastasio 1972:112).

Archaeologists have evidence that the Plateau has been occupied for about ten thousand years (Daugherty 1956:93). The aboriginal culture was based on a fishing-gathering-hunting economy. When European fur traders first arrived, the people they found were already involved in trade with each other and with other tribal cultures surrounding the Plateau (Anastasio 1972:136). Aboriginal trade was made possible by a complex network of rivers and smaller streams that enabled communication between communities. Trade was facilitated by the use of a standard of valuation, the *higua* (dentalium) shell, which served as a kind of money. After the fur trade began, the beaver skin was also used as a standard currency (Ross 1986:109).

PROTO-HISTORIC EUROPEAN INFLUENCE

A number of European influences reached the Plateau before Meriwether Lewis and William Clark entered the area in 1805. Possibly the most important of those influences was the arrival of horses, which most likely were derived from the Spanish horses in the Southwest and came to the Plateau through trade or capture. It has been estimated by various sources that horses reached the Plateau area around 1730 and were well established in the culture by 1800 (Anastasio 1972:127).

The availability of horses made trade and transportation very much easier. Travel was no longer restricted to foot and canoe but could now proceed overland for long distances. The use of the horse increased the number of interactions between groups and facilitated trips to the Plains, which influenced so much of Plateau history (Anastasio 1972:127–28). As

Eugene Hunn (1990:24) points out, "The horse was mobility epitomized. It did not radically change Plateau life so much as it accelerated existing patterns by enhancing this mobility."

Epidemics of European origin were another indirect European influence that reached the Plateau in the proto-historic period. These spread throughout the two American continents soon after Christopher Columbus made landfall, killing native populations in appalling numbers (Dobyns 1983:8). In the Plateau, population reduction before actual contact with Europeans may have been as great as 45 percent from only two epidemics of smallpox, which occurred between 1775 and 1802 (Boyd 1985:334). Elizabeth Vibert (1995:197, 199, 220) believes that the smallpox epidemics of the 1770s and 1800 led to a series of religious prophet dances in the Plateau as an attempt to cleanse the world spiritually and rid it of the mysterious disease. Thus, the Plateau felt the impact of European influences before the first physical contact was made by the Lewis and Clark expedition.

Eventually, a series of epidemics of smallpox, measles, malaria, and other diseases reduced the Columbia Plateau native population by more than two-thirds between 1775 and 1875 (Boyd 1985:398). A small group called the Tunaha, a branch of the Kutenai Indians, was almost eradicated by an early smallpox epidemic (Boyd 1994:14). A visitor, Dr. John K. Townsend, reported in 1834 that whole villages in the lower Columbia valley had been depopulated, with dead bodies lying around them, and commented that entire tribes had disappeared. Townsend observed what was probably a malaria epidemic, which is estimated to have reduced the already decimated population by 75 percent between 1830 and 1833 (Cook 1972:183–84).

Another precontact influence in the area was indirect trade with Europeans. A series of European ships from several countries visited the Northwest Coast peoples, with whom the Plateau people had friendly trade relations. The first European ship to explore the Northwest Coast, in 1602–3, was Spanish. Later ships came from Russia, Great Britain, France, and the United States. In 1792 Captain Robert Gray, an American, entered a few miles into the then unknown Columbia River in his ship, *Columbia Rediviva*. He named the river after his ship and traded with the natives. By the time Lewis and Clark set foot on Plateau soil in 1805, about 130 British and U.S. ships alone had traded or were trading along the Pacific Northwest coast. Some of the goods obtained from various European and American ships filtered inland to the Plateau Indians through their regular trade with the coastal Indians (Reichwein 1988:146–47; Roe 1992:1).

CONTACT: EXPLORERS, FUR TRADERS, AND MISSIONARIES

By 1803 the Pacific Northwest had become an international focus of rivalry between the United States and Great Britain. This was one of the reasons why President Thomas Jefferson commissioned Lewis and Clark to explore the regions of the West, including the Plateau (Reichwein 1988:147). After crossing the continent from the East in 1805, the members of the Lewis and Clark expedition were the first outsiders to enter the southern part of Plateau country. They followed the Columbia River down to the Pacific Coast, meeting and writing about the indigenous peoples who lived along the river.

The exploration did not confirm U.S. ownership of the country. Lewis and Clark were soon followed by British and Canadian fur traders. The Montreal-based fur traders of the North West Company established posts among the eastern Salish Indians (Anastasio 1972:114) in order to exploit the fur-bearing animal resources of the Plateau, especially beaver. The first post was established among the Kutenai Indians in 1807 by David Thompson, the geographer and trader for the North West Company. He established other trading posts, and the North West Company had a monopoly on the fur trade until 1811. In that year the Pacific Fur Company, owned by the American John Jacob Astor, set up a station on the coast named Fort Astoria (Vibert 1997:46). Two members of the U.S. party (one of them Alexander Ross, who later wrote a description of his experiences) traveled up the Columbia River where it met the Okanogan River. At that confluence of waters, Ross and his companion established Fort Okanogan and set up business (Bloodworth 1959:7–8). They became rivals of the North West Company, contesting not only for furs but for the eventual ownership of the country itself.

The fur traders were unhappy with the Plateau Indians. Many Indian groups had little interest in the fur trade, and the Europeans considered them lazy (Vibert 1997:121, 120). Governor George Simpson of the Hudson's Bay Company blamed the Indians' lack of interest on their abundant food supplies. The Indians saw no profit in European trade goods once they had a supply of guns, tobacco, and beads (Vibert 1997:122). The plentiful salmon runs and roots filled the Indians' subsistence needs very well and allowed them to ignore the fur trade. They hunted occasionally in order to buy a gun or other item but did not hunt as extensively for the fur trade as the traders would have liked. The European traders believed that gambling, horse-racing, and other pastimes impeded the hunting of furs for the world market (Vibert 1997:141). The Plateau people consequently avoided being integrated into the capitalist system in any irreversible manner. Because the availability of furs through the activity of Indians was limited, the traders mostly were forced to hunt for their own furs (Stern 1996:29, 84).

The War of 1812 between the United States and Great Britain ended the Astor venture on the Plateau, and both of his posts were sold to the North West Company of Canada. The North West Company later merged with the London-based Hudson's Bay Company in 1821 to become the paramount European-derived institution in the area, dominating the fur trade for the next twenty years (Burns 1966:12; Maxwell 1987:28). In 1826 the Hudson's Bay Company established a fort at Kettle Falls (Maxwell 1987:28), the location of the second most productive fishery in the Plateau.

Missionaries arrived soon after the fur traders. The Reverend Samuel Parker, a Presbyterian, journeyed through the area in 1835–36, scouting out sites for missionary stations (Parker 1844). His most famous colleagues, Henry H. Spalding and Marcus Whitman, established missions among the Nez Perce and Cayuse Indians, respectively (Burns 1966:23). Jesuit missionaries followed in 1840 (Burns 1966:18), establishing missions for the Catholic Church (Raufer 1966:45).

When the Northwest international boundary was established between the United States and Canada in 1846, Euro-American settlers (who had settled in the Plateau in small numbers before this date) swarmed into the territory in large numbers, creating friction with the native peoples. The Euro-Americans arbitrarily occupied Indian lands, signaling the beginning of the end of Indian autonomy (Burns 1966:28–29). This also ended the Hudson's Bay Company's fur trade south of the international line, but the unavailability of suitable furs and the decrease in the price of beaver furs had already greatly reduced its trade (Vibert 1997:48).

These two foreign influences (the fur trade and Christianity, but especially the latter) explain at least in part why the Indians so readily lost their autonomy and their country. For instance, the Catholic fathers attempted to protect the Coeur d'Alene from the influences of incoming settlers and miners by relocating them elsewhere. With the best of intentions, they encouraged the Indians to abandon some of their hereditary lands, which were rich in gold and other minerals, leaving them to the Euro-Americans to exploit (Diomedi 1978:64–65). The Jesuits hoped to create a Reduction as they had in Paraguay and in other parts of South America. A Reduction was an autonomous Christian community of Indians that was independent of the rest of society. Towns were planned among the Rocky Mountain missions, including schools and infirmaries. To accomplish this, the Indians were required to settle in one location and farm, giving up their gathering, fishing, and hunting occupations (Burns 1966:41, 50).

Why did the Indians allow the missionaries so much influence over their lives? Part of the answer lies in the Plateau people's view of Christian missionaries. Native prophets were influential figures in the indigenous religion. They received visions that instructed them to preach to the community to uphold standards of morality. The prophets were expected to reform people through the Prophet Dances. Thus, the Plateau people were familiar with proselytizers *before* Christian missionaries appeared in their country (Spier 1935:8, 12, 19). They were accustomed to religious personages, even from distant tribes, who pressed them to reform their lives and habits, just as the Christian missionaries did. Whether these prophets represented a new factor in the traditional religion, were a reaction to the horrific loss of population to European epidemics, or were part of an ancient tradition is controversial but irrelevant here. The important point is that when Christian missionaries arrived on the Plateau they were given a sympathetic hearing by the Indians, who probably regarded them much as they would have regarded any of their own prophets (Ackerman 1987:64).

Consequently, when the missionaries urged Indians to give up polygyny, change the nature of gender relations, give up "nomadism" for small-scale farming so they could make converts conveniently in one place, change from an egalitarian political structure to a hierarchical one, and make other structural changes to their society and economy, the Indians at first followed the recommendations as they might have followed those of their own prophets. What resulted, however, was social dysfunction, leading to Indian weakness in the face of the Euro-American political challenge for their land

and their way of life. Once missionary hegemony was established, even Indian marriages were not considered legal unless performed by the priest himself, and children became classified as "legitimate" or "illegitimate" depending on the circumstances of their birth. The weakening of the extended family, possibly an unintended consequence of Christian conversion, led to the creation of neglected orphans (Ackerman 1987:65–67, 72). Schools were established for these and other children where they could conveniently be taught Christianity and other European cultural traits (Hunn 1990:39). Missionaries of every Christian denomination were intent on settling the Indians into farming communities. Their purpose was to "civilize" the Indians and make them accessible for proselytization.

Why did the Plateau people persist in Christianity in view of the developing problems in their culture? It is likely that they thought Christianity was similar to their own religion but more powerful. Even today (as discussed in chapter 6) religions have arisen among the Indians that combine the Plateau guardian spirit religion and Christianity. Further, the epidemics of European origin and the incursions of Euro-Americans into their territory may have led them to search for new ways to cope with these events. By the time the Plateau people began to make a connection between the foreign religion and the loss of their culture with its consequent social problems, they were already on reservations. Many hoped that living on reservations would relieve the pressure on their remaining land and culture, but this did not happen (Ackerman 1987:73). These pressures weakened the indigenous people when it came time to treat with the Euro-American military presence.

WAR

Euro-American immigration to the Plateau began soon after the establishment of missions in the Oregon Territory. The Indians became alarmed at the increasing number of Europeans in their midst. They noted the unfamiliar diseases occurring among many tribes and the factions arising within many groups, originating from conflicts between Christian converts and adherents of the traditional Indian religion (Trafzer and Scheuerman 1986:25–27).

Dr. Marcus Whitman, whose mission was located at Walla Walla on the Oregon Trail, always welcomed white immigrants, who often stayed a few days before continuing their journey. By 1846 many Cayuse and other Indians regarded Whitman with suspicion because of the immigrants' presence. They feared the loss of their land and were terrified of the new diseases that appeared among them. Measles was among the diseases brought into the Plateau, sometimes spread by the Indians themselves. In 1847, when a flood of white immigrants arrived at the Cayuse Mission, they appeared to have brought measles with them. The Indians noted that whites did not die from the disease, but it caused a deadly epidemic among Indians, killing adults as well as children. Emotions soared among the Indians, leading to the Whitman Massacre in 1847. Whitman, his wife, and eleven other whites were killed (Boyd 1994:7, 42). Further violent incidents between white settlers and various groups of Indians followed (Trafzer and Scheuerman 1986:25–27) during the next year. As a consequence, some Catholic missions and all Protestant missions in the Plateau were suspended for a time (Reichwein 1988:158–59).

The Oregon Territory was incorporated as part of the United States in 1848. In 1853 Washington Territory was created, which included the present state of Washington, northern Idaho, and western Montana. Major Isaac I. Stevens was appointed the first governor of the new territory and also the acting superintendent of Indian affairs. Indian unrest was common at this time. Outsiders were arbitrarily and illegally driving the Indians off their lands, taking their important root grounds, and depleting the game at their fishing and hunting sites. Miners were particularly troublesome, and many violent incidents occurred with this group (Bloodworth 1959:22–23). Stevens was instructed by the U.S. government to negotiate with the tribes for their lands to accommodate the white settlements that were already present and to concentrate the Indians in finite portions of the territory.

Stevens invited the Plateau Indians to the Walla Walla Council in 1855. Over 6,000 Indians attended, but not all tribes had representatives. During the council, which lasted from May 29 to June 11, 1855, Stevens urged the Indians to sign treaties giving up much of their land, in return promising them reservations for their own exclusive use. Only a few chiefs were in favor of making such a treaty with Stevens, while most others were indecisive. After much persuasion, treaties were signed that ceded land to the U.S. government in exchange for the land on three reservations. Sixty thousand square miles of land were ceded (Bloodworth 1959:24–25;

Hunn 1990:50; Mourning Dove 1990:152–53). Since none of the Plateau peoples had a titular head who had the authority to sign away lands, the signing itself aroused intense dissension among the tribes. Some tribes did not appear at the council but lost land anyway. The lands of some Nez Perce were signed away by other Nez Perce, leading to a schism that persists in contemporary times (Walker 1968). Many of those who were present felt betrayed (Reichwein 1988:169); as a result, several tribes went to war. The consequent hostilities are known as the Yakama War, 1855–58 (Bloodworth 1959:25; Reichwein 1988:170), since the Yakama and Klickitat were the first to engage in hostilities, or the Treaty War (Miller 1990:xxix), since the fighting was a direct consequence of the ill-considered treaties (Reichwein 1988:170). The many incidents of hostility included the killing of miners who encroached on Indian lands, the hanging of Indians by Colonel George Wright at what became known as Hangman's Creek (which is still remembered with anger on the Colville Reservation today), quarrels over the stealing of Indian cattle by some whites, and the defeat of Colonel E. J. Steptoe by a combined group of Spokan, Palus, Coeur d'Alene, and other warriors (Bloodworth 1959:27).

Despite occasional Indian victories like the defeat of Steptoe and his company, events turned against the Indians. The Yakama War of 1855–58 and the Nez Perce War of 1877 (Burns 1966:284, 382), with skirmishes before and in between these dates, did them no good. Most of the Columbia River country was finally taken formally for the Euro-Americans, while reservations were created for the Indians (Burns 1966:79). The Indians were forced onto the reservations, which often were located a good distance from their homelands (Gidley 1979:34). Even then they were not left in peace. For example, the Colville Indian Reservation was created by an executive order of April 9, 1872, by President Ulysses S. Grant. Only twenty years later, in 1892, half of the Colville Reservation (the fertile "North Half") was sold under pressure to the U.S. government by the act of July 1, 1892 (27 Stat. 62), leaving the Colville Indian Reservation tribes with some of the most economically sterile parts of the country (Bloodworth 1959:44–45, 53). A more detailed history of the Colville Confederated Tribes is presented in chapter 5.

The period from the first white explorers in 1805 to the influx of Euro-American settlers in the 1850s was of short duration. Robert Burns (1966:2) noted: "The sweep and proportions of this westward movement are dramatic, but what stuns the imagination is its pace. Individuals could and did live through the entire process . . . for example, the Lewis and Clark expedition had ventured into the unexplored Northwest regions. The last survivor of that expedition, born before the American Revolution, died in 1870 . . . A Flathead woman who saw its coming was alive as late as 1890."

The impact of this movement on the native cultures was intense; but because that impact started less than 150 years ago and the Plateau people have formal oral traditions that preserve their history (Ackerman 1994), traditions have been maintained to the present that might otherwise have been lost.

FIRST OBSERVATIONS ON GENDER

Some of the fur traders, missionaries, and early settlers left writings describing various aspects of Plateau culture. Among these observations were a few notes on women's activities, giving us a glimpse of the gender system extant in the culture before extensive change took place.

The women's economic roles were most often noted. Father Joseph Joset (n.d.), an influential Jesuit missionary from Switzerland who arrived in the Plateau in 1845, declared, "The women are haughty and independent." He attributed this to the fact that a significant part of the diet—fish—was processed and owned by the women: men had no right to that commodity. He further remarked that women gathered roots and berries, which became their exclusive property. With any surplus they gathered, they "bought all they needed, even horses" (Joset n.d.). Since a woman owned all the foods in the larder and indeed the lodge itself, Joset further noted that a man was dependent on the "kindness of his wife." If the husband helped himself to provisions in the house without his wife's consent, he would consider himself a thief (Joset n.d.).

In 1834 the Reverend Samuel Parker, a Presbyterian, was the first clergyman of any denomination to enter the Plateau (Burns 1966:18). He described a Plateau woman's work in disparaging terms, noting that she cut and gathered wood, unpacked horses, erected and dismantled lodges, gathered roots and berries, dressed skins, and fashioned them into clothing. Because this labor was heavy, he made the unwarranted judgment that it was degrading and further concluded that women had a low position in the society (Parker 1844:197). In the 1850s Father Nicholas Point, a Jesuit missionary to the Coeur d'Alene, observed the same activities but reached an opposite conclusion regarding the status of women. He also described the root digging of the women and the processing of the roots in an earth oven. To succeed at the latter task, he noted, "a great deal of care, skill, and experience is required. Hence, success at this undertaking is a mark of distinction for the women" (Point 1967:166).

During the fur trade period, women bartered for goods at the trading posts. "There are scattered references in the (fur trade) journals to women trading grass mats, the pelts of small mammals, roots, berries, and a variety of other items they produced themselves, in exchange for knives, metal awls and needles, kettles, cloth, and so forth" (Vibert 1997:237). Thus, women had control over the fruits of their labor and could dispose of them at their own discretion.

After the Indians took up farming at the urging of the missionaries, Fr. Alexander Diomedi, a Jesuit working among the Colville Indians around 1877, noted: "I once spoke to the chief and told him that it was not proper for him to make his wife run the self-binder; he ought to do that himself and let her work in the kitchen. He replied; 'I began to do it, but I very soon broke a piece and had to lose two days going to Colfax to replace it. My wife is a good deal smarter about that than I am, she can do it very well; I do not think it is too heavy work for her, nor does she complain of it'" (Diomedi 1978:79).

Domestic arrangements were of particular interest to early observers. Polygyny was deplored by the missionaries, because they believed it debased and enslaved women. Mary Richardson Walker, the wife of a missionary, wrote: "Wives are to them what slaves are to the planters as it is their business to provide provisions" (McKee n.d., vol. 2:408). Walker was correct in observing that women provided food. The important point is that they owned the food and distributed it as they saw fit—factors hardly indicative of slavery. Nevertheless, the mere fact that Plateau women labored hard at tasks unfamiliar to Euro-Americans and Europeans led many, like Parker and Walker, to conclude that women occupied a low status in Indian society. Hubert H. Bancroft (the eminent historian of his day), who had access to the same evidence, though secondhand, concluded otherwise. He said of Plateau women: "In the married state the wife must do all the heavy work and drudgery, but is not otherwise ill treated, and in most tribes her rights are equally respected with those of the husband" (Bancroft 1883:277). As we shall see, his view was accurate.

Some men had two to five wives, but they had little influence and no control over them. Many polygynous marriages were unstable, because unrelated co-wives were often jealous of each other and preferred divorce to sharing a husband indefinitely. Alexander Ross, a fur trader in the area from 1811 to 1825 who designated himself as "one of the first commercial adventurers to the Columbia River" (1986:21) and who married an Okanogan woman, Sara Timentwa (Mourning Dove 1990:156), remarked that Okanogan co-wives could not share a residence. In fact, he said that co-wives rarely lived together. That "would be utterly impossible" because they would not tolerate each other. Ross noted that the husband was obliged to go from camp to camp to visit his wives, each of whom resided with her relatives. If the wives met accidentally, brawls and squabbles were the usual result (Ross 1986:281). While Ross spoke of the Okanogan, all Plateau tribes practiced polygyny. Polygynous marriages were notoriously difficult to maintain over time, though many women did share a residence with their co-wives and husband (as discussed in chapter 4). Unrelated wives married to someone prominent, like a chief, often swallowed their pride to share a famous husband. Only co-wives who were sisters could easily live in the same household peacefully, whatever their husband's status.

Ross (1986:280), in an attempt to identify the dominant authority within the family, concluded: "Each family is ruled by the joint will or authority of the husband and wife, but more particularly by the latter." (For the wife's managerial rights within the family, see chapter 5.)

Bancroft (1883:277) remarked that Spokan women sometimes proposed marriage, and after marriage a Spokan male often joined his wife's group "because she can work better in a country to which she is accustomed." He continued: "Either party may dissolve the marriage at will, but property must be equitably divided, the children going with the mother" (Bancroft 1883:277).

Asa Bowen Smith of the Kamiah (Nez Perce) mission protested: "The marriage vow is usually not considered at all sacred among this people. Women are taken & put away at pleasure & there is no law to call them to account for it" (Drury 1958:137). Smith obviously assumed that divorce was a privilege exercised only by men and seemed to be unaware that women left their husbands at least as frequently as husbands left wives. Divorce was at the discretion of either gender.

Smith's incorrect assumption is further evident when we read Joset's comments regarding a woman's autonomy. Joset spoke approvingly of the fact that a man could not gamble away his wife's property since it belonged exclusively to her. Still, this right presented an obstacle to the missionary's objectives. He complained: "How difficult to establish Christian subordination. How often a passionate woman would fill the camp or the whole tribe with disorders: when angry she always could drive the man away, for she could always tell him, 'I don't need thee'" (Joset n.d.).

Joset remarked further that an angry woman "could take her ax and forcibly drive her husband away" (Joset n.d.), thus confirming that the right of divorce was exercised by both men and women. Bancroft (1883:278) declared flatly that Nez Perce men and women both had the absolute right of divorce and that women commanded great respect among the Spokan and Flathead.

Observations regarding the role of women in religion and politics are even sparser than those on economics and domestic arrangements, but there are a few. Spalding, the missionary to the Nez Perce, casually noted that women as well as men practiced as shamans (Drury 1936:323). Susan Allison, an early settler in British Columbia, actually witnessed a shamanic ritual conducted by a Similkameen female shaman. She noted (Ormsby 1976:34): "In the centre of the camp there was a blazing fire, and a little distance from the fire lay the sick one. With a mat separating her from the patient stood the doctor—a very powerful one, I had been told. She sang and swayed from side to side without changing her place, making gestures with her hands, filling her mouth with water which an assistant passed to her, and spitting." Allison left due to the cold but was later told that the shaman had removed a snake from the body of her patient, who was expected to recover (Ormsby 1976:34).

Women participated in war, an aspect of life that may be classified as political. Father Peter DeSmet, the famous Jesuit missionary, recorded that Flathead women served as assistants in warfare: they retrieved arrows and intervened in the battle if a relative's life was endangered (Chittenden 1905, vol. 2:578). Point (1967:192) said of women's battle role:

Several women rivaled the bravest of the men in courage. In the midst of the fray an elderly woman, hatchet in hand, hurled herself so violently between her son, whose horse was tiring, and a Crow on the point of reaching him, that the pursuer, despite his giant stature, judged it prudent to move away. Another younger woman went about on the battlefield gathering up arrows for those of her warriors who had run out of them. Another, who had advanced too far in pursuit of the enemy, made such a swift about face, at the very moment several arms were outstretched to grab her, that she galloped back to her own lines leaving the enemy stupefied. Still another, after having spent some time pursuing several Crows, returned saying, "I thought these great talkers were men, but I was wrong. They are not even worth pursuing."

Point (1967:158) further mentioned a female warrior in passing: "All the Pend d'Oreilles warriors rode out, led by Kuiliy, a young Pend d'Oreilles woman renowned for intrepidity on the field of battle." Unfortunately, he did not further describe this woman.

Another warrior woman was Colestah, wife to Chief Kamiakin, who participated in the Battle of Four Lakes and Spokane Plain against Colonel George Wright in 1858. She armed herself with a stone war club and fought by her husband's side. When Kamiakin was wounded, she rescued him and—being a medicine woman—used her healing skills to cure him (Trafzer and Scheuerman 1986:87–88). Other warrior women are described in chapter 4, but it is apparent that women had the option of becoming not only assistants in warfare but warriors in their own right, either regularly or on an occasional basis.

Plateau women apparently took part in peacetime politics as well as war. "It is no rare occurrence to see a woman step in during council and severely upbraid the chief" (Joset n.d.).

These earliest observations of Plateau women's roles by Europeans and Euro-Americans are unfortunately sparse. The early observers reported only what they saw, sometimes merely in passing, but they tell us that women had economic rights, had a great deal of domestic authority, were autonomous in their personal lives to a large extent, and could be shamans with extensive power. Their political power is also noted, though not in detail. Thus, at least some credence can be placed in the later claims that gender or sexual equality prevailed in traditional Plateau culture (Ray 1939:24; Walters 1938:96).

CHAPTER 2

Methodology and Background

Two problems arise in any study of sexual or gender equality: what is an adequate definition of gender equality, and how does one demonstrate its presence or absence?

Any kind of gender status, equal or unequal, is difficult to evaluate or measure. Even the concept of status can be questioned, since it is a composite attribute, varying from one sphere to the next or according to age (Duley and Edwards 1986:30, 32). Micaela di Leonardo (1991:16–17) also sees gender status sometimes as control over resources, sexual autonomy, political power, or other factors. Thus, it is not surprising that disagreements on the definition of gender status are common in the anthropological literature. In order to establish the presence or absence of gender equality on the Colville Indian Reservation, methodical use of an adequate concept of gender equality to guide the field research is imperative.

This chapter presents a definition of gender equality and describes a methodology, based on the definition, that measures or evaluates gender status for as many factors as possible.

Two contrasting definitions of gender equality have been published, one by Louise Lamphere and the other by Alice Schlegel. Lamphere (1977:613) says: "A situation of sexual equality would be one in which all men and women (regardless of social group or strata) could and actually did make decisions over the same range of activities and people, that is, exercise exactly the same kinds of control." This definition is phrased in such a manner that gender equality cannot occur in a society that has a gender division of labor, or even in one with largely identical gender roles. The Western Bontoc of the Philippines (Bacdayan 1977) come closest to Lamphere's concept of gender equality in that they have almost identical gender roles. Even they, however, would have to be disqualified by her definition since women bear children, and the roles of men and women differ at least in that one respect. By Lamphere's definition, then, no human society could qualify as sexually equal.

Schlegel's (1977b:8–9) definition of gender equality is more useful and was adopted for this study. She writes that gender equality consists of the equal access or different but balanced access of both genders to power, authority, and autonomy in the economic, domestic, political, religious, and other social spheres. She defines power as the ability to exert control, authority as the institutionalized right to make a decision and expect obedience, and autonomy as the right to independent action without control by others. These factors are seen as the means by which gender equality can be measured within a social sphere.

Schlegel's definitions of authority and autonomy were adopted to guide my field investigations, but M. G. Smith's concept of power was particularly useful for Plateau research and was used throughout the study. Smith (1960:18–19) writes that power is "the ability to act effectively on persons or things, to take or secure favourable decisions which are not of right allocated to the individuals or their roles."

Power may be expressed through coercion but often is evident in persuasion, influence, manipulation, bargaining, suggestion, or even bluff (Smith 1960:19). Since authority and power are interdependent, they are often confused. Power may be available within the body exercising authority, but it is also distributed outside that body and is exercised by the use of influence and manipulation. In contrast, authority is exercised through rules and traditions, while power is not fully governed by rules. Authority expresses consent; power expresses dissent. Consent and dissent occur in any social system; thus, power and authority are simultaneously in operation (Smith 1974:104). Essentially, authority is always centralized (in the Plateau case centered in the chief), but policy decisions are made through the use of power (represented in the Plateau not only by the chief but by

the council or individuals through the use of influence and persuasion).
Therefore, authority and power, though often intertwined, are analytically
distinguishable (Smith 1974:29) and are analyzed as separate categories
in this work. The distinction between power and authority is also recognized by H. Moore (1988:210n4).

Both power and authority may be associated with force, but the force
associated with authority is an allocated right. Force not associated with
authority is called rebellion (Smith 1974:30). As we shall see, political
authority in the foraging societies of the Plateau did not have much force
at its disposal, and power was more often expressed through persuasion,
manipulation, and influence. Smith speaks primarily of political power, but
power is a factor in other social spheres as well (as demonstrated below).

In my opinion, Schlegel's definition of gender equality as the equal or
balanced access of men and women to power, authority, and autonomy in
four social spheres may be applied to societies stratified by class, provided
gender equality exists within each social stratum. Societies with complementary gender roles (in which men and women have different, but balanced, access to rights in each social sphere) may also be defined as having gender equality. Consequently, Schlegel's concept of gender equality
is more fertile than Lamphere's and provides avenues for research.

Schlegel's (1977b:8) definition of gender equality was used to formu-
late the methodology for my fieldwork. The collected field data were
divided into the four major spheres of culture noted by Schlegel: economic,
domestic, political, and religious. The data collected for each sphere were
then analyzed to determine if they represented power, authority, or autonomy, as defined above, for each gender within a particular sphere. This
enabled a qualitative evaluation to be made of the relative status of men
and women.

Before fieldwork, I did a preliminary analysis of general Plateau culture
based on the above method, as an exercise to see how data on gender
could be analyzed. This method yielded a three by four table with twelve
separate components (see table 1). Data for each of these components
were extracted either from the published ethnographic reports on the
Plateau or from data that I thought the component should encompass in
the culture. For instance, I found nothing in the published ethnographies
that could be construed as power within the economic sphere. Later field
study in the traditional culture also failed to turn up anything that might

TABLE 1

Power, Authority, and Autonomy in Four Social Spheres

	ECONOMIC SPHERE	DOMESTIC SPHERE	POLITICAL SPHERE	RELIGIOUS SPHERE
POWER	The ability to deny economic benefits to others or the ability to exert influence informally on economic matters.	The ability to influence domestic matters (influencing spouse or other household members).	The ability to influence others in actions pertaining to the group (persuading the chief, making speeches).	The ability to influence others through religious powers; either positive or negative (sorcery).
AUTHORITY	The right to make decisions about economic matters and have them obeyed (e.g., the Salmon Chief's distribution of fish).	The right to make decisions within the household (women control food, both parents decide on marriage partner for a child).	The right to make decisions for others and have them obeyed (chief's appointment of other political officers, making political decisions that are assigned to the office).	The right to make religious decisions and have others follow directions (shamans).
AUTONOMY	The right to control the distribution of the products of one's labor outside of the family (trading processed foods and handicrafts).	The right to control one's life (second marriages, divorce, freedom of movement).	The right to independent political action (voting, speaking publicly).	The right to seek religious expression (seeking guardian spirits, using one's religious power independently).

be called economic power (since power is not guided by rules, it could be more difficult for consultants to recall examples of power, if they occurred at all). In contrast, examples of economic authority were numerous. For instance, the Salmon Chief regulated access to salmon fishing and distributed fish according to certain rules, and the Hunting and Gathering Leaders were obeyed by individuals participating in those economic endeavors. Economic autonomy was evident in the pursuit of trade. Each person chose or did not choose to produce goods for trade and traveled to trading centers and exchanged goods without interference by others.

In the domestic sphere, power was evident only through the influence exerted on others. As an example, a family member might mediate disputes among other family members, or one spouse might persuade another to some action. Authority in the domestic sphere consisted of the right to make decisions within the household. Thus, women owned all food brought into the house and directed the consumption of it, and both parents had the right to decide on a marriage partner for their child. Domestic autonomy consisted of the right to control one's personal life, including control over one's choice of (second) spouse, divorce, and freedom of movement.

Political authority is institutionalized and wielded by one who is recognized as having the right to do so. In the traditional Plateau societies, the chief's decisions, judicial and otherwise, were all examples of authority. Political power was expressed mostly though persuasion, example, and influence. A good speaker or respected hunter had influence over others through his or her individual qualities. Political autonomy is easy to identify in the Plateau. Voting and speaking publicly were entirely individually motivated actions and represented autonomy in the political sphere.

Religious power in the traditional culture seemed to be represented by shamans who used their talents in an antisocial manner. Lesser practitioners of religious power also used their abilities antisocially (e.g., the use of love medicine on a married person). Religious authority, in contrast, was represented by shamans and prophets, whose use of religious power was socially approved. Lesser wielders of religious power also had some religious authority (e.g., a woman with the spiritual ability to bake roots in an earth oven properly, as described in chapter 3, advised other women who undertook this activity independently). As I interpret it, the practitioners of socially approved religious power wielded authority because they were recognized as a source of good advice, which others followed. Religious autonomy in Plateau culture consisted of the right to use the talent derived from guardian spirits without interference by others.

The definitions and associated examples of these twelve components were used as a guide in classifying field data. All observations and interview data were placed in tables under the proper component. This process resulted in a summary statement of degree of participation by each gender in a particular sphere. The summary statements in the tables provide a means whereby the status of both genders may be evaluated—a method for qualitatively evaluating overall gender status. The methodology was applied to the traditional culture of the Confederated Tribes of the Colville Indian Reservation (based on field data); an early reservation phase of the culture, when people farmed the land; and the contemporary phase of Colville Indian Reservation culture, in which the people are involved in the economy of the larger industrial society.

THE FIELD STUDY AREA

The Colville Indian Reservation (see map 2), the major field study area for this research, is located in northeastern Washington in Ferry and Okanogan Counties. The border to the west is formed by the Okanogan River and to the south and east by the Columbia River, Grand Coulee Dam, and Franklin Roosevelt Lake. The northern border is located at 48.5 degrees latitude (Wight, Mitchell, and Schmidt 1960:77). The study was also conducted in areas adjacent to the reservation where consultants reside. Towns visited in the course of the study include Nespelem, Omak, Malott, Inchelium, Keller, Belvedere, and surrounding rural areas.

The Colville Indian Reservation was established in 1872 (Gidley 1979:30). Eventually eleven bands or tribes (also referred to as "ethnic groups") were settled there: the Chelan, Colville, Entiat, Lakes, Methow, Moses-Columbia, Palus, Sanpoil-Nespelem, Southern Okanogan, and Wenatchi tribes, plus the Chief Joseph band of the Nez Perce. Other Indians present today include in-marrying individuals from other Plateau tribes, such as the Yakama and Coeur d'Alene, and individuals from outside the Plateau, especially the Plains Indians. Note that the "Colville tribe" is only one of the groups among the Colville Confederated Tribes who live on the Colville Indian Reservation. When the term "Colville" is

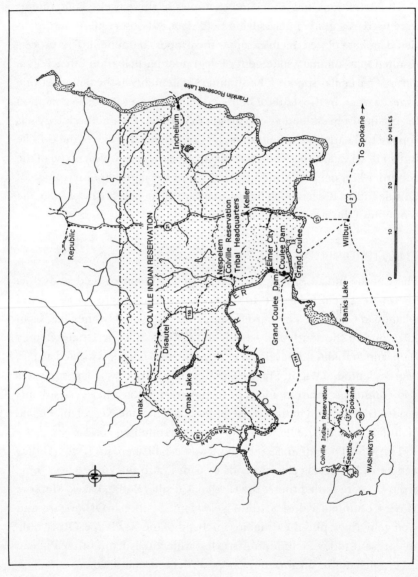

2. The Colville Indian Reservation. Map by R. E. Ackerman.

used on the following pages, it refers to the entire reservation unless otherwise noted.

The Okanogan Valley, where the town of Omak is located, is the homeland of the Southern Okanogan people. Many Okanogan still live there today. The Methow, Chelan, Entiat, Wenatchi, and Columbia were formerly located outside contemporary reservation boundaries. All of these groups were removed to the Colville Reservation from their native territories. The Sanpoil tribal homeland is in the present-day Keller area (see map 2). Many members of the Colville tribe and Lakes tribe (U.S. group) once lived near Kettle Falls, Washington, now also outside reservation boundaries. These groups today cluster around Inchelium. The Nespelem were fortunate to be allowed to remain in their ancestral area around the town of Nespelem, Washington, but they were forced to share it with the Nez Perce band headed by the famous Chief Joseph. His group was forced out of its homeland in Oregon, suffered detention in Oklahoma for several years, and was eventually placed on the Colville Reservation (Gidley 1979:40–42). Accompanying Chief Joseph was a remnant of the Palus band who also settled on the Colville Reservation.

At the present time, due to intermarriage and scattered employment opportunities, people do not necessarily live on their ancestral lands even when available. People of Sanpoil ancestry might live in Omak, commute to Nespelem for employment (a distance of thirty-seven miles), and be married to someone of Lakes ancestry from Inchelium. Despite this movement, most people still identify with one or more ancestral tribes. To complicate the situation further, the Canadian-U.S. border divides two tribes: the Okanogan and the Lakes. Members of these two groups continue to visit, exchange gifts, intermarry, and hold celebrations in common, but the alien political entities that are interposed between them make such interaction more difficult than in the past. The difference in U.S. and Canadian inheritance laws, for example, makes the consequences of marriage across the border unattractive to many, since the Canadian government recognizes only the patrilineal line in its definition of "Indianness."

THE RESERVATION SETTING

The offices of the Colville Confederated Tribes and the headquarters of the Bureau of Indian Affairs are situated near Nespelem, Washington, the approximate center of the reservation. Four voting districts exist within the reservation. From west to east, they center around the towns of Omak, Nespelem, Keller, and Inchelium (see map 2). The small city of Omak lies just outside reservation boundaries, with an Indian population of about 10 percent of the total. Omak is a bustling town, the shopping center for the area. Nespelem, Keller, and Inchelium are far more rural. Indians who own sufficient land ranch and farm for a living. Horses freely roam the side roads in Nespelem, and fenced cattle range at the edge of town.

The Colville Confederated Tribes, organized in 1938, are governed by the Colville Business Council, a body of fourteen persons elected from the four districts noted above. Council members are elected for a two-year term, and the competition for these offices is keen. In 1979 about half of the approximately 7,400 tribal members lived off the reservation, many in the nearby towns of Grand Coulee, Coulee Dam, and Omak. All tribal members have the right to vote in reservation elections, whether they reside on or off the reservation, and receive equal benefits of tribal membership, such as per capita payments.

RESEARCH INVESTIGATIONS

I used the usual anthropological methods—participant observation and consultant interviews—to collect information. For instance, I watched the style of gender interaction among young adults playing basketball and attended ceremonies and powwows that yielded information, especially on community cohesion. I chose consultants based on availability and recommendations from various acquaintances and friends on the reservation. My sample of fifty-one consultants (see table 2) was deliberately skewed toward the older segment of the reservation population, who constituted the most knowledgeable sources for the traditional way of life. Some consultants were interviewed many times, and all are identified by tribal affiliation, age, and gender.

I interviewed both genders, since I saw this project as investigating a gender *system*, not only *female* status. I do not subscribe to the feminist theory that being a woman is necessary to gain knowledge about and empathy for other women, a kind of sisterhood in shared oppression (Wolf 1996:13). Having already conducted research among the Nez Perce and Tlingit Indians and a Yup'ik Eskimo village before coming to the Colville

TABLE 2

Consultants by Age, Sex, and Tribe

Sex / Age	Sanpoil M	Sanpoil F	Nespelem M	Nespelem F	Colville M	Colville F	South Okanagon M	South Okanagon F	Methow M	Methow F	Chelan M	Chelan F	Columbia M	Columbia F	Nez Perce M	Nez Perce F	Wenatchi M	Wenatchi F	Lakes M	Lakes F	Entiat M	Entiat F	Others M	Others F	Totals by Age M	Totals by Age F
Age																										
90–99													1									1			1	1
80–89														1											0	1
70–79	1	4						2		1	1			1		1			2						4	9
60–69			1			1		1	1					2				2						1	2	7
50–59							1							1					1						2	1
40–49		1			1			2	1																2	3
30–39		1				2	3	3						1		2						1			3	10
19–29		1			1	1	2																		3	2
Totals By Tribe	1	7	1	0	2	4	6	8	2	1	1	0	1	6	0	3	0	2	3	0	0	2	0	1	17	34

Reservation, I knew that the roles and status of men and women would be different from those of Euro-Americans. Nor did I ever think that I was more powerful than the women I interviewed, an idea explored by Gunseli Berik (1996:56). Even in 1979, when I began this project, the thought would have made me smile. The Colville women individually and as a group are far more competent and self-assured than many Euro-American women, due to their emphatically different cultural training. Further, I had no power over them due to the money I dispensed for interviews. Only older consultants accepted fees for interviews in any case, because they had little income. Younger employed people did not accept fees but still talked to me willingly. Only four Colville people in a field career lasting over twenty years on that reservation refused to talk to me for various reasons, mostly ideological.

The consultant group of twenty-five elders, sixty years of age and older, provided information on the traditional culture of their respective tribes. Much of the old mode of life persisted in their youth and did not disappear until Grand Coulee Dam was completed in the early 1940s. The people easily accepted a number of outside influences and had integrated them into the aboriginal culture before the reservation period (as discussed below), but the economic, political, religious, and domestic arrangements of the culture were still recognizably Plateau, even after many of their native lands had been lost. After the Indians were forced onto the reservation, the impact of Euro-American culture was severe in some social areas, such as religion and marriage forms; but when a choice was possible, the people accepted Euro-American influences only so long as they did not interfere with their traditional practices. Consequently, the elders who were interviewed were able to describe the traditional, though modified, Indian way of life. Their accounts of the culture repeated much of what has been published by earlier ethnographers (e.g., Cline 1938; Ray 1932, 1939), but the consultants were able to discuss issues pertaining to gender status that were not addressed in previously published works on Plateau culture.

All reservation tribes except the Palus are represented in the consultant sample (see table 2) by at least one individual in the sixty years plus age group. (I was misinformed at the time of the initial fieldwork that the Palus were not one of the confederated tribes. Because of this error, I failed to make a point of interviewing the few Palus who lived on the reservation.

The Sanpoil are considered the same group as the Nespelem.) Not all age groups are represented in some tribes due to the lack of availability of consultants of that age. Since some tribes are more numerous than others, more individuals from these groups were included in the sample.

One-third of my interview sample consisted of males and two-thirds of females (17 and 34, respectively.) Among the sixty plus age cohort, more women than men were interviewed because more women survive to old age. This was evident at tribal dinners, where the elders were honored at a separate table. The sex ratio in the rest of the sample is similar, however, and other factors limited access. These factors did not include reticence on the part of male consultants to speak to a female investigator. On the contrary, a tradition of easy communication between men and women prevails on the reservation, which was of benefit to me. I received many leads from men to other possible consultants, often male. The sex ratio in the younger groups is explained by the fact that fewer men are employed in office work, where interviewing is easily possible. Instead, many men were employed in the lumber industry and farming and were not readily accessible during work hours. The younger group of both genders resisted being interviewed in the evenings after work.

Consultants were sorted by age, which provided a method of perceiving if gender equality was undiminished or was eroding over time. Considering the gender of the consultant revealed which gender, if either, was dominant in any sphere of life and whether the information given by one gender contradicted that of the other.

I do not identify consultants by name in order to protect their privacy. In fact, a few people refused to be interviewed without the assurance of confidentiality, which I readily gave. Privacy may be considered old-fashioned in some quarters; but in small communities it is wise to conceal identity to avoid dissension. A few people consented to have their names used in a general way, which I have done in the acknowledgments. I did not use "key" informants. My intention was to interview as many people as possible to avoid errors.

It should be noted that "gender equality" is a European or Euro-American concept. It was not a concept always familiar to the individuals I interviewed, particularly the elders. While younger adults understand the term, having had to cope with the lack of gender equality outside of their culture, the study of gender equality is of interest primarily to Euro-Americans

who have not experienced it in their society. I can only describe gender
equality from a Euro-American viewpoint since it is the only one that I can
honestly claim. Euro-Americans are so immersed in class structure that
even some anthropologists tend to see hierarchy everywhere. They dis-
agree about the nature of hunting-gathering societies, asking whether they
are sexually egalitarian or even egalitarian. Sherry Ortner is among those
who would answer in the negative. She notes that the "apparent benevo-
lent authority of elders or the apparent altruism and solidarity of kin are
often grounded in systematic patterns of exploitation and power" (Ortner
1995:179). Ortner cannot look at the simplest society without seeing a
politics that is as complex and sometimes as oppressive as those of capitalistic or colonial societies (Ortner 1995:179), though she denies that capitalism has permeated every corner of the world (Ortner 1984:142). I
would agree on the complexity of politics in Plateau societies but not on the
oppression (as I hope the following pages demonstrate). Brian Hayden
also takes Ortner's viewpoint on lack of equality in a Plateau culture, as
discussed in detail in the next chapter. Most anthropologists, however,
agree that hunting-gathering societies are indeed egalitarian (Atkinson
1982:239–40), a stance with which I agree. Colville people take the principles by which they live for granted, including egalitarianism and gender
equality, and sometimes fail to recognize their uniqueness in this domain
when compared to the dominant culture surrounding them.

Colville people do recognize the descriptions of their culture, however.
From the beginning, the tribal council asked me to submit all of my work
to various members of the tribe for review before I published. This has been
done with all my writings, including this manuscript; while two minor
details have been corrected, my general description of their culture has
been accepted.

CHAPTER 3

Traditional Plateau Culture

The traditional Plateau culture described in this chapter provides a background for the gender status described in later chapters. The aboriginal culture, strictly speaking, occurred before 1855. In that year the Plateau peoples were pressured into signing treaties in which many people were forced to agree to leave their native lands and live on reservations. Though cultural change certainly occurred before 1855, and even throughout the Plateau's prehistory, the treaties and subsequent events after 1855 diverted the evolution of some aspects of the culture onto an alien path.

I define the traditional culture as being made up of those cultural elements derived from the aboriginal culture. Some of these elements did not last long under Euro-American pressure (like polygyny); others remain to this day (like the extended family) or evolved in the Plateau tradition (like the kinship system), so not every cultural element accommodated to Euro-American models. The subject of this book, gender equality, is a traditional element of Plateau culture that has survived and adjusted to the new conditions. I see traditional culture as an inheritance from the past, either unchanged or adding modern elements that are harmonious with the indigenous culture.

The traditions described in this chapter are those closest to the aboriginal culture that we know of, but the reader should remember that many of these descriptions were recorded after the people were placed on reservations.

SUBSISTENCE

The aboriginal Plateau peoples (see map 3) were gatherers-fishers-hunters. Fishing provided more food than hunting, and gathering was at least as important as fishing. The diet in most of the area consisted of approximately half vegetal and half animal foods, a situation that has implications for the gender system. Fishing, especially for salmon, provided one important staple of the area, while the abundant wild roots (especially camas [*Quamasia* sp.] and bitterroots [*Lewisia rediviva*]) formed the other equally important staple. In addition to these foods, berries, additional plant foods, deer, and other large mammals were important elements of the diet (Ackerman 1971:598; Anastasio 1972:119, 122; Post 1938:12).

The Indians followed an annual round, often within their own village territory; but they also visited the village territory of other groups, sometimes distant from their own area, in order to fish or dig roots. This practice was particularly useful if a local resource failed. In late fall they settled in their own permanent winter villages, situated near streams for the relative warmth that the water and lower elevation provided.

Few economic activities were pursued during the winter. The bulk of the food during this period came from stores accumulated during the rest of the year, though a little hunting was done to relieve the monotony of dried foods. The winter was a time to hold the Guardian Spirit Dances, ceremonies attended not only by local residents but by people from nearby villages (Ray 1932:28).

The Sanpoil, Nespelem, and Southern Okanogan bands or tribes are among those that live on the Colville Reservation today. In the past, while they still followed what presumably was their aboriginal annual round, they left their winter villages around April to go to their fishing camps and root digging grounds (Post 1938:11). This was not a mass movement of the entire village. Instead, small groups of families (perhaps four or five) left at different times and traveled together. Only the very old remained at the winter villages the year around, attended by one or two people (Ray 1932:27).

Digging for roots did not become general until the very important First Roots Ceremony was held in the early spring soon after the resources

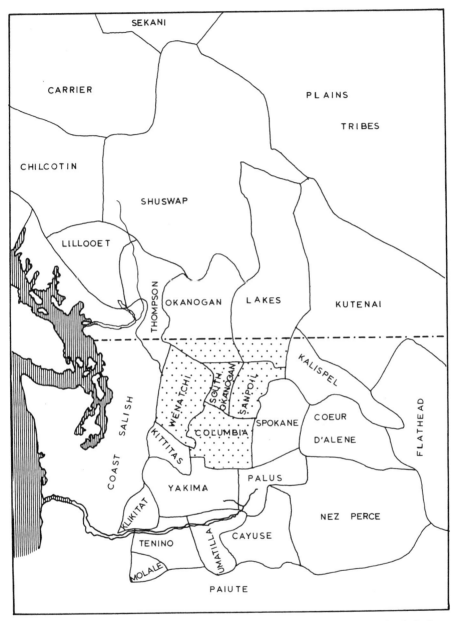

3. The Plateau Culture Area by Tribes. Tribes in the stippled zone are included on the Colville Reservation. Adapted from Ray (1939:11) by R. E. Ackerman. Permission granted by author.

ripened. This ritual was one of several sacred First Foods Ceremonies, which all had gender implications. The First Roots Ceremony was primarily a female ritual but was necessarily simple since people were scattered in small groups at this time of year. Four to five women, according to Ray (1932:97), were appointed by the chief or an elderly man of the camp to collect and cook the first ripening foods that were the object of the ritual. After the food was prepared and the people of the camp were gathered, prayers were said to the Creator, followed by consumption of the food. General digging could then proceed without further ritual. A similar ceremony was held with the ripening of each important crop (Ray 1932:97), the purpose being to ensure that the harvest would be good that year. A contemporary First Roots Ceremony, which somewhat deviates from Ray's description, is described in chapter 4.

Areas where roots grew were sometimes fired to increase the yield (Teit 1900:230). Women spent arduous hours collecting the roots and drying them in preparation for storage. When a very large quantity was collected, a circular pit was dug two and one-half feet deep. Four to five flat stones were placed on the bottom of the pit, followed by a large amount of dry fir-wood and then a quantity of small stones. The wood was kindled and burned until the ember stage, at which point the small stones dropped down to the bottom of the hole. Sufficient damp earth was shoveled in to cover the top of the stones, followed by about half a foot of branches. Other layers were laid until the hole was nearly full. The roots were placed on top, covered with fir branches, a layer of dry pine-needles, and another layer of fir branches. Then everything was covered with earth, and a large fire of fir-wood was kindled on top to provide heat. The roots remained in the earth oven for twelve to twenty-four hours, depending on the kind of roots cooked (Teit 1900:236–37). Obviously, this was an exacting task in getting everything layered correctly and fired properly; and, as noted in chapter 1, women who could do this skillfully were honored for it. Some women had a guardian spirit to ensure their consistent success in this endeavor.

When one area was exhausted of roots, the women moved camp to other areas. Throughout the year other plants were collected and processed for winter use (Ray 1932:27). Ray (1932:99–105) lists fifty-two important roots, fruits, stems, nuts, seeds, lichen, and other plant foods collected by women. Richard Post lists thirty-six such foods (1938:29–30). While the women performed this heavy work, the men were as yet relatively unoccupied (Ray 1932:27).

In the Sanpoil and Nespelem areas, the men's time for heavy work began with the salmon runs in May. Each village owned a fishing site where the salmon passed as they moved upriver. Fishing was regulated by the Salmon Chief (not a political office), a person whose guardian spirit gave him the talent for this occupation. Before the Salmon Chief permitted general fishing, the Salmon Ceremony was performed by him and male elders whom he appointed. The ceremony is in the same category as the First Roots or First Fruits Ceremony. The ritual in the Salmon Ceremony consisted of a five-day period during which the first fish caught were consumed in a formal ceremonial fashion. After the ceremony was completed, fishing became general but was regulated by the Salmon Chief. While the men fished, the women did the important work of butchering the catch and hanging the meat on fish racks for sun-drying (Ray 1932:28, 69–71, 75). Women never fished for salmon, which was a male occupation; but they made fish nets and used them to fish (Post 1938:14), presumably for nonanadromous fish.

The fishing and root digging camps were abandoned in the fall, when much of the population moved to the mountains to hunt deer. The hunting parties included not only men but a large number of women, who made up to one-third of the hunting party. Their functions included running the camp, drying the meat the hunters brought in, and, in some areas, helping to drive the deer (Ray 1932:78).

Around mid-October winter villages were again inhabited. Mat houses were rebuilt, and the extended family was reunited (Ray 1932:28).

Famines were rare in the area (Ray 1932:107) since the available fish and plant foods were more than sufficient for the population (Anastasio 1972:120, 122). James Teit (1906:199) mentions a famine among the Lillooet, probably in the early 1800s, caused by the salmon failing to run upstream the previous season. He also refers to an unidentified plague the year before the salmon failure, which caused a great mortality. If a salmon run failed in one spot, the usual remedy was for people to travel elsewhere to get salmon for the year. I speculate that with a perhaps lingering illness and a dearth of personnel among the population this option was not easily available that year, and people starved. In the absence of such unusual events, famines were probably rare all over the Plateau.

Meat (Post 1938:22) and fish (Ray 1932:70) were distributed, but plant foods were not usually shared. Food shortages occurred on an individual basis, due to illness or a lack of industriousness. Food of all kinds was shared with individuals who had none, no matter what the causes of their destitution (Ray 1932:107). All stored foods, including meat and fish, belonged to the women (Griswold 1954:117; Walters 1938:75, 91).

SOCIAL STRUCTURE

Political Organization

Politically the Plateau Culture Area was described as consisting of autonomous villages or bands (Ray 1939:8). Ray notes that among the Sanpoil "tribal organization in the ordinary sense was lacking entirely" (Ray 1939:6); but he later (1960:773) refers to groups throughout the Plateau as tribes rather than bands. Angelo Anastasio (1972) also believes that Plateau polities displayed more complexity than that characteristic of simple band organization. His work describes political and economic interactions of a sophisticated type (1972:152–92).

I also have concluded that there were tribes in the Plateau area, at least in the past. I base this judgment on some peculiarities in the political organization. In true band structure, the headman or headwoman is chosen by consensus. Authoritarian leadership by the headman is condemned or simply ignored (Service 1962:51–52). The office of chief in Plateau political organization is quite different. The chief inherited his position, providing he was competent at the time. Further, he was never deposed. The chief held his position for life, even if he became senile (Anastasio 1972:181–82). The band headman, in contrast, held his position only as long as his fellow band members were satisfied with his performance. When he became old or otherwise disabled, another headman was chosen by consensus.

Further evidence for something other than a band society on the Plateau is the existence of subchiefs, heralds, the chief's spokesman, and messengers, all appointed by the chief (Ray 1932:111; 1939:22). Specialized offices such as these are not found in real band societies.

Bands and tribes do have a number of characteristics in common. Both are essentially egalitarian. Leadership continues to be personal except that the headman becomes a chief. In both band and tribe, each village or social entity is economically and politically autonomous. Feuds plague both levels. In order for band to become tribe, foreign war must provide external competition necessitating some internal unity, which leads to the creation of integration on a tribal level. In addition, pantribal sodalities, such as clans, must be present, which unite individuals across communities (Service 1962:113–14). In the absence of identification of these two cultural elements, only bands have so far been recognized in the central Plateau, though Ray (1939:10) identifies tribes on the eastern periphery and other places in the Plateau.

War among interior Plateau groups has been recorded for the recent past (Ray et al. 1938:397; Teit 1906:238–39, 1909:546–48) and occurred in prehistoric times. There was no trace of sodalities in the literature, however, except among the Lillooet, whose obvious clan organization exists due to Coast Salish influence (Teit 1906:252).

My recent investigations have revealed the existence of a sodality in the Plateau: the nonunilinear descent group. This is a basic institution, which explains how the complex areal society described by Anastasio (1972) actually works. These sodalities are not patrilineal or matrilineal descent groups. Instead, descent is traced through both parents. In brief, the bilateral (traced through both sides of the family) "extended families" so often referred to in Plateau ethnographies are actually nonunilinear descent groups. Each of these groups traces its descent through either males or females five to seven generations back to the founding ancestor of the group—the key element in identifying a nonunilinear descent group (Ackerman 1994). These groups were neither matrilocal nor patrilocal. A young married couple could choose to live with either set of parents, and their respective nonunilinear descent group, or could switch back and forth.

Each nonunilinear descent group has another order of relatives, a kindred, who do not belong to the localized nonunilinear descent group or "extended family." These kindreds reside in other communities, often distant ones. To the members of related nonunilinear descent groups, the kindred offers friendship, hospitality, economic and emotional support, the opportunity for trading goods in life-crisis ceremonies, and, finally, an option to change residence to another community if desired. Because of this complex kinship network, full siblings may belong to different ethnic groups or tribes, since they have a choice of changing affiliation from one

nonunilinear descent group to another and consequently changing affiliation from one tribe to another. In addition, any one person was and is
likely to have a number of half-siblings in other tribes because of the
numerous marriage partners their parents often had, thus extending their
kin network. Siblings, half-siblings, and cousins of any degree all stand in
the sibling category, even today. Thus, the kinship network, which for any
one individual can number hundreds of individuals, allowed similar cultures to develop within the Plateau, created a kind of political or sympathetic unity, and also allowed people to make comfortable marriages in
distant communities. These kinship groups existed in the past and persist
into the present, providing an explanation for the social complexity that
Anastasio (1972) perceives (Ackerman 1994).

Consultants indicate that each village in the past included at least two
nonunilinear descent groups. I suspect that several continuous groups of
villages contained different branches of the same nonunilinear descent
group and that this group of villages made up a tribe in the recent past.
Residence changes between villages within a group of villages were easily
accomplished and required no demonstration of commitment, since in
the Indians' view this may have been no change of residence at all. This
group of villages shared identical religious observances and other unique
cultural markers (Ackerman 1994). For these and other reasons, and
despite the fact that the term is not a precise one, I refer to most Plateau
ethnic groups or bands as "tribes."

Why did tribes seemingly disappear in the Plateau? I believe that this was
because of the reduction of population due to epidemics of European origin. For instance, two smallpox epidemics raged through the area in proto-
historic times, reducing the population by at least 45 percent (Boyd 1985:
333–34). These were followed by other epidemics, such as "childhood diseases," more smallpox (Boyd 1985:335, 338), and malaria from 1830 to
1833, which swept away an estimated three-fourths to seven-eighths of the
remaining tribal populations (Cook 1972:172). I conjecture that the population losses loosened the bonds of tribalism. Robert Thomas Boyd (1985:
335) also states that social units became somewhat simpler after the epidemics struck. This seems reasonable, for if we suppose that the United
States were to lose half or more of its population due to epidemics, who
would listen to City Hall, much less Washington, D.C.? People would be
thrown back to their local communities for survival, retaining, perhaps, a

sentimental tie beyond their local districts. It seems reasonable that this may be the reason why obvious Plateau tribal ties were destroyed.

In contact times each village was governed by a chief and council or assembly (which included all adults in the village) and sometimes by a sub-chief and other officials, as noted above (Ray 1939:22). The village was autonomous—thus the problem with the term "tribe" for some scholars. Despite political autonomy, neighboring villages were always bound to each other through kinship, friendship, language, and common culture, bonds that were reinforced by constant social interaction (Ray 1939:9).

Individuals or families often visited neighboring villages; and when a change of residence was needed or desired, the next village was often chosen. Among the Sanpoil, each village experienced a large turnover in population because of the constant movement of families and individuals (Ray 1932:109). Indeed, constant movement between villages was characteristic of the Plateau peoples as a whole (Ray 1939:7–8), enabling individuals and/or families to move elsewhere when a temporary loss of a resource in their native village occurred (Ackerman 1994). Different languages proved to be no barrier to such movement. A bilingual village composed of Kittitas, of the Sahaptian language group, and Wenatchi, of the Salish language group, existed near present-day Leavenworth, Washington (Ray 1939:8).

While neighboring villages used adjoining territories in common for hunting and gathering purposes, fishing sites were recognized as belonging to a particular village. Despite this ownership, relatives from other communities and even strangers were welcome to use a village's fishing station; but the host village, through the Salmon Chief, regulated access to the stations so that everyone could participate in the fishing (Ray 1939:16; Walker 1968).

Political chiefs came to office by strict inheritance in only three groups. What Ray (1939:18–20) calls "loose heredity" was the more common principle of succession in the Plateau: the chief was succeeded by his most able son, who was not necessarily the eldest. If the chief had no son or the son was unsuitable for the office, then the chief's brother or brother's son was likely to be chosen.

Theoretically any man (or woman in four tribes) in the village was eligible to be chief provided he exhibited the proper characteristics: good judgment, skill in arbitration, and able management of resources (Ray 1932:22; Walters 1938:95). In practice, descent from father to son was most common in the past, but the possibility of choosing anyone in the village as chief appears to be no idle principle. Southern Okanogan elders relate that about 1910 the son of the deceased chief of a Southern Okanogan village was passed over in favor of another individual because of the latter's knowledge of English as well as other attributes. The general consensus was that he was more capable of dealing with the problems arising from white incursion onto their territory.

Plateau societies were egalitarian, and class structure was absent. Ray (1939:25) identifies egalitarianism as one of the two dominant cultural patterns of Plateau culture. Even ranking was absent within the social structure. The other dominant trend was pacifism, which I address below. Ray says: "Sanpoil insistence upon the equality of men was of an impressive order. Class distinctions were unthinkable . . . when a new chief had to be selected any man was eligible" (Ray 1932:25).

Class differences would not develop in societies like those in the Plateau because "[i]n egalitarian societies, . . . it is impossible to alienate people from their right of access to basic resources" (Etienne and Leacock 1980:9). Anyone in Plateau societies had the right to resources, and no one could deny that access. Further, stratification is limited in hunter-gatherer societies because an accumulation of wealth would be a hindrance to a nomadic lifestyle (Duley and Edwards 1986:37).

Despite what was once taken for granted in anthropological knowledge, there has been a recent challenge to the concept of egalitarianism in the foraging cultures of the Plateau and elsewhere. Some archaeologists are playing with the idea of complexity in hunter-gatherer societies, claiming to see stratification in a number of places (e.g., Hayden 1992 in the Plateau; Sheehan 1997 in Alaska) where it has not been discerned before. Brian Hayden found house pits of varying sizes at the Keatley Creek site in Frasier River Lillooet (Stl'atl'imx) country, which he attributed to the existence of social inequality (Chatters and Pokotylo 1998:79). In an article written with James G. Spafford, Hayden concludes that the Keatley Creek people were divided into poor families and "great houses." The poor were attached to the larger houses, they believe, as servants or tenants. Hayden and June Ryder believe that the archaeology of this area of the Plateau suggests the possibility of a chiefdom level occurring around 1000–950 A.D., based on the theorized monopolization of the salmon runs (Pokotylo and Mitchell 1998:100). How this could occur in a foraging society is puzzling, especially in the light of Mona Etienne and Eleanor Leacock's (1980:9) comment above. If stratification was attempted, could not the "disenfranchised" move elsewhere? This was the usual remedy in later periods in the Plateau when there was some political dissatisfaction with a chief. While salmon resources are easy to procure in a few favorable spots, they tend to be available in lesser numbers in many places, and if people moved upstream they would be hard to control. A landslide that dammed the Fraser River 1,100 years ago blocked salmon streams, thus restricting access to the resource and theoretically destroying the stratified culture postulated by Hayden and others (Pokotylo and Mitchell 1998:100).

Hayden (1992) refers to Teit as an authority for characterizing the Lillooet as having hereditary elites with wealth and private ownership of key resources, but he fails to give a reference. He cites markers of stratification such as wealth, trading, slavery, polygyny, seasonal sedentism, and high populations (Hayden 1992:3–4). These indices can occur in many nonstratified cultures, and other factors have to develop for stratification. Teit (1906: 252–54), whom Hayden cites, does indeed describe the Lillooet as having clans of the Northwest Coast type. The word "chief," however, was applied to any person who gained influence for whatever reason: wealth, perhaps, but mostly wisdom, oratory, and generosity (Teit 1906:255). All these factors earn prestige throughout the Plateau. Teit (1906:255) says: "The child of a 'chief' or rather of an influential person of this kind could attain a rank equal to that of his father, only by his own exertion and worth." These people formed a nobility of merit, while the hereditary chiefs (which fall into the Plateau pattern) formed a nobility of "rank" (Teit does not define that word: I doubt that it is a description of complexity in Hayden's terms). The hereditary chiefs were the main political officers of the community, even though the influential men called chiefs might have much prestige and influence within the community (Teit 1906:255). Hayden does not provide a persuasive description of a stratified society.

Hayden also assumes the presence of political complexity on the basis of such factors as storage areas and the possible presence of clans (Hayden 1992:19, 10). I have defined clans (nonunilinear descent groups) in the Plateau above, and I see no connection with stratification. Storage is a necessity in areas where winter prevents the collection of food. By Hayden's definitions, there are precious few egalitarian foraging groups anywhere in the world.

Hayden's (1992) collection of articles on complexity includes one by Dorothy Kennedy and Randy Bouchard, ethnographers who have written some excellent monographs and collected reliable data. Their Lillooet consultant stated that fishing spots were used exclusively by members of one family who "owned" the fishing spot; but after that family had enough to last the year, anyone could use that location (Kennedy and Bouchard 1992: 308). In addition, a village owned clusters of sites (Kennedy and Bouchard 1992:310), presumably where anyone from the village could fish.

Robert Tyhurst (1992:397), also in this collection, notes: "For salmon, it is interesting that the notion of salmon fishing sites of any kind being owned by families or by larger kin groups is not well remembered by older Lillooet members." Tyhurst seems to dismiss that testimony, however. He says that this datum contradicts older and reliable ethnographic information, but he does not give a reference for this ethnography.

Steven Romanoff distorts Plateau social organization by ranking occupations and placing hunters above fishers in prestige: a startling theory. He gives as a reason that fish were not easy to preserve (not true). Romanoff sees the existence of stewards (such as the Salmon Chief, who distributes salmon) as an index of rank society (1992:471). He does not include gatherers in this scheme, who provide at least 50 percent of the foods to their communities.

Land was held in common by a Plateau village, and everyone had access to its resources. There were "family-owned" pieces of land like berry patches; but in reality they were "owned" only under the usufruct system. If a family failed to use the resource several years running, then anyone could move in and use it or could ask permission of the steward ("owner") to use the land. Not all land seemed to be assigned to individual families. Ray (1939:21) says of the Plateau that a strong ethic of equality and sharing of food prevailed, and my own field experiences support his comments. Hayden and most of his contributors (1992) give us a distorted view of what the foraging Plateau peoples are like, without any persuasive evidence to prove their contentions.

There are alternative explanations as to why some of the Keatley Creek houses were larger than others. They could have been ceremonial houses used by the entire community, or they could have been women's houses. The latter explanation seems likely: Alice Fletcher (1892) learned of the existence of women's houses among the Nez Perce around 1750, which had disappeared by the time she visited.

Alan Marshall (1977:136, 139) also notes the existence of not only women's houses but men's houses among the Nez Perce in the past. These were actually sweat lodges, one for each gender. Unmarried men and women resided in their respective sweat lodges. The women's lodge was the location where young men could court the unmarried girls. Women's houses have also been noted for the Chilcotin and Southern Okanogan (Ackerman 1982), as described in the next chapter. In summary, though I view the Plateau societies as relatively sophisticated, I do not believe that there was ever a chiefdom level in any Plateau culture recently or in the distant past or on the Northwest Coast, which had ranking, but no chiefdoms.

While there was a difference in wealth and prestige among Plateau families, it led to no institutionalized political or social advantages—necessary factors in order to have a ranked or stratified society. Plateau chiefs were often noted to be "poor," as they were obligated to provide food for those who had none. Village members frequently gave food to the chief to use as emergency supplies for other village members or for the maintenance of the chief's family (Ray 1932:110–11; Walters 1938:95). Shamans, either male or female, were the most likely individuals in the society to be wealthy (Ray 1939:25–26), since they received generous gifts from their grateful patients or clients.

Being wealthy meant owning luxury items, obtained through trade or gifts, and numerous horses. These items could be accumulated by any vigorous and ambitious individual who acquired them by gathering extra resources from the land, making artifacts for trade, or drying food to trade for the goods he or she wanted. Since only luxuries were defined as wealth, the uneven distribution of "wealth" was acceptable. Access to food was not an index of wealth, for everyone without exception had access to the resources of the environment. No one could or would prevent that. Perhaps the most important index of an egalitarian society is the ready availability of the basic needs of life. Even food and shelter were shared with those who were unable to contribute to the common welfare due to illness or incompetence. No one went hungry so long as there was food in the group. Prestige also was not a scarce good. Any individual with talent of any kind who used it responsibly and who was an overall good citizen also accrued prestige. Furthermore, the Plateau had an *ideology* of equality (Ray 1932:25), which was expressed throughout the culture. This ideology will become evident in the pages below.

The chief's authority was limited. The assembly elected him, and he consulted the assembly on all important matters in most parts of the Plateau. Women sat in council or assembly in central Plateau groups (Ray 1939:24), where they had a right to speak and a right to vote (Ray 1932:112) and exerted great political influence (Ray 1960:780; Teit 1930:161).

Ray (1932:25) characterizes Plateau societies as pacifistic, a trait they displayed to an impressive degree in the central Plateau. Only on the southern and eastern boundaries of the Plateau in contact times did large-scale intensive warfare appear in the area. Ray (1939:40) regards Plateau warfare with the Plains as an adoption of the Plains pattern, with its notions of individual glory. Since the objective of both Plains groups to the east and Shoshonean groups to the south was to seize Plateau territory (Anastasio 1972:192; Ray 1939:40) and drive away the original inhabitants, the hostilities constituted war, in my opinion, not raiding. The fighting between the two groups was rational because it was over a real issue: the ownership of land. Warfare *within* the Plateau, however, was kept to a minimum through extensive intermarriage. For instance, protracted hostilities between the Coeur d'Alene and the Spokan were characteristically settled through the arrangement of a marriage between a Spokan chief and a Coeur d'Alene chief's daughter. The exchange of people in marriage guaranteed peace (Teit 1930:119–20), because one did not fight relatives.

In addition to the warfare taking place on the edges of the Plateau, raids and feuds occurred within the region in contact times. The raids were not sustained warfare and took place between groups with relatively great distances between them. One infamous incident was a raid on the Sanpoil made by Nez Perce warriors, an event that is still alluded to and resented today by Sanpoil elders on the Colville Reservation. After one raid, the Sanpoil chief successfully appealed to his people to forego retaliation for the killings and stolen property, calling on them to remember their pacifistic ideals (Ray 1932:25). Pacifism was useful in this culture as a means of sharing material goods, through both trade and resource extraction (Suttles 1987), and it was reinforced by the complex web of intermarriages that Plateau peoples cultivated.

Feuds probably occurred with more frequency than raids. Since these involved individual families with a murder to avenge, they were difficult to settle. Chiefs attempted to negotiate a settlement by persuading the victim's family to accept blood money instead of the death of the murderer. The fear, of course, was that the affair would escalate into general bloodshed if not promptly settled (Ray 1932:113, 1939:36–37). Ray believes (1939:35) that, despite feuds and raids, warfare within the Plateau was nonexistent, especially when contrasted with the constant hostilities among the Plains peoples.

RELIGION

If central institutions (Schlegel 1977b:19) exist in Plateau culture, religion is truly such an institution. It was and continues to be the most important part of a Plateau individual's life.

The guardian spirit was and is the central concept of the traditional Plateau religion. Large numbers of guardian spirits existed, appearing most often in the form of animals, but they also appeared as plants, inanimate objects, and physical phenomena such as clouds and thunder (Ray 1932:169). Guardian spirits were obtainable only before puberty, and the training of a boy or girl was pointed toward the acquisition of such a spirit during a spirit quest.

Very young children might receive a guardian spirit vision spontaneously as young as four, according to elders; but this was unusual. The more common procedure consisted of sending a child after the age of six and before the advent of puberty to isolated locations such as mountain tops or secluded expanses of water for his or her spirit quest. The child spent a series of isolated one-night quests in many Plateau societies (Ray 1939:68–69) or, consultants say, several days and nights in succession among the Nez Perce. The child was alone and fasting, abstained from sleep and water, and wore only a minimum of clothing. While in this state of physical deprivation, the supplicant saw a spirit in the guise of a human being. The guardian spirit bestowed on the child two gifts: general good fortune and a particular talent (Ray 1939:69, 87). After bestowing the talent, the spirit transformed itself into its animal form or other entity, thus revealing its true nature. According to Nez Perce consultants, the deer guardian spirit might bestow good luck in hunting, the rattlesnake spirit gave the ability to destroy enemies, and the gopher spirit offered success in hiding from and evading enemies. The same guardian spirit conferred different abilities on different people (Ray 1932:183, 185). These talents were given along with a song and less often a dance step (Ray 1939:69), which were and are a form of prayer.

After receiving the vision and gifts of the guardian spirit, the child returned home and expunged his or her experience from memory until maturity. During the course of a Guardian Spirit Dance many years later, the spirit would take possession of the person, who went into trance and started dancing. Established shamans of either gender always hosted these dances. Their major function was to nurse neophytes through their first spiritual possession. The shaman used his or her power to learn the nature of the neophyte's spirit and then whispered its identity into the ear of the dancer. Only then did the young person learn the identity of the spirit.

An interesting psychology is revealed in this process. By the time of the neophytes' first trance, when they were in their late teens or early twenties, their talents and preferences were already known to themselves and to the community. It turned out that the nature of the guardian spirit was almost always appropriate for the abilities and personality that the young person displayed. Whether the person received the abilities from his or her guardian spirit—which was and is the Plateau world view—or whether the guardian spirit was unconsciously chosen to reflect the individual's psychological needs and talents (Ray 1939:69–70)—which is the Euro-American world view—is really quite irrelevant. The Plateau religion fitted a person extremely well to succeed in life.

In adulthood, the guardian spirit was always on hand in time of need. If the salmon runs stopped, a person with salmon power invoked his or her spirit, discovered how to rectify the situation, and effected the return of the salmon. An example of the use of spirits is narrated in a Nez Perce story I collected in 1965.

A Nez Perce woman was captured by the Bannock Indians but managed to escape. They were pursuing her, however; "she heard the men coming about dawn, and there was no hiding place. Then she heard the chipmunk spirit say, 'Child, there is a rock, throw yourself in there. Let the storm cover you.' She crawled under the rock, a very small place because she herself had become small and hid. Then she chanted, 'Come rain, come rain.' The rain came, fog, the Bannocks came close but did not see her." She was able to escape.

This kind of event occurred even in contemporary times. Around the 1960s, two Nez Perce men were thrown in jail at Lewiston, Idaho, but managed to escape. They were being pursued, when one asked the other, "What do you know?" (meaning what spirit do you have that can save us). "One stopped and called a storm down on them to hide them, and they got away."

Another example of the exercise of power was described to me on the Nez Perce Reservation by a woman in 1965:

> A woman was going to be doctored. They all went over. The Indian doctor was smoking. He gave directions that the sick woman should be laid on the couch, so they carried her in . . . The doctor sang and pounded with a stick, and repeated the song five times. Then he sang another song. "This work is not my power. It was given before the white man, and white man's medicine. We are going to work through this power and spirit." He found her problem was her leg. He put his hands in water, then on her leg, and then blew on her leg because her stepmother had rattlesnake power. The stepmother had tied her leg with an invisible rattlesnake. He took it off and blew if off. [The patient's] grandfather knew Otter [another spirit], which can be a jealous spirit. This spirit had taken two people in the family through death and was about to take her as well. So the doctor took the Otter spirit off too. He worked on her a long time. "It's not my power or will, but the spirit." He said that if his spirit were with them, the sun would be there at noon the next day with a black cloud near it, and it would shower. If all this happened, she would be well. The next day, they saw the sun with a black cloud and it showered as prophesied, so all was well. It really showered. The patient got well and got married, is living in Ohio now. She married a hospital technician.

A film was made of Ida Nason, a Wenatchi-Entiat elder, recalling her life (University of Washington 1985). In it she talked about her mother, Tixanap, who was a healer or shaman. Tixanap obtained her power through her father, also a healer. As night approached, he deliberately left a rope behind and sent his daughter after it. She found the rope, but her father continued to send her into the dark for five nights (five being a magic number). During that experience, she saw a vision for the first time. It was powerful enough that she eventually became a healer like her father.

When Tixanap reached maturity, she became ill and could not walk. A spirit illness was usual after attaining maturity but before identifying the guardian spirit. Her father gave a Guardian Spirit Dance during the winter. He put up a pole in the longhouse where the dance took place, built five fires, and put red color on her face. Tixanap sang for five nights. She used the pole to pull herself up and began to dance. The audience helped her sing her shaman's song. She came into full knowledge of her guardian spirit and became well.

The women of the family reprimanded Tixanap's father for helping her and not helping his son. In defense, he noted that Tixanap was bright, willing, and energetic, whereas her brother slept all the time and thus was poor material for becoming a healer (University of Washington 1985).

Though many talents awarded by guardian spirits seemed to be gender-specific, this was not consistently so. Some women acquired hunting or salmon fishing abilities or war power from their guardian spirits. Those with hunting power could choose to hunt but usually delegated this power to a man, most often a husband or brother (Cline 1938:159); or if their ability lay in predicting the location of animals, Colville consultants said that they informed the Hunting Leader where to find the animals. Some men acquired female-type abilities from their guardian spirits. Post (1938:26) records that a few men were granted the talent to mix fresh berries with roots so that they dried properly, an exacting task usually performed by women. Spiritual abilities (referred to as "powers" by the Indians) belonging to individuals were resources for the entire community. One person's salmon or hunting talent benefited everyone, and the chief called on these persons as needed.

Almost all people had some spiritual power conferred on them by their guardian spirits. The only difference between ordinary individuals endowed with guardian spirit power and shamans or healers was that the shamans' guardian spirits (which might be identical to those of others) endowed them with stronger talents or powers. These most often included curing abilities (Ray 1932:185), but consultants say that the curing abilities could be perverted for killing. As John Ross (1996:19) notes, "Though all sorcerers were shamans, not all shamans were sorcerers." The shamans' strength could tempt them to kill, but if they did so too often, they would lose power, which might even turn on the shamans and destroy them.

A category of medicines existed that required no spiritual powers. The knowledge of herbal medicines to cure things like coughs or rashes was handed down from one generation to the next within a family. No spiritual intervention was needed to ensure their efficacy. Nancy Turner et al. (1980: 17) mention a tea made from a fungus for people with tuberculosis, a solution made from horsetails to wash children's skin sores (1980:18), pine pitch juice that was swallowed to alleviate a sore throat (1980:29), and an infusion of roots for a young girl who was "run down" (1980:68). Two kinds of healing occur in Okanogan-Colville culture. The first is practiced by some older people who have learned the use of certain herbs from their immediate forebears and who teach this knowledge to their descendants. The second type of healing is done by shamans, who use their power in ritual to cure, as described above, though they too use plants to aid their cures occasionally (Turner et al. 1980:150). My Nez Perce consultants mentioned a number of herbs that they learned about from their elders (herbs for curing headaches, herbs to cure a fussy baby, love medicine, etc.). Mourning Dove (1990:68) also notes that women knew medicinal herbs for childhood stomachaches, toothaches, and indigestion. These, apparently, fell into the category of "home remedies."

Neither virtue nor good character was a prerequisite for attaining spiritual powers. Indeed, the only vices that prevented one from obtaining a guardian spirit were laziness, cowardice (fearing and rejecting the vision), and a lack of concentration (Cline 1938:137).

An individual might undergo several spirit quests and acquire more than one spirit. Some unfortunate persons, however, might fail to receive any vision at all, dooming them to an adult life of poverty and incompetence. Consultants say that such a male would have no economic skills for hunting, fishing, or gambling. He would be inept socially and in courting. Such a woman would be unable to find many foods or be unable to process them skillfully for storage. She also would be unfortunate in gambling or love, endeavors that are highly valued even today. These people, though rare, were looked on by others with pity, not scorn. They were cared for by other members of the village when their luck was especially poor and would not be personally blamed. Blame was directed instead at the parents, who failed to guide the child's education in supervising his or her vision quest properly. For the Plateau individual, finding a guardian spirit was literally a quest "for his identity and meaning in life" (Jilek 1974:102).

THE LIFE CYCLE

Birth and Childhood

Children were highly valued and welcomed within the nuclear and extended family (nonunilinear descent group). Great effort was exerted to protect and educate a child to maturity. Beginning with the pregnancy, the expectant parents observed a number of taboos to safeguard the unborn child, especially the first one. Subsequent children were in less spiritual danger. Both parents took great care to be respectful to shamans so no harm would occur during the birth. Taboos were also observed after the birth of a child.

When labor began, the woman retired to the menstrual hut with an older woman to attend her, normally a relative. Most deliveries went well; but if trouble developed, a shaman was called. Shamans of both genders specialized in birth, but any shaman was effective during a difficult delivery (Ray 1932:124–26).

A child born to a young single woman was accepted by the mother's kin without condemnation. Such a situation was neither a social nor a psychological handicap in a child's life; nor was the mother criticized. She either kept the child or allowed it to be adopted by a married couple (Ray 1932:146, 127–28). If she kept the child, it was easily integrated into the nonunilinear descent group.

Grandparents exerted great influence on children, whether raised within their households or not, and often gave the child its first name (Ray 1932: 131). The love between grandparents and grandchildren was intense. Grandparents were the primary comforters and disciplinarians. Parents often sent a child who was involved in some mischief to the grandparents, whose admonishments were usually more influential than those of the parents. If children needed an unusual amount of comfort from some disappointment, they turned to or were sent to their grandparents.

Physical punishment of children was never applied within the nuclear family or extended household. Instead, in reservation times when families were scattered on allotments, a parent or grandparent requested the services of a "whipman" or "whipwoman," who was appointed by the chief. The whipman's function was to visit families in turn and punish misbehaving children for past or current misdemeanors. When people lived together in villages before they were placed on reservations, the whipman punished children as a group. If several children were playing, and one of their number misbehaved or picked a quarrel, not only the guilty parties but all the children were whipped (Ackerman 1971:596). Crying during the whipping was discouraged with additional blows. As a rule, the whipman's blows were fairly light and never drew blood. Sagebrush or willow limbs were used among the Sanpoil and Nespelem (Ray 1932:131). Along with the whipping, the whipmen dispensed admonitions for good behavior—they were regarded as teachers. This system of punishment and education must have created a great deal of peer pressure for good behavior among the children themselves and must have taught communal responsibility. It also trained them for endurance and stoicism under conditions of stress.

The institution of the whipman as the disciplinarian of children disappeared on the Colville Reservation relatively recently. Contemporary Nez Perce and Umatilla individuals have told me that the custom has survived on their reservations as of 2002. Significantly, individuals who are in their fifties and sixties on the Colville and Nez Perce Reservations remember their childish terror of the whipman's visits without resentment. It is also significant that this communal form of punishment allowed the parents to escape their children's resentment by not having to inflict physical correction themselves. Parents were never supposed to hurt a child; if they lost their temper and did so, the child as an adult might justifiably shame them for it. Instead the community, in the person of the whipman, inflicted the highly effective punishment on children. Since the discipline was impersonal, no long-term resentment seems to have developed among the children when they became adults. Indeed, the memories of their misdeeds and the following punishments evoke laughter.

Grandparents supervised the training of young children in the past. They aroused the children at dawn, led them to the river, broke the ice if necessary, and made them plunge into the cold water to bathe, a practice believed to promote endurance. Endurance was also taught by encouraging children to run long distances as fast as possible (Ackerman 1971:595). These educational practices may have been instrumental in preparing a child for the guardian spirit quest.

The concern involved in raising the young in Plateau society resulted in what must have been a nearly constant haranguing of children by their elders, judging by what consultants say today. The effort and attention expended on their development was impressive. No evidence has surfaced indicating that these methods were a burden either to children or to their elders.

The ties between grandparents and children were stronger than those between parents and children. Even today on the Colville Reservation I observed that children may live with their grandparents for a few years or indefinitely though their parents maintain a stable and secure home nearby. The grandparents' rights tend to be paramount over those of parents.

Puberty

Only girls, not boys, were isolated at the time of puberty in the Plateau. By the time children reached puberty, both boys and girls ideally would have had at least one successful vision quest, since visions were not possible after this point in life. During a girl's isolation at her first menses, however, she might win an additional spirit or acquire the only guardian spirit she would ever have.

When her first menses appeared, a Sanpoil girl was isolated in a menstrual hut for ten days. She ventured out for exercise only at night when she was unlikely to meet anyone else. After puberty, she was expected to isolate herself during subsequent menstrual periods. Sometimes this expectation was not met, as a series of remedies were available to erase the possible ill effects of infringements of the taboo (Ray 1932:134–35).

Marriage and Divorce

First marriages for both genders were always arranged by parents, sometimes without consulting the wishes of the young people. According to Ray (1932:139, 140), the boy's mother made the proposal to the girl's mother. If they agreed, the two fathers made their arrangements. After a few days the girl was escorted to her husband's home to take up residence there. At least as often, the young couple took up residence with the girl's parents, since the culture was ambilocal rather than patrilocal (Ackerman 1994). A few days after residence was established, the "marriage trade," an exchange of gifts that symbolized the gender division of labor, took place. The groom's family presented food and other goods traditionally provided by a male for his family to the girl's relatives, including dried salmon, deer meat, buffalo robes, buckskin, and other items. Some time later the bride's family presented to the groom's relatives those items that a woman tradi-tionally provided for her family. These goods included camas and other roots, dried berries, and female handicrafts (Ackerman 1971:600). The marriage trade marked the beginning of a relationship between the two families (Ray 1932:141).

Another account (Mandelbaum 1938:113) notes that the usual pro-cedure in arranging marriages was for an older male relative of the prospective groom to approach the girl's father for the proposal. If an agreement was reached, horses were presented to the girl's father, a return gift was given, and the young couple then took up common resi-dence. Presumably, the marriage trade took place afterward, as described above. My field data correspond more closely to the description given by Ray, however.

A different method of choosing marriage partners occurred during the "marrying dance" (Teit 1930:191). This took place with the entire community as witness. Young unmarried women among the Coeur d'A-lene danced in a circle in one direction, while young unmarried men formed a circle around the women, dancing in the opposite direction. When a young man passed a woman he wanted to marry, he touched her with a stick on her shoulder. If she did not want him, she dislodged the stick. If she let it remain in place, he danced alongside of her. They were then considered married. Thompson Indian women could choose a husband during this dance by seizing the man's sash and follow him, dancing (Teit 1900:353). The marrying dance was noted to occur among the Coeur d'Alene, Thompson, Shuswap, Lillooet, Okanogan, Yakama, and Klickitat people (Teit 1930:191). The two customs of the marrying dance and the puberty blanket (described in chapter 5) indi-cate the society's seriousness in making sure that the next generation would be born.

Residence after marriage was definitely patrilocal, according to Ray (1932:140). He noted frequent exceptions to the patrilocal rule among the Sanpoil-Nespelem, however. Very often a young couple remained with the girl's family. It is reported that among the Okanogan a polygynous man might have several wives and, to avoid quarreling, would leave each with her own family and take turns visiting each wife (Mandelbaum 1938:118). In these cases, the children were living matrilocally. May Mandel-baum (1938:103) and Teit (1906:255) write that a young couple had the

choice to live with either set of parents (ambilocality). My field data note
that, essentially, no particular rule of residence seemed to exist and ambilocality was the prevailing practice.

The kinship system was bilateral everywhere in the Plateau area—that is,
kinship was traced equally through both mother and father. Marriages were
not permitted between third or more closely related cousins, according to
Ray (1932:139), or even between sixth cousins, according to Mandelbaum
(1938:112). Some contemporary Colville Reservation tribal members state
that any degree of relationship between two individuals prohibits marriage.
This rule almost always necessitated marriage outside of the village in the
past, leading to kinship bonds between neighboring communities. Marriages also occurred between members of different tribes separated by
some distance (Anastasio 1972:149). Distance did not lead to isolation
from consanguineal kin for the daughter or son who married into another
tribe. Young relatives could be visited at their new homes or seen at the fishing grounds in the spring.

Premarital sexual relations occurred in traditional times and seem to
have been encouraged. Despite this, elders occasionally arranged marriages for young people that did not please them. A girl who faced an
unwanted marriage might sometimes elope with her lover. If the young
people were able to evade pursuit for a few months, they were considered
married and could return to their home (Ray 1932:142). Elopement may
have been quite common in traditional times: many consultants describe
such incidents in their lives and in those of their friends, but it is difficult
to estimate the frequency of elopements at this late date.

A young man or woman who found an arranged marriage unsatisfactory had the right to divorce (Mandelbaum 1938:117). Their parents had
no say as to whom they would marry the second time, since the first marriage conferred adult status on them. A woman's desire for divorce was
not hindered by economic concerns. Elders note that she did not need a
man to supply her with meat and fish since she could live on what she gathered and trade her surplus for fish and other commodities. Further, as the
female head of a household, she had the right to participate in the communal distributions of meat and fish. Her natal extended family also helped
her. Ray (1932:143) reports that the prolonged absence of a husband or
the complete lack of one presented no economic difficulties for a woman
and her children. With divorce easily obtainable and acceptable, and

involving no economic burdens, a large number of people went through several marriages in a lifetime.

Polygyny occurred, but such marriages were usually unstable. Since warfare did not have a severe effect on the male population, and no great age difference existed between most spouses, polygyny could have been possible only through a continuous process of winning and losing marriage partners. A consultant of Ray's (1932:143) could not name any man who had married only once. My field data indicate the same pattern for women as well as men. This pattern of frequent marriage and divorce is extremely common among hunting and gathering groups (Leibowitz 1978:182).

The levirate and sororate were traditional practices, but Mandelbaum (1938:117) and Ray (1932:144) suggest that they were optional. Today Colville Reservation elders insist that the two customs were mandatory in the past (see chapter 4).

Death

Burial took place the day after death. A preferred spot for interment was a talus slope where the body could be covered by gravel or rock. Close relatives of the deceased cut their hair at shoulder level and wore it loose. The spouse observed a longer mourning period than the deceased's other kin and was unable to remarry until the hair had grown to its original length. All possessions of the deceased and the surviving spouse were given away, including clothing. In the past the dwelling itself was destroyed. The survivor was left with only the clothes in which he or she stood (Mandelbaum 1938:128). Consultants say that the purpose in destroying all goods that a married couple had used together was to eliminate the path that would enable a lonely ghost to return for the soul of the surviving spouse.

Mourning by the widow or widower was maintained until the relatives of the deceased visited and ritually dressed the survivor in new clothing. This signaled a return to normalcy and the possibility of remarriage if the survivor wished.

AREAL INTERACTION

Though Plateau peoples were foragers (actually collectors in Lewis R. Binford's [1980] classification) and in many ways resembled other typical foraging groups, their lives were more socially complex than that term might suggest. Anastasio (1972:185) believes that formal and informal social and political mechanisms operated in the Plateau that united the entire area into one social entity. We have seen that neighboring groups used resources in common, strangers could participate in resource extraction, and the rule prohibiting marriage between relatives created a complex network of kinship ties across the Plateau, composed of a system of localized or village-based nonunilinear descent groups and far-flung kindreds (Ackerman 1994). It also has been pointed out that peace was an ideal within Plateau boundaries (Ray 1939:35)—and we shall see that this was a functional ideal. All these factors support Anastasio's construct of the Plateau as one social entity, facilitating the areal social interaction and trade described below.

Anastasio extracted the presence of a number of activities uniting the Plateau people from historical sources recorded between 1805, when the Lewis and Clark expedition entered the Plateau, and 1855, when the first treaties were signed, which eventually forced Indian groups onto reservations. The latter date also marks the time of the disruption of the social network uniting the Plateau (Anastasio 1972:112). The social network included activities called "task groupings" (Anastasio 1972:152), which are defined as activities with a specific purpose and a limited time duration. The purpose of the task groupings was to organize the extraction of natural resources not only by local neighboring groups but by groups and individuals from any part of the Plateau Culture Area. While the Plateau overall has a similar ecology, variations exist within it due to differences in topography, climate, and location (Anastasio 1972:117). For instance, though salmon became available in season throughout most of the Plateau, their quality decreased as they progressed upstream. Salmon appeared at The Dalles and Celilo Falls in mid-April in a fat and therefore desirable condition. When they appeared at Kettle Falls two months later, they were considerably leaner. Consequently, many Plateau people traveled to The Dalles and Celilo Falls in early spring to get their annual salmon supply there and at the same time to engage in trade with other visitors to the area (Anastasio 1972:122).

Other people followed the salmon run up the Columbia River to Kettle Falls near the present-day Canadian border, where the salmon appeared in mid-June. These two locations, The Dalles and Kettle Falls, were the most important trading spots in the Plateau area because of their excellent fishing sites. Other fishing sites also were used as marketplaces, where brisk trading took place. The most important fishing sites in the Plateau were The Dalles, Celilo Falls close by, the junction of the Snake and Columbia Rivers, and Kettle Falls (Anastasio 1972:122–23). These sites attracted large numbers of people. One aggregate of people observed in 1814 was estimated to number three thousand men plus their families (Anastasio 1972: 158), indicating how plentiful the salmon must have been to sustain such large numbers of people in one location at the same time.

Certain areas that produced substantial wild crops of roots also attracted task groupings. Roots provided up to one-half of the diet in many Plateau tribes and were reported never to have failed. Thirty to forty days of labor were needed to gather a year's supply of roots in some areas; but in Nez Perce country, the prime area for roots, only four days of labor were required to obtain a year's supply (Anastasio 1972:119).

Hunting bison and fighting Plains Indians constituted another task grouping that attracted large numbers of people to Flathead tribal territory (Anastasio 1972:163). The economic component of bison hunting was important, for bison skins were highly valued in trade; but the political factor of Plateau presence on the Plains was equally significant. The Blackfeet raided the Bitterroot Valley and other areas west of the Rocky Mountains several times during the period 1805 to 1855, and further incursions were feared (Anastasio 1972:192; Teit 1930:318–19). The Flathead tribe was seen by other Plateau groups to provide the first line of defense for the entire Plateau against the Plains tribes on its eastern boundary (Anastasio 1972:194).

Some of the Flathead bands lived east of the Rocky Mountains before they acquired horses (Teit 1930:303). Once mounted, they exploited the buffalo more intensively than they had before. This led to protracted warfare with Plains tribes, and the Flathead east of the Rockies were forced to take refuge with their kin west of the Rockies. The Flathead male population was ultimately decimated by the hostilities and was replaced by Plateau men from other groups marrying into the Flathead (Anastasio 1972:192–93).

Because of the dearth of warriors, the Flathead were eager to have other Plateau peoples assist them in keeping the Plains tribes at bay. Independent groups of warriors and their families originating from all points of the Plateau traveled annually to the Plains to hunt the buffalo and fight the Blackfeet. At least 1,000 Plateau Indians were estimated to be on the Plains at one time between 1805 and 1855, since smaller numbers might not have survived the warfare. Traditional enmities that existed between some Plateau groups had to be suppressed while on the Plains and indeed at all task groupings (Anastasio 1972:130–35, 146).

Locations where people gathered regularly for any reason, even warfare, served as trading centers. Trade between Plateau and Plains groups took place between battles. Trade between the Plateau Sahaptins and Shoshoneans of the Great Basin also took place between their battles (Griswold 1954:48, 125).

Certain social mechanisms, including kinship relations, eased interaction at the sites where people gathered. Since hostilities were forbidden at task-grouping locations within the Plateau (Anastasio 1972:165), intra-Plateau pacifism may have arisen from this prohibition or was at least buttressed by it, making interaction across tribal lines possible. The exchange of goods with its associated social ties also served as an important mechanism uniting Plateau groups. Most of the intra-Plateau trade took place between trading partners and friends, with relatively little of the trade being impersonal and commercial. With personal ties as a mechanism, great quantities of goods were exchanged informally. On the formal level, many items were presented at birth, first hunting, and first root gathering feasts, at first participation in public dances, and at celebrations, name-giving ceremonies, marriages, deaths, and the termination of mourning. Many goods changed hands at gambling contests as well (Anastasio 1972: 170, 172).

Intertribal political problems, ongoing or incipient, were settled at the task-grouping locations, and village chiefs camped together for this purpose (Anastasio 1972:158, 182). The chiefs thus constituted a council that attempted to settle the personal quarrels between individuals occurring across tribal lines during the previous year. Political differences arising between groups were also addressed and settled, such as disputes over river boundaries. Thus, the chiefs were dealing with pan-areal problems. At such a meeting in 1854, the problem of white encroachment was addressed and strategy fashioned to deal with it (Anastasio 1972:182–83, 191–92).

The task-grouping locations also served as centers for the dissemination of information. The latest news from within and outside the Plateau was eagerly shared and conveyed home. Information was even exchanged with enemies under warfare conditions. Thus, the news of events was relayed quickly to all parts of the Plateau (Anastasio 1972:172). Due to this information network, Plateau peoples were aware of the societies on the Northwest Coast, the Plains, and the Great Basin. When the Euro-Americans and Euro-Canadians arrived to trade for furs, their cultures became familiar to Plateau people, who also learned about the Iroquois and Hawaiians who arrived with them (Anastasio 1972:191).

Since individuals had to seek spouses who were of no known degree of kin to them, over time two neighboring villages might be so intermarried that young people would have to look farther for spouses. Kinship consequently united even widely separated groups. Chiefs deliberately sought marriages for their children among the offspring of chiefs in other communities in order to ensure peace between their groups (Anastasio 1972:146, 181).

Polygyny and serial marriages may have been among the factors responsible for the social unity of the Plateau. Because some men had wives, ex-wives, and children in several villages (as described above), their children had half-siblings in several communities whom they could depend on as part of their kin network. Since half-siblings were always considered friends and allies, the serial marriages and polygyny, though often disruptive in one generation, would have positive consequences in the next. The kinship network across tribal lines created an area-wide community (Ackerman 1994).

Two confederacies of Plateau tribes were known in the contact period. The Yakama Confederacy included the Yakama, Kittitas, Wanapum, Klickitat, and Palus tribes. The Columbia Confederacy consisted of the Columbia, Wenatchi, Entiat, and Chelan tribes. Little is known about the political structure of these confederacies, or indeed if they existed prior to the horse, but their presence indicates that a more elaborate political organization than that of village or band level occurred in the Plateau (Ray 1960:771, 773). The data gleaned from historical sources and the complex web of kinship across tribal lines suggest something more complicated than band-level political integration. As explained above, I believe that most of these groups had tribal organization.

Extra-Plateau Trade Networks

Trade within the Plateau was extensive even before the introduction of the horse, as rivers provided an easy means of transportation throughout much of the area. Trade was a strong unifying factor within the Plateau. It "encouraged local specialization in . . . production and diminished the cultural distinctiveness of participant peoples" (Stern 1993:20). Trade also united the Plateau peoples with their friends on the Northwest Coast and their enemies on the Plains and in the Great Basin. The Upper Chinookan–speaking tribes of the Dalles, the Wasco and Wishram, controlled the trade between the Plateau and the lower Columbia area. These two tribes, along with the Lower Chinook on the coast, dominated the important areas of the Columbia River—The Dalles portage two hundred miles inland, the Cascades portage at the beginning of tidewater, and the coastal area around the mouth of the Columbia River (Griswold 1954:7, 33, 150).

The trade network extended even farther. Products originating in Alaska and California reached the Columbia River. In exchange, Plateau goods reached Alaska and California and points in between (Griswold 1954:8–9). Facilitating this trade was the Chinook trade jargon, which was used from California to Alaska. A standard of exchange, dentalia shells (*Dentalium pretiosum*), was used in all of these areas. They had many of the attributes and functions of money: they were rare and difficult to obtain, they could be exchanged for goods at a set rate, and they were portable and durable. The shells served as payment for services as well as for goods. Dentalia varied in size from one-quarter inch to three or four inches in length, the larger shells being more valuable (Griswold 1954:8–9, 5, 59, 62).

Items traded from the Plateau to the coast included dressed deer skins, buffalo robes (traded from the Plains), dried pounded salmon that could be kept for several years, dried meat, berries, roots, wild hemp, and other items native to the Plateau. In return, the Plateau people obtained from the coast dentalia shells from Vancouver Island, California shells, canoes, sea mammal furs, eulachon, dried seal meat, cured shellfish, whale meat and blubber, and handcrafted items (Griswold 1954:9).

People within each area of the Plateau, Northwest Coast, and Plains participated in the trade through the production or procurement of natural items available in their areas and scarce elsewhere. Thus, saltwater fish were traded up the Columbia River and dried salmon were traded down to the Coast. The Northwest Coast Nootka produced and exported excellent canoes and dentalia shells (Griswold 1954:29, 24, 20), the Copper River people of Alaska exported copper, the coastal Makah produced dried halibut and whale products, and the Quinault traded sea otter skins (Griswold 1954:31, 25).

Salmon formed an important part of the trade. As they are oilier and therefore more desirable near the mouth of the Columbia, they were caught there and traded fresh upriver. The tribes of the Plateau, due to their semiarid climate, were able to produce pounded dried salmon, which lasted indefinitely and was highly valued in the wet Northwest Coast area, where it was hard to produce. Though pounded salmon was highly prized, it required much labor and was a Dalles specialty. The importance of this commodity is indicated by the estimate that The Dalles people alone annually produced a million pounds of pounded salmon for trade (Griswold 1954:26–27, 28, 37).

Trade goods from the Plains reached The Dalles through the efforts of the Nez Perce and other tribes that hunted buffalo every year (Griswold 1954:40). The Nez Perce traded horses and Plateau and coastal foods to the Plains people. In exchange, they received dressed buffalo hides, feather bonnets, catlinite, obsidian, buffalo horn, and the highly prized buckskin clothes (Griswold 1954:41–42).

Thus, the peoples whose gender status is to be examined constituted a relatively sophisticated and complex mercantile society. The data regarding gender status must be understood in the context of that sophistication. These people were concerned with societies, events, threats, and trends that occurred well outside their village and tribal territories.

CHAPTER 4

Gender Status in Traditional Colville Reservation Culture

The traditional Colville Reservation culture described in this chapter is defined as being made up of those cultural elements derived from the aboriginal culture, which prevailed before 1855. Some of these cultural elements remain today, like the extended family and the guardian spirit religion; or evolved in the Plateau tradition, like the kinship system. Gender equality is one of those traditional elements of Plateau culture that has survived and adjusted to the new conditions. Traditional culture, in my view, is an inheritance from the past, either unchanged or with the addition of modern elements that are harmonious with the indigenous culture. We shall see in chapter 6 that traditional culture is not incompatible with many aspects of Euro-American culture.

The concept of gender equality differs by culture, if it is consciously formulated at all. The Inuit, for instance, view maleness and femaleness as transitory. After a person dies, a newborn of either sex will inherit his or her name and personality and keep that identity throughout life. Thus, Inuit names are gender neutral, and gender is not seen as an inherent attribute of a person (Guemple 1995:27).

The Blackfeet distinguish animate beings from inanimate beings; gender is irrelevant in terms of status. Having religious power is the important quality. Women have more innate power because of their reproductive ability, but men can acquire power as well. Gender status in Euro-American terms appears to be irrelevant in that culture (Kehoe 1995:124).

The Euro-American concept of gender equality includes individual autonomy, personal choice, and independence as well as other qualities. Independence is especially highly valued. Cultures that are communal in nature, like the Plateau culture, however, view it differently. Certain independent behaviors are compatible with their equality, but not others, such as lack of generosity in sharing food or neglecting one's elders who need care (Duley and Edwards 1986:40–41).

My description of traditional gender status on the Colville Reservation is frankly based on comparisons with Euro-American culture. Since most middle-aged and younger Colville residents do not speak their native languages, I did not get an indigenous concept of gender status. The older people seemed to be confused by my explanations of the object of my research, gender status; but some finally appeared to understood after discussion. The younger people who had experience working off the reservation understood me readily.

The following description is based on my field data obtained on the Colville Reservation from 1979 to 1980, with additional field research occurring between 1981 and 1986. The information comes from men and women who were sixty and older in 1979. My field data are supplemented by references from previous ethnographic studies. The mode of life that I describe here existed mainly from about 1890 to 1920, the time of the parental generation of contemporary elderly consultants. Many of the gender practices described lasted well after 1900 and were followed by my consultants in their youth. The gender system is a traditional one—which is not surprising since the reservation was formed in 1872, perhaps one to two generations before today's elders were born. Cultural changes had taken place before this period, but adherence to indigenous cultural norms was more usual. The consultants' accounts of the traditional gender system agree with one another across tribal or ethnic lines, although a few variations are noted.

As an aid for examining the power, authority, and autonomy of each gender in the various social spheres, I prepared tables outlining the relative access of men and women to power, authority, and autonomy in each of the spheres (for an example, see table 3 below). The reader may note that the placement of some items under one category or another seems arbitrary. The methodology employed here is useful but not perfect, and there is certainly room for disagreement in regard to the placement of some items in the tables. The distinction between power and authority in particular is blurred in some examples. When such blurring occurs, I offer explanations for a particular placement. The main purpose of the exercise is to evaluate gender status on the Colville Indian Reservation: a disagreement as to where certain practices fit in a table should not affect that evaluation.

The tables are divided into columns for males and females. Activities pertaining to each gender are placed in the relevant columns. Those opposite each other indicate balanced or complementary access to rights in a particular sphere. An activity placed across the mid-line of the table indicates an identical right of men and women in a particular sphere.

THE ECONOMIC SPHERE

Power in the Economic Sphere

The testimony of consultants reveals no power or influence operating in the economic sphere of traditional Plateau culture. I asked such questions as: Could anyone prevent someone else from extracting resources from the environment? Were men or women able to expropriate goods from others? The answers were all negative. Thus, economic power may not ever have been present in the traditional culture, or incidents of it may simply not have been remembered. As noted above, however, there was much evidence that the opportunity to accumulate wealth was available to all adults in the Plateau, limited only by an individual's energy and ambition. No evidence surfaced that any one individual was able to prevent any other from pursuing economic gain; nor was there evidence that anyone was able to keep the fruits of another's labor. Even the fruits of a child's labor belonged exclusively to the child.

This was similar to the Dakota Indian culture, in which no one had the right to "forcefully impose their will on another. No person had the right to command or appropriate the possessions of another without that person's permission" (Albers 1985:119). This trait holds for most foraging societies.

Authority in the Economic Sphere

Since authority is defined in this study as the right to make decisions and have them obeyed, the division of labor based on gender with its socially defined rights and responsibilities is relevant to an understanding of authority assigned to each gender. Consequently, the gender division of labor was reexplored with consultants.

The Gender Division of Labor

The gender division of labor described by members of the Colville Confederated Tribes in the 1980s corresponds well with that recorded in the ethnographic literature of the Plateau. The men fished and hunted, and the women collected vegetal foods. Fishing and gathering are said by consultants to have provided the largest quantity of food. They were unanimous in stating that a typical meal consisted of half meat or fish and half plant foods. In contrast, Ray (1932:77) states for the Sanpoil, today resident on the Colville Reservation, that fishing was paramount in dietary importance and game was approximately equal in quantity to vegetal foods in the diet. A more recent study (Hunn 1981:129, 132) confirms that vegetal foods made up about 50 percent of most Plateau diets; but in the southern half of the Plateau, where vegetal foods were particularly abundant, as much as 70 percent of the diet was derived from plants.

It is notable that even if Hunn's percentages for the southern Plateau are correct, Nez Perce consultants who live there also claim that their traditional diet consisted of somewhat over half plant foods (Ackerman 1971:598). Their testimony suggests that the concept of a diet derived from half male and half female sources may have an ideological basis. Unfortunately, there is no actual way to be certain of food proportions without weighing foods used in actual meals and judging their nutritional content. This is now impossible, since none of the Plateau tribes has access to these foods on a daily basis today. Nevertheless, it is significant that in the perceptions of Colville Reservation and Nez Perce consultants the diet was made up of half protein and half plant foods. Only one consultant suggested anything different. He estimated that in the Chelan area, where hunting was very productive, the typical diet consisted of slightly over one-half fish and game, while the rest of the diet was made up of plant foods. This ideology or fact of equal food production by men and women endows both genders with authority due to their equal importance in obtaining subsistence foods.

Fishing   Earlier ethnographies report that only men fished for salmon, while women alone had the responsibility of preparing the salmon for storage (Post 1938:17; Ray 1932:28, 70). It should be added that once a woman put her labor into preparing the salmon, it belonged to her; she made the decisions on its use autonomously. A fair number of these salmon were used by women in trade.

Men captured salmon by several methods, the salmon weir being the most efficient. Weirs, however, could not be placed anywhere. For instance, locations where they could be placed along the Okanogan River were few (Post 1938:12). Consultants say that much labor went into the construction of a weir. Even with the use of a horse and wagon in the 1920s, a male consultant recalled that the materials needed to build the weir took about two weeks to collect. After transporting these materials to the river, it then took ten to twelve men (with the incidental assistance of boys) a week to build the structure. All this labor was considered worthwhile, for a weir with its fish traps could catch up to 200 salmon per night.

Once the weir was in operation, but before general fishing could commence, it was necessary to perform a ritual called the First Salmon Ceremony (Post 1938:15). This was one of the First Foods Ceremonies designed to thank the powers of nature for the food and thereby to insure the availability of the food for the rest of the season. The Salmon Ceremony was celebrated by a group of men made up of elders and the Salmon Chief, who totally consumed the first salmon of the season in a ritual manner. Women were not allowed to take part in this ritual, for reasons discussed below. As of 1986 only the Lakes tribe on the Colville Reservation still had the salmon to conduct the ceremony. Many people go to the Yakama Reservation to attend that Salmon Ceremony, since the Yakama still are able to get salmon.

After the Salmon Ceremony was completed, the fish caught in the weir were distributed daily to the people by the Salmon Chief. The fish were parceled out according to family size: large families received more fish. Weir fishing continued throughout the fishing season.

After the weir had been operating for some time, platforms were built for dipnetting and spearing. The catch through these methods of capture was kept by the individual fisherman, who distributed the fish as he chose, usually among his family and relatives. There was thus a reward for being a good fisherman despite the communal distributions of fish.

The work was long and laborious. Since the fish ran only in the afternoon and at night, the men rested in the morning. The fishing platforms were occupied at least until midnight with the aid of torches. A Methow consultant noted: "As long as the fish were running, we fished. A dipnet could catch two to three fish at a time. They were very heavy. Since the dipnet was such hard work, you had to pace yourself." Only three platforms were available in one section of the Okanogan River near his village, he said, and the Salmon Chief regulated each individual's turn at the platforms so that everyone would have a chance to use a dipnet. The dipnet was a successful, though laborious, method of capture. Around July or August, when everyone had enough fish to last the winter, the weir was dismantled so the remaining salmon could go upstream to spawn.

The fishing activities of the men were obviously of prime importance to the economy. Even though the women did the crucial work of processing the salmon for winter storage, those scholars who look for evidence of women's subordination might point out that women had no role in the actual fishing. A few consultants, however, reported a new detail in the gender division of labor related to fishing. Despite a prohibition that prevented women from approaching the weir at any time, whether menstruating or not (Post 1938:17), they had an indispensable role in the building of the weirs. Only women could obtain the thongs or lashings that bound the tripod poles of the weir together. Men knew that the lashings came from a tree, but they were forbidden to know which one. While Post (1938:13) fails to note that the tripod lashings were provided by women, he records that they were made of willow bark. One female consultant confirmed this. Before my conversation with her, one of my male consultants thought that the willow source was incorrect. Since the lashings were 1 1/4 inches wide, he speculated that they were fabricated from a slice of a jackpine tree. He noted that men and boys were not allowed to accompany the women while the raw materials were being gathered. The very locations and nature of the material were supposed to be unknown to them. As a result, men were unable to build the weirs by themselves—they needed the cooperation of women, thus endowing women with a crucial role in the important salmon fishing. This arrangement suggests an ideology of balance or complementarity between men and women.

Under unusual circumstances, certain women were allowed to approach the weir. When a fish run failed despite the Salmon Chief's best spiritual efforts, he might invite a female shaman endowed with strong salmon power (who routinely avoided the weir like other women) to assist him in reestablishing the fish run. Her assistance consisted of going to the weir and clearing away the debris that collected around the fish traps, a routine chore usually performed by boys every morning. During this task, she undoubtedly invoked her guardian spirit and prayed for the fish to return. My consultant commented: "This was a method that never failed."

Another role that women had in connection with salmon weirs is mentioned by Post (1938:12): "The first step in the building of the weir is the announcement by a man (occasionally a woman) that he will build one at such a time and place. This announcement usually occurred at the winter dance." It seems likely that the woman mentioned in passing by Post had salmon power (like the woman discussed above), because the men who directed the building of a weir also had salmon power. These female shamans would be suitable persons to build a weir.

Considering the exceptional participation of women with salmon power in building a weir and insuring a fish run and the necessary service of other women in providing materials to build a weir, salmon fishing was apparently not a male monopoly in traditional culture but rather a common enterprise undertaken by both men and women.

Gathering Gathering vegetal foods was exclusively the task of women. To dig the roots that formed a principal and much-favored staple of the diet, the women used digging sticks, which they fashioned themselves and owned exclusively (Ray 1932:98). Camas roots, which were and are highly valued in those areas in which they grow, have a very high protein content: 5.4 ounces per pound of the roots. Steelhead trout (*Salmo gairdneri*) has 3.4 ounces of protein per pound (Marshall 1977:62), making scientific sense of the high value that the Plateau people put on the plentiful camas.

Like salmon fishing, gathering could not commence before a religious ceremony was held, the First Roots or First Fruits Ceremony. The purpose of these ceremonies was to thank the powers of nature for the food. There is also an element of renewal or maintenance of the established natural order in the ceremony (Post 1938:17). One consultant said it was a sin to dig roots or gather berries without having the appropriate ceremony first—"it would be like stealing the food."

The First Roots Ceremony began with preparation for the first root digging of the season. A Gathering Leader who was elected to that office for life, with a group of women also appointed for life, made the decision about when the roots or other foods were ripe enough to collect. The women left the settlement as a group to gather the first food of the season. They chose an area, made the proper prayers, and collected a quantity of roots. Then they returned to the community and prepared the food for consumption. Prayers accompanied most stages of this process. A feast followed the next day, with many kinds of food being prepared by the community. The feast was preceded by praying and drumming. The end of the feast was a signal for all of the women of the community to begin their annual root digging for the year. A First Roots Ceremony that I attended in 1993 was preceded by extremely wet, muddy conditions, but this did not deter the women who obtained the first roots. The roots were judged to be ripe and were gathered, and the ceremony followed.

Ray (1932:98) states that individual groups of women followed a Gathering Leader, who chose the location of digging each day. Perhaps this communal digging was remembered during the period of Ray's fieldwork, but consultants in the 1980s remembered only that women dug individually or with friends after the root feast. They further noted that the Gathering Leader had a status similar to that of the Salmon Chief and that she had been endowed by her guardian spirit with a special talent to find roots. She was chosen by the assembly, not appointed by the chief or an old man as Ray (1932:97) says.

First Roots Ceremonies and feasts are still held today on the Colville Reservation, but only by the Nez Perce, Sanpoil, Lakes, and Wenatchi tribes. The Moses Columbia tribe participates in the Nez Perce ceremony. A Yakama woman residing on the Colville Reservation noted that Root Feasts there are similar to those that take place on the Yakama Reservation today. Helen Hersh Schuster (1975:432–37), who works among the Yakama, notes that a group of seven women dig the roots. One (apparently the leader) says a prayer referring to the roots as the "oldest food" before they leave camp. Then the members of the group, who are fasting, go to the mountains to dig roots for the ceremony. After returning to camp, they prepare the roots for the next day, when the feast takes place. This ceremony must be very similar to those in the past. What is noteworthy in the First Roots Ceremony, aside from its religious significance, is that the Gathering Leader everywhere in the Plateau is endowed with authority similar to that of the Salmon Chief, since she performs a similar religious and economic function. This point has not been made in previous ethnographies.

While it was not necessary for the average woman to have a root spirit to find roots, consultants say, those women endowed with such a religious power located roots more readily than other women in a bad year. Furthermore, these women were reputed to be faster and more skillful in digging roots at any time because of their spiritual power. It was said that the guardian spirit Gopher, being a good digger, often served as a representative of the root spirit.

While gathering food of any kind, women were often accompanied by their infants and small children. One Nespelem elder, when asked if taking small children handicapped her work while she dug for roots or gathered, denied that it did. She said of a toddler: "If they could walk, they went along. There was no hurry. If there is a baby, the oldest girl in the family takes care of it. I used to leave my baby with my cousin in-law. When the baby started walking, I dug roots while she played. With the car, it was even easier [to take children]. I trained my girls to dig when they got older, but they played too. The boys wandered around."

If no one in the family was available to look after an infant, it was placed in a cradleboard and kept nearby as the mother worked. Toddlers played near their mother, and older girls (from age eight) began their training for gathering under their mother's direction. As noted above, sometimes an older girl back at camp such as a daughter, sister, or cousin looked after a younger child while the mother was digging; but this was not an indispensable service. A mother apparently was not handicapped in her work by the presence of young children.

A woman gathered as much food as possible. If she had a very large family and was unable to gather enough food to last the winter, she could expect help from other village residents.

Gathering began before dawn. The woman packed her infant and went to the picking or digging grounds and did not return before mid-afternoon. She then went to fetch firewood and water, assisted by the young girls of the family. Plateau women were physically strong and habitually bore heavy burdens.

Gathering plant foods required an extensive knowledge of the botany, plant habitats, and the best time to harvest the plants. Even more exacting was the preparation of roots for storage. The roots had to be baked in an earth oven, a process that required careful tending (Post 1938:26). Teit (1930:185) reports that Coeur d'Alene women prevented men, especially unmarried men, from approaching their earth ovens while the baking was in progress, because the roots were at risk of not cooking properly in the proximity of men.

Roots were not found in quantity near the winter villages. They had to be dried or baked in the spring and summer camp areas, cached, and transported to winter quarters at a later time. Women carried the loads in four to five Indian hemp baskets weighing about 30 pounds each (120 to 150 pounds total), which they tied into a cluster to carry on the back. In comparison, fur trade voyageurs were expected to carry loads of 180 pounds (Stern 1993:127). The women did not consider carrying such burdens to be a particular hardship. Obviously, transporting these loads became far easier after horses became available.

Women set their own pace in their annual work, traveling as they needed or wished without regard for their husbands' movements. They did not require direction from men to conduct their work; nor did men need direction from women in their economic tasks. Each was an independent agent, a status that individuals consciously cultivated. This is also true for the Dakota Indians, who expect each sex to be self-sufficient in subsistence activities (Albers 1985:120).

Hunting Communal deer hunts lasting one to two weeks took place in the late fall and early winter after the fishing and gathering were completed for the year. Hunting was less important than fishing and gathering but provided the only fresh food from November to early spring, and the meat was valued for this reason. Hunt Leaders led the hunting parties and organized the activity. They filled an authoritative position similar to those of the Salmon Chief and the Gathering Leader and acquired their talent of frequent hunting success from a guardian spirit. Each Hunting Leader in a village led at least one hunt during the fall. Men planning a hunt went through a ritual sweat bath for ten days and

refrained from sexual relations throughout the ritual period and the duration of actual hunting.

Women (presumably those who were not menstruating) always accompanied a fall hunting expedition and constituted one-third of the number
(Ray 1932:78). They made camp, cooked, helped drive the animals when
needed, and collected a few more vegetal foods when other responsibilities allowed. After the men killed an animal, the women packed the carcass to camp, where they butchered and dried the meat.

Hunting parties regularly shared meat. The first deer of the year killed
by each hunter in camp was distributed among those at the camp by a
young boy or an old man, directed by the hunter. This was a First Foods
ritual, similar to those of the Salmon Ceremony or the First Roots Ceremony. Thereafter, the deer were shared in a different manner. After the
meat was butchered, one woman from each household or a man, if he had
no wife, sat in a circle to receive a portion of the catch. A man was selected
to divide the meat: he was not necessarily the Hunt Leader (Post 1938:22).
Meat did not have to be shared with people not in the hunting camp, with
one exception. The hoofs, lower legs, head, and lungs of the deer were
dried and kept separate by the Hunting Leader's wife. After returning to
the winter village, she boiled these parts and invited the elders of the village to dinner. This was an obligatory custom, insuring the hunter's success in the future (Ray 1932:92).

Consultants generally agreed with Post's (1938:22) account of the meat
division. The man who actually killed a deer kept the head and hide, and
the meat was divided with the others in the hunting camp whether they
actually hunted or not. Thus, old men no longer able to hunt came along
to help run camp and dry the meat so that they could share in the kill.
Divorced women without male relatives in the area would also help run
the camp with the same objective. My consultant commented: "This was
completely acceptable."

One consultant stated that a hunting party he participated in killed fifteen deer in one and a half to two weeks. Four deer were sufficient to last
the winter for a family of four. Post (1938:22) suggests that the division of
meat was uneven (the families of participating hunters receiving more),
but the reference is somewhat ambiguous.

The sharing of meat in a hunting camp may be expected in a group
where everyone's efforts were necessary for success. The fact that women

received the meat (Post 1938:22), however, brings into question some ideas on how men supposedly obtain exclusive political power in all hunting and gathering societies. It is theorized for all such cultures that men accrue political power through meat distribution to other males, thus placing obligations on them (Friedl 1975:22). The Plateau practice of men distributing meat to women does not support this theory. A consultant pointed out that the woman receiving meat actually represented a family, and the meat was for them. This is true, of course; but elsewhere it is noted (Walters 1938:75) that if a woman acquired a surplus of meat during the season she used it for trade or in any way that she wished. No one had the authority to countermand her decision on how to use the food brought into the household.

To explore the extent of male power accrued through the distribution of meat in the traditional culture of the Colville Reservation, consultants were asked if good hunters attained more political influence than other people. One, a Chelan Hunt Leader himself, agreed that such men were more influential politically because "they had ambition in getting out and bringing in meat; they liked getting out. But women too who were good providers had lots of influence. Some women had ambition; they were listened to by the chief. These types of people are equally important because they too had ambition and brought in much food."

When asked if people were grateful to good hunters for distributing meat, he said it was just a system; it was not done because they were generous. "It is harder to get roots. I tried digging with my wife sometime and my hands got tired. Women did a lot of work in the past. Some women were better providers than others. If a woman like that married a poor hunter, she was the main provider for the family."

Thus, women's work was highly valued and definitely prestigious. Successful women had the same kind of political influence as successful men, even though plant foods were not usually distributed in the manner of meat and fish. The chief listened to both men and women who were economically skillful, no matter which economic skill they possessed. Like a hunter or fisher, a woman could be a good provider or a poor one. The type of skill (fishing, gathering, hunting) was not a factor in the respect that accrued to a "good provider."

Girls were encouraged to marry good hunters or fishers, but it was not necessary to do so in order to have sufficient food for the family. Even a

man who was a poor provider could have two wives because of the communal distribution of fish and the availability of plant foods. Good providers,
however, were able to marry the more attractive women and to keep plural
wives without easily losing them, because of the prestige they had. It was a
matter of pride for women to be able to give food and not have to ask others for it, even if it was readily available. Furthermore, when a man hunted
or fished alone, he was under no obligation to share the game. Thus, some
economic advantage was available in marrying such a man. In contrast, a
woman who was a good provider could marry a poor hunter or fisher, for
she could collect extra food and trade for what they needed.

Good hunters had prestige, but no more than good fishermen or good
gatherers. The work of both genders was equally valued—consultants were
unanimous on this point. Even though fish and game were shared and
vegetal foods were not, the prestige accruing to men and women because
of their economic skills was identical. Vegetal foods were shared in only
one situation. If the chief found that a family was short of provisions (usually in the winter), he announced the need and asked for food from those
who could spare some. The women then brought out their dried meat,
fish, and vegetal foods and gave them directly to the family needing them.

Hayden (1992:541) misinterprets Plateau culture when he states that
there is little sense for generalized hunter-gatherers to collect extra supplies because they might have to give them away during shortages in other
households. If there is a surplus and a way is found to preserve surplus
food, he says, the sharing ethic will be curtailed. A capitalistic society has
an understandable ethic to hoard goods for individual use, because there
is no ethic of sharing between households. This is not the case among
Plateau societies. They have the advantages of sharing and community living. Having the reputation of generosity is extremely prestigious in Plateau
societies. In Goodnews Bay, Alaska, a Yup'ik Eskimo village where I conducted research in 1965–66, this was made explicit to me by a man who
hunted for more meat than his family needed so that he could be generous with members of his community.

Methow consultants say that women did not hunt large game in the past
but only killed rabbits and birds. Post (1938:24) notes that Southern
Okanogan women collected small game if they came across it. A Moses-
Columbia woman states that women hunted and fished (not for salmon)
for their own use in the past. Mrs. S. S. Allison (1892:307) noted, "In early

times the women were nearly as good hunters as the men, but since they have grown civilized they have given it up lest the white settlers should laugh at them, for they are highly sensitive to ridicule."

One anecdote related by Teit (1930:244–45) concerns an Upper Thompson woman who had shamanistic powers over mountain sheep. The "chief" (perhaps the Hunting Leader?) was afraid they would not be able to capture any of these animals, so he addressed her: "Well, you may know something. I will give the leadership of this hunt to you; you shall be hunting chief." (The phrase "know something" refers to religious power.) She accepted the leadership, with the result that the hunting party was able to kill a large number of sheep.

This example, of course, was not a case of women actually pursuing and killing an animal themselves; but the story illustrates the possibility of one gender being able to cross over into the other's realm occasionally. Such cross-gender economic behavior was not seen as a threat by either gender. The conflicting evidence regarding women actually hunting and killing game allows no solid conclusion to be made regarding the hunting of large game by women in the past. Men traditionally did not collect plant foods unless they were away from camp hunting and wanted some fresh vegetable or fruit to eat on the spot.

Women made baskets and mats, dressed hides, and sewed clothing during the winter months. They chopped wood, packed goods, and prepared the sites for tipis. At the same time, they trained their daughters for these tasks. Men started training their sons about the age of eight. The boys accompanied their fathers so they could learn male economic tasks. One young Sanpoil woman summarized the division of labor by saying that hunting, fishing, and warfare were the "only" things men did, while women performed all other tasks.

Men and women did not share any economic tasks, but they did share the responsibility to feed their dependents. While each had control over the timing of his or her labor and controlled the surplus production of that labor, they recognized their responsibilities to their families and communities.

Ceremonial Recognition of the Gender Division of Labor

The importance of each gender's economic contribution was noted formally in ceremonies that honored a child's future economic role. When

a boy killed his first deer or caught his first fish, it was presented to his grandmother. She prepared a small feast for close relatives during which the meat
or fish was completely consumed. The boy did not partake of this food but
was honored as the provider of it. A comparable feast was held for a girl
when she independently collected her first roots or first berries. The foods
she gathered were ceremoniously consumed during the feast, and she was
praised as the provider. Gifts were given to the elders attending these dinners, and sometimes one of them gave the child a new name. A girl might
have her first ceremony performed about the age of eight, while a boy might
get his first deer about age twelve. The ceremonies were held for each new
species of important food caught or gathered by a child. These rituals were
also noted by Ray (1932:133) and Mandelbaum (1938:108).

Taboos   The subject of taboos (rules or laws according to consultants)
constitutes one of those categories whose proper placement is ambiguous
in the framework of this study. It is as reasonable to place them in the religious sphere as in the economic one. Taboos are discussed here in connection with the economic system because they are so intimately intertwined and because consultants offered economic as well as religious
rationales for these customs.

For instance, the menstrual taboos that once existed were believed to
protect a number of economic practices. Unfortunately for the study of
the traditional gender system, the practice of menstrual taboos disappeared at least fifty years before 1978, when I first entered the field. Thus,
while the taboo is remembered to have occurred, details are not available.

Isolation at first menses was remembered by elders, but none of the
women interviewed had ever experienced it. Neither did any experience
isolation during subsequent menses. Nevertheless, prohibitions related to
the menstrual taboo were remembered in general. One was even practiced in recent times: the prohibition against women approaching fish
weirs during the salmon season.

Consultants recalled that girls and women refrained from touching
men's weapons and fishing implements at all times, and girls were taught
to avoid areas where men manufactured them. If a girl failed to observe
these taboos, not only was the men's hunting or fishing ability adversely
affected, but the girl herself risked becoming an indolent individual who
would never acquire the skills necessary to fulfill her female role.

Similarly, men avoided touching women's tools. A male consultant noted: "As a boy, I was told not to touch the women's baskets. If I fooled with the root digging outfit, I was told I would never learn to shoot straight." He was also told to avoid touching the women's material (probably prepared skins in the past), so he would not lose the ability to hunt or fish. Thus, men and boys too would be unable to fulfill their gender role. Boys under fifteen were not to approach root ovens at all, or this very important baking process would fail. Further, the women had the right to demand that not only boys but men of any age had to avoid the root-oven area completely in order to protect the root-baking. One Moses Columbia woman equated this taboo on men with the menstrual taboo on women.

Aside from the menstrual taboo, these restraints were no longer rigidly required of either gender once they reached maturity. If an adult woman touched a man's weapons during her menses, his hunting or fishing ability would still be temporarily harmed, but ritual measures could be applied to undo the damage. Ray (1932:135) notes that a great number of these measures existed and concludes that women often broke the taboo. One consultant observed that menstrual taboos did not constitute a superstition, as horses are known to bolt when they smell blood and other animals are affected as well.

Women used the menstrual hut for sweat baths; consequently, men had separate sweat baths in different locations. The menstrual hut was also used for childbirth, as the blood spilled during the process was considered unlucky. The baby was not considered dangerous, only the blood itself.

One female elder remarked that menstrual huts were also used as a place where women could work on their handicrafts in uninterrupted peace. This purpose was not generally remembered, however, and I was unable to verify this use of the menstrual hut through the testimony of other people. Walters (n.d.) and Mandelbaum (1938:124) do note that Southern Okanogan women built a longhouse for themselves where they worked. It was about seven feet deep and lined with mats on the floor and sides. The roof was flat. A ladder made of a notched log was used to gain access to this structure. Men never entered this place, for their religious power would have been damaged. Women did all their weaving there. It is likely that this edifice was the menstrual hut, at least among the Southern Okanogan, who along with the Chilcotin and Nez Perce were the only recorded Plateau tribes with communal menstrual huts (Ray 1939:54).

Single and widowed Nez Perce women lived in their menstrual lodge called Al-we-tas, "the abode of those without husbands" (Fletcher 1892). In this house they wove mats, made garments, and performed other tasks. The Nez Perce no longer used these houses after about 1750. The function of the women's houses appeared to be slightly different between the Nez Perce and Southern Okanogan if the scant information available is reliable.

Marshall (1977:136, 139) also notes the existence of not only women's houses but men's houses among the Nez Perce in the past. These were actually sweat lodges, one for each gender. Unmarried men and women resided in their respective sweat lodges. The women's lodge was the location where young men could court the unmarried girls.

Men went through a ritual cleansing (the sweat bath) for up to ten days before every hunting expedition and also before fishing. During this time, and for the duration of the fishing season or the hunt, they refrained from having sexual relations (Ray 1932:78; Mandelbaum 1938:119). This is a common practice in many cultures (e.g., see Hoebel 1966:241). What appears to be unique to Plateau culture but may simply be unreported in other foraging cultures is that the Gathering Leader and her companions also performed the same ritual sweat baths for five days (five being an auspicious number) before they gathered the first foods in the spring for the First Foods Ceremony. All consultants agreed on this point. A Yakama woman residing on the Colville Reservation elaborated further.

> My grandmother was a [Gathering] Leader, dug for the first feasts. You had to live clean to dig for the first food. You had to take a sweat bath for five days before going out digging for the first feast and for everyday digging too. A woman kept away from her husband before she went to get roots. No woman smells before hunting on the men, and no man smells on women before digging for roots, or the roots would go away. You need clean bedding and a clean body for digging. So, all my kids were born in June. Sometimes you forgot, and had to go through sweat bathing again, get clean clothes and bedding. My mother had to sleep by herself too when she was digging.

Thus, point for point, Plateau women and men followed the very same taboos when they undertook their respective major economic tasks. This consultant still lives with these restraints and cites as proof the fact that all of her children were born in the same month.

This custom was remembered by two others, a Moses-Columbia woman and a Nez Perce, and was tentatively confirmed by a Coeur d'Alene woman. The young Nez Perce woman said that abstinence is necessary every time before digging because men or women who have had sexual relations have an odor that is not conducive to successful gathering, hunting, or fishing. She mentioned as evidence one man who did not follow the rule and was therefore a failure as a hunter and fisher. Three other women from other tribes denied that any such custom existed, however, although they conceded that the practice of ritual cleansing and sexual abstinence was followed by the Gathering Leader and her group when they dug roots or picked berries for the First Foods Ceremonies. A Sanpoil elder said that all women did sweat bathe before digging the first time of the season and wore new clothes as well. They kept away from their husbands but not throughout the digging season, only the first time. A Coeur d'Alene woman said that every woman prayed when she dug roots the first time or gathered the first berries of the season. Interestingly, most consultants were not surprised when told of the Yakama woman's testimony. A few commented that the Yakama were strict about such things. It seems likely that the practice of season-long abstinence was widespread in the past since intermarriage spread such customs throughout the Plateau; but apparently the custom has been attenuated along with many other taboos.

Supporting evidence for this kind of prohibition appears among the Thompson Indians in connection with sunflower roots (*Balsamorrhiza sagittata* Nutt.), which are difficult to cook. Teit (1900:349) reports: "Women, while cooking or digging this root, must abstain from sexual intercourse." He mentions no such prohibitions for the digging of other roots.

An elderly Northern Okanogan consultant noted that an animal could smell blood; thus, it was important for women to stay away from their husbands when menstruating. She herself even washed her family's clothes separately, according to gender. She offered the explanation that the odors of men and women are different and should never be mixed, even those of boys and girls. To do so would dilute both maleness and femaleness.

The menstrual taboo in Plateau culture thus appears to be not a stigma but a marker of femaleness, balanced by similar restrictions for men that mark maleness. Menstruation is not seen in Plateau culture as an index of female inferiority. While the taboo does signify pollution and female inferiority in some cultures, in others it is the blood itself that is dangerous because any flow of blood is dangerous. It is "out of place" (Buckley and Gottlieb 1988:26). Thomas Buckley and Alma Gottlieb (1988:14–15, 24) argue that menstrual taboos are cultural constructions whose meaning varies from one society to another. In Plateau culture I interpret menstrual flow as an uncontrollable magical force that is capable of destroying or distorting the spiritual powers around it. It is a kind of "wild card," capable of anything. Consequently, women in this condition had to isolate themselves to protect the members of the community, whose well-being depended on the timely intervention of their guardian spirits to help them survive. The presence of "out of place" blood would destroy the successful operation of their spiritual powers.

Further, in Plateau culture all of the ritual precautions—including avoidance of the other gender's economic tools, the role of women in the building of fish weirs and ensuring of the fish run, the avoidance of root ovens by males, and particularly the similar ritual cleansing and sexual abstinence undertaken by both genders before they performed their major economic tasks—suggest that menstrual taboos were not unique prohibitions in the culture. The mere existence of taboos cannot indicate that women held low status in the Plateau, since menstrual taboos were only one of a series of prohibitions applying to both genders. Indeed, the consequence of the various taboos seems to have been a careful definition of each gender, effectively hammering them into place. It would seem that the following of taboos was more definitive of gender than the kind of work that each gender performed, since men and women occasionally carried out the work of the other gender.

The Value of Male and Female Economic Roles

Though women's work on the Colville Reservation and in the Plateau generally appeared in the past to be as important as men's to an outsider, the question is whether the people themselves recognized that importance. To explore this significant theoretical point, all elders of both genders were asked which foods were more important in the traditional diet: meat and fish acquired by men or roots and berries collected by women. Consultants of both genders *unanimously* stated that all four of these foods were equally important. These responses were exciting, because it is rare

to get unanimous testimony in fieldwork. Several consultants were bemused
by the question. They commented as follows:

> Meat cooked without berries or bitterroots is poor. Fish is always
> cooked with berries. Bitterroots with fish. Salmon eggs with choke-
> cherries. All these foods equal in importance. They are mixed with
> each other.

> There were prayers over the first roots and berries in the spring
> just like the first salmon or first deer.

> Meat and fish were about half the food. The roots and berries and
> other greens were the other half. Bitterroots and sarvisberries were
> the most important plant foods; as important as meat and fish.

> Bitterroots and berries are as good as meat and fish. They are the
> same as taking holy water during communion. Bitterroots and
> berries are called "chief" because they take care of the people, just
> like a chief. Meat, fish, roots, and berries are all important, all the
> same.

> All those foods—all important. It is impossible to choose.

Since the foods collected by the women were highly nutritious, they must
have added to the importance of the female economic role. One historical
anecdote related by a consultant concerned a woman and her daughter
who escaped a raid and fled into the Cascade Mountains for refuge. They
remained there from August to March, living exclusively on roots found in
a cache. Not only did they survive, but their energy remained unimpaired
on that restricted diet.

I asked if people ever worried about lack of food in the past. One woman
said that even though her husband drank too much they never went without food. Another said that there was always Indian food to be obtained
from the land. If anyone ran low on food supplies, it was because of care-
lessness—that is, failing to put up enough food for the winter. Some circumstances prevented people from foraging for food. If there was a death
in the family, the mourners were required to abstain from hunting, fishing,
or gathering. Other village members helped to support such families during the mourning period. Since a surplus was easy to acquire, and often
routinely accrued, it was relatively simple to take care of people who for
one reason or another were unable to obtain food.

When a description of men's work was solicited from consultants, virtually every woman spontaneously observed that "men didn't work," or "men didn't do much work, they just provided food," or "men didn't work, they only hunted, fished, and went to war. Women did all the work." (It should be remembered that fishing and hunting were arduous, and warfare was perilous.) No resentment of men was expressed along with these comments. Actually, women were well off as a result of this division of labor. They owned almost everything in the house because of the effort they exerted in transforming goods into usable items for the family. They built the house, they dried food, and they cured rawhide and turned it into clothing. Labor expended on an object made the laborer the owner. A man could give a fresh cut of meat to others; but once it was processed it belonged to his wife because of the effort she made in drying and storing it. As a consequence, men owned relatively little except their personal possessions, like weapons and clothing. Horses were their most important possession.

The women's concept that men did not work was explored with consultants. After discussion, women conceded that men did work: "It was hard for men to haul deer long distances back to camp." Men, however, had more leisure time than women and were exposed to their wives' anger occasionally because of their "laziness." Despite the strenuous effort involved in fishing and hunting, they were considered pleasurable activities. Thus, "men didn't work" is only an insider view; obviously, men were involved in important economic pursuits. This emic or insider evaluation has some contemporary consequences (discussed in chapter 6). The most perceptive comment regarding the traditional gender division of labor came from a young woman in her twenties: "Men did fun things [in the past]; they killed deer, but they needed to drag it back. That was a lot of work. Women had to cut the meat up, skin it, make clothing, had to gather. Women's work wasn't duller, just busier."

Indeed, most economic activities in the past were accompanied by excitement, ritual, a sense of holiday, and companionship for everyone so that work, though often exacting, was associated with enjoyment as well as a sense of accomplishment.

How many people could a man and woman supply with food? A man said that his mother gathered enough vegetal foods to supply her husband and herself, three elders who could not work, and three children, while his father was able to supply enough meat and fish for this same group. A woman said that in the past she was able to support seven to eight people easily, plus feed many visitors who dropped by and stayed several days. Before she was married, four women in her family worked all summer to acquire extra fish to trade commercially and more for the "marriage trade." One elder noted that while women's work was never done and they were busier than men, she calculated that men and women obtained about equal amounts of food. Women perhaps produced a little more than men. Thus, the work of one individual in his or her prime was indeed productive.

The economic contribution of women within traditional Plateau culture, then, was as significant as that of men, was well recognized by both genders, and was highly and equally valued. The structure of the sweat house reflects that equality. Four of the poles in the sweat house symbolize the seasons, four symbolize the cardinal directions, four symbolize the sacred colors, and four symbolize the four foods: roots, berries, salmon, and meat (Louie 1991:165). The first two foods are the products of women's labor and the last two the products of men's labor. The salmon, roots, berries, and venison make up the four Great Foods made at the time of Creation (McKeown 1956:44). That these four foods should be represented in the sweat house, which is a Plateau religious institution of prime importance, is significant. Plateau people value their religion above all else, and to have integrated the gender division of labor into their religion points directly to the equal value they place on men and women. Since some anthropologists claim that women, women's work, and the products of their labor are not highly valued within any culture even though they are objectively important (Ortner and Whitehead 1981:16; Rosaldo 1974:19), this is a significant point.

Autonomy in the Economic Sphere

Economic autonomy in the past most often consisted of making or preparing goods for trade and then traveling to some area other than home territory to make an exchange. Trade depended entirely on individual initiative. Both men and women were heavily involved in the activity and were absolutely independent from spouses and other family members in its practice. Women, as the proprietors of food, dealt mostly in that commodity. They also traded items such as basketry, cured skins, and decorated skin clothing. Since men owned most of the horses in contact times, horses were their major commodity. Men also fashioned weapons, fishing implements, feather regalia, and other handicrafts for trade. It is interesting to speculate concerning the extent of men's trade before horses were introduced into the area. Could male trade have been minimal? Women often accumulated more material wealth than men in contact times unless the men had large herds of horses (Schuster 1975:131).

Men and women packed food and objects for trade on their backs before the introduction of horses. Both served as interpreters to expedite trade. Chinook, the trade jargon, was easy to learn and men learned it quickly. A male elder commented, "Women learned languages quicker than men. I don't know why." Women often served as interpreters in trading transactions.

It was through trade that women most often acquired horses of their own, though they sometimes received them as gifts from consanguineal relatives. They did not acquire herds as the men did, but a few horses were useful in transporting children and vegetal foods and formed part of a woman's personal property. Ross (1986:309), an early fur trader, noted that women rode horses as competently as men.

At the annual fish encampments and other trading locations, relatives were reunited and gifts exchanged. Everyone met new people and greeted established trading partners. Trading partners were not related and came from different areas, so that the goods they exchanged were not similar. Even children participated in trade. A historical anecdote recounted how a Moses-Columbia child traveled to the Plains with her parents. She had prepared dried salmon eggs before the trip to trade for a doll from a Blackfeet girl. While she and the other child were conducting their business, but before the exchange could be completed, fighting erupted between the Plateau tribes and the Blackfeet, much to the girls' mutual disappointment.

Food was highly valued as a trade item. One particularly valued commodity was dried salmon, which women pounded into a powder. While this was a lengthy task, it was a rewarding one, for the fish powder kept indefinitely and was highly esteemed for that reason. A salmon skin filled with pounded salmon powder was said to be equal in value to a good horse.

Gambling constituted another autonomous economic activity. Both men and women played stick games, which effected large exchanges of property at the encampments. Traditionally, gambling took place only between opponents of the same gender because of the fear that the spiritual power that was so important to the success of the games might be subverted by menstruating females.

Another aspect of economic autonomy is personal control over the means of acquiring economic goods. Marilyn Strathern (1988:140) notes that control over resources is a significant factor in egalitarian societies. Further, each gender in such societies owns its own labor. Plateau men and women both had this control over different but significant resources and both "owned" their own labor. Men made their weapons and tools personally or traded for them, and women made their own digging sticks for root gathering. These observations on power, authority, and autonomy in the traditional economic sphere are summarized in table 3.

THE DOMESTIC SPHERE

The domestic sphere is defined here as concerning relationships and activities (economic and otherwise) that take place within the household. The traditional Plateau family was of the extended type and constituted a localized or village-based nonunilinear descent group. One feature of the household was its permeability. It was not a bounded entity but open to other households of the village and to visitors and visiting kindred from other tribes for three seasons of the year. The Plateau extended household was involved with social, economic, political, and even religious processes in the society at large, defined as not only the village and tribe but the entire Plateau itself (Ackerman 1994).

The kinship system was ambilineal (that is, people traced their ancestry through both mother and father equally), reflecting the gender equality of the culture. The household often included an older couple and perhaps one or two of their siblings, also elderly; some of the married sons and daughters of all the elders, along with their spouses and children; and unmarried children. Though Ray (1932:140) says that Plateau families were patrilocal, no set rule surfaced in discussion with consultants, thus making residence ambilocal. Many married as well as divorced women lived with their consanguineal relatives in the past.

Power in the Domestic Sphere

Power in the domestic sphere was expressed through the exertion of informal influence in the traditional culture. Depending on the degree

TABLE 3

The Economic Sphere: Traditional Culture

MEN	WOMEN
POWER	
none recalled by consultants	
AUTHORITY	
each gender provided about 1/2 of food	
men fished for salmon	
men with salmon power built weirs	women gathered material for weir lashings
	women with salmon power insured fish runs
Salmon Ceremony	First Roots and Fruits Ceremonies
Hunting Leaders, Salmon Chiefs	Gathering Leaders
men prohibited from vicinity of root ovens	women prohibited from vicinity of salmon weir
men distributed meat	women received meat
economic skill equals political influence	
boy's First Catch Ceremony	girl's First Gathering Ceremony
boys prohibited from touching women's economic tools	girls prohibited from touching men's economic tools
sexual abstinence before fishing, hunting	sexual abstinence before gathering
foods equally valued and nutritious	
work of both genders considered equally important by both genders	
AUTONOMY	
men owned personal items and horses	women owned personal items and food
traders in horses, weapons, etc.	traders in food, handicrafts
male and female trade equally important	
both genders served as interpreters	
both genders gambled	
men made own weapons and tools	women made own digging sticks

of intimacy between them, married couples advised or influenced each other. Even a chief's wife or wives gave him advice on particular political problems. When disagreements arose within a marriage, a Nespelem woman noted that "a sensible couple talked things over" until problems were settled.

Some women declared that men were "bosses" within the family, while other women insisted that women were "bossier." A Moses-Columbia woman stated: "Women had a lot to say. They controlled food supplies: there were medicine women. Some learned the Chinook dialect [jargon] for trading. Men traded men things, like horses. Women owned horses too, but not many at a time. Women got goods to trade through gathering. They did not do the bidding of men automatically."

Ross (1986:280) summed up the situation well when he noted that the family was ruled by the joint authority of the husband and wife, "but more particularly by the latter." These comments suggest that overall authority was not institutionally assigned to either the man or the woman within the marriage.

The existence of polygyny in traditional Plateau culture may seem to contradict the implication of equality between spouses evident in Ross's comment. Remi Clignet and Joyce Sween (1981:445) ask the relevant question: "Does polygyny enhance female autonomy or ensure male dominance?" They conclude that the answer depends on the type of culture and the circumstances within the family in which the polygynous tradition exists. They point out that an automatic conclusion connecting polygyny to female subordination is a bias of Western culture (Clignet and Sween 1981). The weight of evidence in the Plateau points to the conclusion that traditional polygynous marriages did not appear to handicap women in any way or place them in a subservient position.

Why polygyny did occur in the Plateau is puzzling. Having plural wives did not result in notably greater economic benefits for the husband as in some cultures, and taking a second wife often led to domestic trouble. Even the Plateau people recognized the instability of such marriages. Non-sororal co-wives often regarded each other as rivals and tried to turn the husband against the other wife. Sometimes a woman entered into a polygynous marriage with the intention of driving off the other woman or persuading the husband to leave the first wife, a situation fraught with dispute and tension. One of the women in a polygynous marriage usually became impatient with the situation and left.

Despite the risk of disrupted household peace, many men wanted plural wives for the sake of prestige or vanity. Plural wives announced to the world that a man was handsome and sexually attractive, a reputation that some men actively cultivated. Susan Allison, an early settler, noted that "a

man's looks go a long way with Indians" (Ormsby 1976:64). Despite the fact
that a man was unlikely to keep the same two or more wives throughout his
life, winning women as wives was prestigious; losing a spouse was unimportant (the same was true for women). Further, since shamans, chiefs, good
hunters, good fishers, and successful gamblers could easily provide for more
than one woman at a time, they were the most likely to have plural wives,
though they also had trouble keeping the same wives throughout their lives.
Plural wives were necessary in some cases, since successful hunters and fishers brought in an above-average amount of food, which required more than
one woman to process it. This was not considered the major cause of polygyny by consultants, however. One woman thought the reason was ego,
"macho," because it made a man feel important.

Since it was so difficult to keep peace among unrelated co-wives, serious
men interested in peace and family stability preferred sororal polygyny to
nonsororal polygyny. Jealousy was not as likely to occur among sisters or
cousins (classificatory sisters), and consultants recalled examples of happy,
stable marriages under these circumstances.

Two consultants pointed out that in some instances a wife or co-wives
would choose an additional wife for their husband because she had a particular talent that the family needed (such as a talent for beading, tanning,
or sewing). In these perhaps rare cases, harmony was usual among the wives.

My consultants had never heard of the custom of polyandry. One woman
commented that if it had ever occurred the two men would have killed each
other. Marshall (1977:82) tried to elicit a term for "co-husband" in the Nez
Perce language but was not successful. He comments: "However, de facto
polyandry probably occurred briefly and occasionally"; but he does not
elaborate on this intriguing statement.

First marriages for young people were always arranged by their parents.
If an arranged marriage seriously displeased a young individual, he or she
had the option of eloping with a lover, an act that thwarted the parents'
authority. I interpret this as a use of power. There is no way now to estimate the percentage of marriages formed in the past by means of this
irregular method, except that in the course of fieldwork on three Plateau
reservations anecdotes concerning elopements of particular people surfaced frequently.

The parents' wishes were also thwarted by another irregular marriage
custom, which verged on being acceptable. This consisted of a young man

slipping into a girl's bed after everyone was asleep. If she did not object to his presence, he remained with her until morning. When he was discovered by her family, he had to be accepted as the girl's husband. Many parents were not upset by this behavior. Consultants say that this type of marriage was very common once.

In the past, meals were served to men first, while the women and children dined later. This is a cultural trait that may imply male power or authority. Consultants had no rationale for the custom but denied it occurred because men were dominant. Some pointed out that since women served the meals it was easier to take care of the men before the women ate. The custom fell out of use about 1910.

Wife-beating, a use of power, occurred in the past and was common enough to be noted in the literature (Ray 1932:145). The practice was considered shameful and illegitimate, according to both male and female consultants. When a young man was to marry for the first time, an older man of the extended family advised him on how to treat his future wife. One of the pieces of advice was not to mistreat her. He was told that he should not beat her if he was unhappy with her. Instead, he should leave her or tell her to return to her father. Wife-beatings were viewed as a sign of marital disharmony and indeed did often follow a quarrel between spouses. One aspect of domestic violence that is different from Euro-American culture is that women did not have to endure the violence because of economic circumstances or public pressure. Public pressure went in the other direction: the man was pressured to stop hurting his wife, most often by members of his extended family. A woman had the economic ability to leave the marriage—staying was her choice.

It was not unknown for women to defend themselves against violence. A. J. Splawn (1917:172), an early settler, recounts how the Indian wife of a white man won a fight her husband instigated. It was reported that thereafter she had no more trouble with him. Mandelbaum (1938:116) reports that a woman might leave a husband who beat her.

Rape may be interpreted as evidence for the presence of male power and a concomitant lack of female autonomy. Rape did occur in Plateau traditional societies (Ray 1932:146; Turney-High 1937:83–84), though consultants insisted that it was an uncommon crime and in no way condoned. One incident, narrated by a Moses-Columbia woman, occurred about 1930, when a man who committed rape was brought before the chief for judgment:

The chief asked the people, what should we do with this man? The women wanted to punish him themselves. The chief agreed. The women took the man away somewhere. They held him down while one older woman rubbed her bottom on his face, asking him, wasn't this what he wanted? She was so mad at him that she threatened to pee on him, but he begged for mercy, so she didn't. The chief then told the man he must leave the village.

Note that the women's actions were institutionalized. They were not an illegal posse but acted as the society's agents in punishing the offender. Harry Turney-High (1937:83–84) also describes this custom among the Flathead, another Plateau tribe:

It seems that rape was not punished by the chief or the men of the tribe but was left to the collective anger of the women. There survive memories of the treatment accorded some notorious rapists. In such cases the women of the village plotted to decoy such men into unfrequented places and to fall upon them. Once overpowered they could expect any degree of abuse and indignity at their hands which they could not resent or avenge.

The punishment meted out to Plateau rapists is reminiscent of Bronislaw Malinowski's (1929:274–75) description of similar penalties exacted in the Trobriand Islands. When a strange male ventured too close to the forbidden area of the women's gardens, he was seized by a group of women, who punished him by rubbing their genitals against the man's nose and mouth. Some women urinated or defecated over his body. In the Plateau area, there was no similar punishment of a woman by a group of men for any reason. Rape was never socially condoned.

Suicide, particularly suicide rooted in jealousy, was an occurrence noted among Plateau tribes in several sources. One report attributes this behavior primarily to women and rarely to men (Mandelbaum 1938:127). If this is true, the behavior might suggest that men dominate women psychologically and have power over them. Nez Perce women during my fieldwork in 1965, however, insisted that men more often than women commit suicide due to jealousy. Teit (1906:202) probably obtained a more balanced account and made the evaluation that suicide occurred among both men and women, the cause being shame or jealousy. Suicide thus appears to be an irrelevant factor in the balance of power between men and women.

When a man was considerably older than his wife, he appeared to have more power or influence over her than if they were of similar age. Young girls were sometimes given in marriage by their parents to men a full generation older because of their wealth. The husband's influence prevailed within the marriage because of his age, experience, and wealth. He did not have the authority, however, to keep his wife in the marriage if she wished to leave.

In those marriages in which the woman was much older than her husband, a similar situation prevailed. Casual references to such marriages revealed that they occurred fairly often; but they were not arranged marriages, unless a levirate or sororate was involved. They were mostly undertaken at the wish of the couples themselves. These unions were as successful as any other, and some lasted until the death of the older partner. It was said that sometimes a shiftless younger man sought to marry an older woman so that he could have access to her wealth and be supported by her. This situation, in my view, is essentially similar to that of an inexperienced girl marrying an older, experienced man for his wealth. More often, however, motivations were more subtle. In the successful old woman–young man marriages, the woman was said to have much influence over her young husband. A female consultant related:

> My father-in-law was Canadian [probably a Northern Okanogan Indian]. He was an orphan. His grandmother fed him moss as a baby. He stayed with different people, moved from one family to another. He got on this side of the border and stayed with a cousin. He met a woman who was either separated or widowed, older than him. He went home with her. They had a daughter and a son only so she must have been pretty old. His wife had a grandson when he married her . . . They stayed together until she died.

It was evident that the emotional as well as the economic stability that the wife provided in this story may well have been part of her attraction for the young man in the first place. The women's influence in those cases would have been entirely natural. Richard Lee (1979:454) also notes that older wives among the !Kung had great influence over their young husbands.

Authority in the Domestic Sphere

The discipline of children, whether physical or moral, requires the exertion of authority. In the Plateau, no gender hierarchy of influence prevailed.

Both parents were imbued with equal authority in the exercise of moral discipline (physical punishment of children was not condoned; this was done by the whipman). The father's admonitions were not considered more authoritative than those of the mother. Other relatives also took a hand in discipline and sometimes interceded for a child with its elders. No difference in discipline was imposed on children according to gender.

Grandparents, regardless of gender, had more authority over children than parents and played a larger role in their lives. It was customary for children to be left with their grandparents soon after weaning, while their parents left the area to follow the annual round and perform their economic tasks. Further, residence with grandparents gave children the much needed stability for personal growth if their parents went through a series of marriages and divorces, as was common. Even if the parents remained on the scene, grandparents continued to be very involved with the nurture of children. The greater authority they exerted over them was based on the premise that they had more experience in child-raising than the parents, and they certainly had more time, since the parents became the major providers of economic needs within the extended family as the grandparents aged. Further, the elders of the family were due the most respect and consideration. The grandmother, as the manager of the household, was consulted by everyone on everything going on in the extended family. She was looked upon as a "teacher" by the younger people within the household.

The grandparental role was and is a very coveted one. I met a 38-year-old woman who looked forward eagerly to the impending birth of her first grandchild, so she could take it into her home and raise it. One woman whose mother died young said she had a difficult time raising her children without her mother's supervision, advice, and assistance.

Old age was an absolute advantage for both men and women, since elders were highly respected and had implicit authority. Consequently, women did not conceive of menopause as a stage of life to be feared. Even childlessness was not a problem for a woman, since in the kinship system she was mother and grandmother to her siblings' children and grandchildren and was often called upon to play that role in the absence of the real parents. People even today refer to having several mothers and grandmothers and express great devotion to them all.

Parents (or grandparents) participated equally in the choice of a spouse for their child, often without consulting the wishes of the young people involved. Among the Flathead (Turney-High 1937:87), the Sanpoil, and the Nespelem (Ray 1932:139–40), the boy's mother proposed a marriage to a girl's mother. If she agreed, the two fathers made arrangements. Another account reports that the boy's father made a marriage proposal to the girl's father. The latter consented by accepting the gifts, thus completing the agreement (Mandelbaum 1938:113). Most Colville Reservation elders, including the Southern Okanogan among whom Mandelbaum worked, say that both parents had to agree to a marriage match. It was said to be unthinkable for that decision to be made by the father alone.

Fathers exchanged gifts when a marriage agreement was reached, but field research indicates that only women participated in the "marriage trade," the gift exchange that formalized a marriage. This form of marriage is no longer practiced in the areas I visited and has not been for some time, so it was hard to verify to my satisfaction that only women were involved in this important ceremony. Nevertheless, this is the information obtained on the Colville and Nez Perce (Idaho) Reservations and appears to be true for the Warm Springs Reservation. Many elders said that men never took part in the marriage trade; only one testified to the contrary. A Southern Okanogan woman said that men exchanged gifts too, but with each other. Women exchanged more items because they produced more. A male Methow noted that men did get involved in the marriage trade but not nearly as often as the women. Men's participation was briefly noted by Mandelbaum (1938:116) without further comment. It certainly seems that in some areas in recent times women were dominant in the marriage trade because all of the items used in the exchange were owned by them, even the "men's food" (fish, game), and men might have had fewer things to trade. In the past, the trading might have been more evenly distributed. Marriage trades took place in the fall, since by then surplus food would have been available for the exchange. If it is accepted that only women participated in the marriage trade, which is verified in recent times in certain places, then women had a large part, perhaps the major one, in validating marriages.

Arranged marriages were preferred for young people, because then their extended families were able to enter into formal relationships with one another. Such relationships provided economic, social, and political advantages for both kin groups. Thus, the young people were firmly under their parents' or grandparents' authority in this matter, though this authority could be defied by elopement and other methods, as noted above. Nonetheless, autonomy for the young people was curtailed by the arranged marriages.

My consultants also noted that the levirate and sororate were also required marriages, despite previous reports that they were optional (Mandelbaum 1938:117; Ray 1932:144). The levirate and sororate functioned to retain the established ties between the two affinal groups and, perhaps more importantly, retained orphaned children within the same household in which they had resided with both parents. If their mother died, she was replaced by her sister or cousin, who served as mother to the children. If the father died, his brother or cousin (often residing within the same household) replaced him as husband and father. The grandparents had a vested interest in the levirate and sororate, for the customs insured the continued presence of the grandchildren within their particular household and nonunilinear descent group. Furthermore, the children's lives were then minimally disrupted by the death of a parent. With so much at stake, a sibling or cousin of the deceased accepted the authority of kin in this matter and entered into the levirate or sororate marriage. One elder who entered into such a marriage in her youth indicated no reluctance on her part to take her cousin's place and raise the children of the family. It should be pointed out that Plateau families even today rarely include only one's own biological children. There are stepchildren, nephews and nieces, young cousins, and even orphaned or neglected children taken off the street ("take-ins") who are raised together in one group.

In the past, a man had the right to kill his wife's lover without fear of reprisal from the lover's kin, provided he was sure of his wife's infidelity. Events rarely went this far, however. The husband was normally urged by his relatives to forego revenge and generally took their advice. His usual course was to ignore the affair, especially if he valued the marriage. If he abused his wife or quarreled with her because of her infidelity, she might leave him.

Consultants made allusions to a custom that appears only twice in the literature (Ackerman 1971:601; Turney-High 1937:96) and that is somewhat analogous to a man's right to kill his wife's lover. This custom is called *pokwantam* or *pokwas* in the Columbia language, meaning "she took away her man." It consists of a wife attacking her husband's lover with a group of her friends and beating her, with the hope of frightening her away from the husband. This appears to be an institutionalized recourse for the wife, as the husband never intervenes. The cultural rationale is that, when a romantic triangle develops, it is taken for granted that the husband would not have strayed if the other woman had not tempted him. Often the man is so flattered by his wife's loss of control when she attacks his lover that he remains with or returns to his wife. A myth involving such a triangle is told in which all three protagonists were transformed into boulders that can be seen on the Colville Reservation today. Several women, speaking generally, said that women "might take a lot from a man," but his acquisition of another woman was the breaking point.

Autonomy in the Domestic Sphere

Autonomy in the domestic sphere was extensive for both genders and was expressed in marriage and divorce arrangements, family size, and other modes of behavior.

Though first marriages were arranged for young people, thus limiting their autonomy, second and subsequent marriage partners were chosen by the individual. Marriage then consisted simply of a couple taking up common residence (Ray 1932:142). The only exception to free choice in the second marriage occurred when the levirate or sororate was required, as noted above. Since they were mandatory, according to elders, they represented a restriction on autonomy but affected men and women equally.

Divorce was common and equally available to both men and women. It was accomplished easily since the couple did not own property in common. Each partner simply picked up his or her personal property and left. Consultants say that the woman owned all of the stored food, the mats making up the tipi, the tipi poles, her economic implements, all prepared skins, her clothes, and a few horses. The man had fewer categories of goods: his weapons, fishing implements, clothes, and horses made up his entire property. Young children remained with the mother. Older children could choose between the parents. Marriage in the Plateau, as among other American Indians, was not heavily invested (Albers 1989:137).

The main cause of divorce was said to be the love affair of one of the spouses, in which case remarriage was immediate for at least one individual. Less often, domestic violence or in recent years the alcoholism of one of the spouses led to divorce.

Divorce did not result in economic deprivation for either party. Both genders had the choice of joining the household of their consanguineal relatives or living independently. A woman could easily support herself and her children with the food she gathered and trade some of it for meat and fish (Ray 1932:143). A man may have been somewhat less independent; for while he also could trade meat and fish for vegetal foods, he probably could not have set up a household without a woman's labor to build a dwelling, get firewood, cook, dry food, and so forth. He most likely moved in with some member of his extended family.

If a man left his wife and she was unwilling to part, she had the option to pursue him. An early account describes how a white settler tried to leave his Indian wife and failed. She followed him wherever he went, camped outside his quarters, and asked others to intercede for her with him. Her husband finally yielded and took her back (McKee n.d., vol. 2:564–65).

Women made teas or medicines to regulate family size by boiling various parts of plants. They had plants for conception, contraception, and abortion. Children were desired, but the value of spacing children was recognized. The role that lactation plays in delaying conception was also recognized.

So far I have referred only to two genders, but there may have been as many as four in the past. Terms for male and female versions of homosexuality occur in the Sanpoil language (Ray 1932:148) and may refer to two kinds of berdaches. A berdache assumes a change in sexual status and role (Angelino and Shedd 1955:125). Plateau berdaches were of either biological sex; but little is known about them today, though such individuals linger in the memory of living elders. I was told that gender reversals were sometimes opposed by the family, perhaps due to Christian influence, but opposition was often ineffective. Berdaches were rare but apparently known in every generation until missionaries forbade the practice.

Turney-High (1937:85) mentions male but no female berdaches among the Flathead. A male berdache who lived in missionary times was remembered by some Idaho Nez Perce whom I interviewed in 1965, and the memory of such people is recalled on the Colville Reservation as well. Female berdaches are referred to by Teit (1906:267), suggesting that the numbers of male and female berdaches may have been roughly equal.

Whether individuals of both sexes were viewed as a third gender or an additional two genders was not researched at the time of this study.

Claude Schaeffer (1965) traces the career of Qanqon, a Kutenai berdache born female, in fur trade accounts. Qanqon was a shaman, prophet, warrior, courier, and guide: functions that Schaeffer believes were unheard of among Plateau women. A conventional Plateau woman could perform all of these roles without having to become a berdache, however. Any woman with ability given by a guardian spirit could be a prophet, shaman, or warrior. Since we know that women were traders and interpreters, one serving as courier or guide does not seem unusual. Schaeffer explains the Kutenai berdache's unusual status due to her large size and supposed inability to attract men. Yet he notes that she was married at least once before assuming male status (1965:195, 196). The fact that any Plateau woman could perform all of the roles ascribed to this berdache without abandoning her female status and yet could choose to become a berdache indicates the scope of the autonomy available to individuals of either sex in traditional Plateau society.

Seven examples of berdaches are mentioned in the field notes of Walters (n.d.), unfortunately without much explanation. These included three men who dressed like women and performed female tasks and four women who dressed like men. One of these women was persuaded to give up the berdache status by her relatives when she was about thirty-five. She married and bore children. One surmises that this persuasion to change was effective due to Euro-American influence. These examples of berdaches definitely predate 1938 (when Walters published her formal article) and may actually refer to the generations before 1938.

The presence of berdaches in any culture is an example of the cultural construction of gender (Albers 1989:134): in other words, gender is defined by the culture in question. That this cultural phenomenon occurred in the past among the eleven tribes of the Colville Reservation and other Plateau tribes is interpreted here as an expression of domestic autonomy, since the behavior was self-directed and a choice was made to avoid a conventional marriage. Berdaches are generally excluded from this account of gender equality due to a lack of data, not because they are irrelevant to such an account.

Berdaches, in my view, fall into the same category as other Plateau customs that allow a wide latitude in the definition of self, of "personhood"

(Albers 1989:135). A typical Plateau person acquired at least three names in the course of his or her lifetime. If one's public name seemed inappropriate to one's personality, it was changed (Ackerman 1994:301–2). A person also had latitude in the choice of residence and tribal affiliation. The berdache institution presented an opportunity to change even one's gender. These options available to individuals to change personal identity may have contributed to overall societal stability.

What of interpersonal relationships between husband and wife? Some individuals commented:

> Women made decisions independently. A boy about to get married was advised by his male relatives, "You can't tie a wife down. She can travel, go to town. It is best not to try to control her."

> My husband and I were mates [pals]. When I went huckleberrying for a week, he'd wonder where I was.

> Men and women were not physically close in the past. They were both busy with their separate work, and at home, and the whole extended family was there too.

These remarks indicate the extensive independence that women exercised and the lack of accountability that each marriage partner owed to the other. Personal relationships between marriage partners might have been less intense in the Plateau extended family than would be expected in a Euro-American nuclear family.

Superior prestige was not accorded to a male in this culture. Some believe that all societies award prestige only to socially dominant males (Ortner and Whitehead 1981:12). I take strong exception to the notion that in all cultures men and their roles are valued more highly and have more prestige (Ortner and Whitehead 1981:16). This is not true anywhere in the Plateau and probably not in the Subarctic.

Table 4 summarizes the gender roles in the domestic sphere in the traditional culture. Males appeared to have somewhat more power over women due to the use of violence against wives by some men, though a few women also engaged in this behavior. This was counterbalanced by the explicit disapproval of family violence by the community and the earnest advice given to a young man before marriage to refrain from such behavior. A young man was also counseled that he must not try to control his wife, humiliate her in public, or object to her traveling about to trade, gather, and visit. A wife did not automatically do what her husband wished, though she too was supposed to support his dignity in public. Publicly and privately, a woman had a voice, influence, and rights. She acquired wealth she alone possessed. Her autonomy could be expressed by going through many marriages and divorces. A mechanism making this independence possible for either gender was a person's greater loyalty to his or her non-unilinear descent group, with loyalty to the spouse coming second. This was revealed by the somewhat greater sorrow some individuals expressed when speaking of the death of parents as compared to the death of a spouse. Such an attitude is comprehensible in a society in which the extended family or descent group was so important and in which a spouse did not replace the relationship shared with parents and siblings.

THE POLITICAL SPHERE

Power in the Political Sphere

Political power in the Plateau consisted of exerting influence in decision-making. We have seen that individuals especially skilled in some economic activity had more political influence than others but that this political influence was not restricted to one gender. Sometimes a preferred course of action was conveyed by an individual through oratory while in assembly or council, with the purpose of influencing opinion among fellow village members and the chief. At other times, the opinion of a well-respected person of either gender was solicited by the chief or other village members. This kind of influence was open to anybody in the group who met the other criteria leading to respect.

Chief's wives appeared to have special influence in the political process. Although some individuals denied that a chief's wife or wives routinely advised the chief on political problems, most consultants insisted that all wives gave advice to their husbands as a matter of course, and chiefs' wives were no different. The role of chiefs' wives as advisers was apparently not an institutionalized pattern and thus involved power. The style of advice was said to range from diffidence to a vociferous partisanship in pressing a viewpoint. It was considered natural within a stable marriage for a chief to discuss a problem with his older wife and elicit comment and opinion.

TABLE 4
The Domestic Sphere: Traditional Culture

MEN	WOMEN

POWER

spouses influence each other

no institutionalization of power (dominance) in couple's relationship

polygny	no polyandry

elopements a method to defy authority

meals served to men first

wife beating	easy divorce
rape	punishment of rapist by women

great age disparity in married couple allows older spouse more influence

AUTHORITY

equal authority in discipline of children

equal authority in arranging marriages for children

cement marriage agreement	women formalize marriage through "marriage trade"

authority of kin in levirate and sororate imposed on both genders

man had right to kill wife's lover	woman had right to beat husband's lover; right of divorce

AUTONOMY

right to select second and subsequent marriage partners

equal right of divorce, no economic deprivation

control of family size

berdaches of both sexes

A chief's daughter or sister was also expected to advise the chief and influence other village members as well, if she had the "right kind of personality." One consultant made her point by noting that she could not understand why there was criticism of Rosalynn Carter because she was a source of advice to her husband, President Jimmy Carter. She would want to know what kind of wife any presidential candidate had because the wife would automatically be an adviser.

Families or individuals had the right to leave a village if they were dissatisfied or unhappy with a chief; but that was not usually viewed as a political exercise of power, and most of the time it was not.

Authority in the Political Sphere

Political authority was vested in the chief and the assembly. The assembly, which consisted of all adults in the community, elected the chief in most Plateau groups. "Loose heredity" (Ray 1939:19) narrowed the field of candidates to the chief's family among many tribes; and strict heredity obviated the necessity of an election in other groups, such as the Moses Columbia.

In addition to the chief, political officers included the chief's spokesman and herald. The spokesman office occurred in the south and central Plateau: his function was to repeat the chief's words in a loud voice whenever the chief spoke publicly. The herald was a messenger who rode or walked around the village or camp shouting out the chief's advice or decisions. Both of these officers were appointed by the chief. In much of the Plateau, the two offices were performed by the same individual (Ray 1939:24).

The Sanpoil chief was assisted by a subchief and a lasher, who administered punishment after a judgment was passed (Ray 1932:111, 113). The assembly chose the Salmon Chief (Ray 1932:69), always a male so far as we know, from among those with spiritual power for salmon (though some women also had salmon power, as noted above). Hunting Leaders were chosen by consensus (Ray 1932:77–78) as were Gathering Leaders, according to consultants. It should be noted that even the chief and Salmon Chief were chosen by consensus: this was the Plateau election style.

Ray reports that women were eligible for the office of chief in a few Plateau groups: the Southern Okanogan, Lakes, and possibly the Coeur d'Alene. Female chiefs were also recorded for the Shuswap, Lower Thompson, and Carrier, but they inherited the office from a father, in the absence of a brother, and passed the office to their male descendants to perpetuate the line (Ray 1939:24). Presumably the women exercised all the usual functions of a chief while they held the office.

Walters (1938:95–96) also reports elected female chiefs, not only among the Southern Okanogan but also among the Methow and Chelan groups, which are now numbered among the Colville Confederated Tribes. Her description of female chiefs, however, indicates that they were not the head political officer of these groups but instead had important advisory and judicial functions. These women were called *sku'malt*, "a woman of great authority." The sku'malt was formally elected by the group and was always a consanguineal relative of the chief. When she died, the group chose another female relative of the chief to occupy the office. Although Walters records the name of several of these female chiefs, she presents no detailed description of their functions, perhaps because their functions were not recalled by her consultants. Female as well as male chiefs were presented with food by village residents to be kept as emergency reserves for anyone needing them.

Some variation in function between groups occurred in the office of the sku'malt (Walters 1938:96). In one Southern Okanogan band, consultants say the sku'malt served as an adviser or judge in cases of murder, feud, or other such disruptive crisis. Walters was told that in two other Southern Okanogan bands the sku'malt was the only chief the band had, but she found that this information contradicted the chiefly genealogies she had collected. Among the Coeur d'Alene, women called *sq'o'ma'lt* (a variation of sku'malt) were simply highly respected women whose opinions were valued—they held no office like that of the Southern Okanogan sku'malt. The functions of the Methow and Chelan female chiefs were apparently similar to those of the Southern Okanogan advisers (Walters 1938:97).

My field data on the sku'malt's functions are also slight, as very few contemporary consultants (1980) remember the office. Those who do remember the sku'malt in the Southern Okanogan and Methow tribes state that the woman obtained the office through election by the assembly. She was always related to the chief and was required to have intelligence and wisdom. Further, she was expected to have spirit power "of a special kind" to perform the role. Like other leaders, she characteristically refrained from being overly critical of other people.

Consultants confirmed that the main function of the sku'malt was judicial, although only a few of the cases she judged were recalled by elders. In one of these cases, the sku'malt awarded a man's property to the wife and children he abandoned so that he could not return someday to claim it. This incident occurred during reservation times, and the property referred to may have been land or a permanent house. She also judged "murder cases," possibly the settlement of feuds. The sku'malt served as an adviser on political affairs when requested to do so and also acted as Gathering Leader in the first spring gathering of roots and berries for the First Foods Ceremonies.

A number of problems are implicit in the data derived both from the literature and from consultants. The sku'malt's role did not appear in every Plateau tribe, but the role of the Gathering Leader did. The only Gathering Leader I was able to interview on the Colville Reservation in 1980 was a Nez Perce whose public function was only as a Gathering Leader, since the Nez Perce do not have a sku'malt.

Another problem is evident when the advisory and judicial roles of the sku'malt are considered, for these were chiefly functions. The judicial role was the most important function of a chief (Ray 1939:22). If a woman wielded judicial authority among the Southern Okanogan, Methow, and Chelan, she must have been equal to the male chief in importance. Thus, it seems unlikely that the sku'malt's role was relatively unimportant (Walters 1938:97), even though her role is largely forgotten today. It is possible that Euro-American officials were influential in the gradual demise of this role, since consultants say that the federal government eventually assigned all judicial functions to the male chiefs.

The possibility of women serving as chiefs in the same way as males (Ray 1939:24) cannot be dismissed lightly, despite scant confirmation in the field. Only one elder, in her nineties at the time I interviewed her in 1979, remembered a woman who served as a political village chief. The narrator was a descendant of the people she talked about (five generations before her), and the story was part of her descent group's history. The female chief was a Chelan named Kwy-hin-meetkw, who filled the office after her husband died, and it was expected that she would occupy it only until her son was validated as the new chief. Before validation could take place, her son was killed in a snowslide while on a hunting trip. Her son's loss so infuriated Kwy-hin-meetkw that she blamed her daughter-in-law for his death, with the rationale that he died while trying to provide meat for his wife. The mother, in her role as acting chief, removed herself and her people from the area (this was in winter), leaving the daughter-in-law and her three small children to starve.

The daughter-in-law and her children suffered severely from the cold as well as the lack of food. A sympathizer among the villagers, however, secretly left them provisions. These kept most of them alive, but the food was inadequate. One of the boys did not survive. The rest of the family was saved from starvation only by the same sympathetic village member, who returned secretly and transported them to the woman's relatives in another community. This young woman later married her deceased husband's cousin in the levirate, and her surviving son succeeded his grandmother as chief of the Chelan after he became an adult.

The political aspects of this narrative include the following points: (1) a wife could succeed the chief and perform all the functions of a chief; (2) she could literally wield the power of life and death in what was perhaps a temporary office; (3) the other band members could say nothing about abandoning a woman and children in winter; and (4) she was succeeded by the grandson she tried to kill. Other questions of a nonpolitical nature include her seeming irrationality in blaming her daughter-in-law for the son's death and the condemnation of her own grandchildren to death. Several individuals, descendants of the surviving daughter, were not able to elaborate further on the points raised above, as this occurrence took place five generations before. The important point of the history for this study is that a woman acting as chief wielded all the powers of a real chief. Did she use her temporary position as a means to seize permanent power, or did she hold that position by right? Chelan consultants insist that women were never chiefs except when substituting for a deceased husband. Kwy-hin-meetkw must have served as chief of the Chelan for at least fifteen to twenty years before her grandson succeeded her, however, because he was a young child at the time of the historical incident related above. Thus, dismissing the idea of female chiefs in some Plateau tribes is overhasty, and Ray's (1939:24) remark that female political chiefs occurred at least among the Lakes, Southern Okanogan, and perhaps Coeur d'Alene is likely to be correct. In fact, in 1994 a consultant mentioned in passing the name of the female Lakes chief that was referred to by Ray, but I was not able to write it down. More fieldwork on this point may be productive.

Supporting the above argument is the story of a supernatural entity called Scomalt in Okanogan folklore. This woman governed an island and had godlike aspects, since she could create what she liked. She punished the people of her island for wickedness and drove them to the mainland, where they became the ancestors of all Indians (Ross 1986:273–74).

Female chiefs are not unusual in North America. In the Northeast alone, female chiefs and other high female officials occurred among the tribes of

Massachusetts and Rhode Island (Salwen 1978:167), the Iroquois (Fenton 1978:315), the Shawnee (Callender 1978d:627–28), the Sauk (Callender 1978c:650), the Kickapoo (Callender, Pope, and Pope 1978:661), the Miami (Callender 1978b:685), and in the Great Lakes area (Callender 1978a:617, 618). They are mentioned among a South American tribe, the Mehinaku (Gregor 1977:164). The memory of other female leaders persists in the Plateau. These include the Gathering Leaders described above, who are analogous to the Hunting and Fishing Leaders of the men.

Chief's wives who served as political leaders when necessary are well remembered today. Kanitsa, mother of Chief Moses of the Columbia, often served as leader in place of Chief Shooktalkoosum, her husband, who was gone for long periods fighting the Blackfeet on the Plains. Kanitsa's authority was derived from her position as head wife in the chief's household, but since she was a prominent chief's daughter as well her prestige was enhanced within the household and the tribe (Ray 1960:780). The chief's head wife had no title despite her actual and potential authority.

A chief was often polygynous because of the large amount of food needed by his household, as he had obligations to feed the entire village during assemblies, funerals, and feasts. Consequently, plural wives were an advantage in the collection and preservation of large amounts of food necessary for these events.

The chief's widow, presumably the first wife, managed political affairs in at least the Southern Okanogan and Sanpoil tribes during the year of mourning observed for the death of a chief. At the end of the year, the widow and/or daughter nominated the chief's successor. It was said that their right to nominate the successor was absolute. The assembly, however, could choose another person if it wished.

The Columbia tribe ordinarily had no need to nominate and elect a chief's successor since they had a system of strict inheritance. The person in line for the succession was obvious, and he simply took charge. In recent years, however, no obvious successor to the office was evident. Instead, two direct female descendants of the deceased chief "named" (appointed) the successor on at least two occasions. Others said that the assembly had to confirm the women's choice. It is possible that this pattern of female nomination and assembly confirmation is implicit in Plateau culture and may be an older pattern than that of strict inheritance among the Columbia. In 1987 I interviewed a Coeur d'Alene chief's daughter who had "nominated" the next chief after her father died. The successor was not a close relative, so he was not an obvious candidate for the office; but she judged him to be a talented man with much needed leadership qualities. The members of the tribe were consulted to confirm her choice, and they accepted. The interesting point for this study is the prominent role women played in the selection of a chief in most Plateau groups, whether the selection could be defined as a nomination or an actual appointment. Women thus performed a crucial role in the chiefly succession.

The political authority and initiative of women is also implicit in the oral history related to me of a woman who sought to make peace between an Okanogan band and a Shuswap group. Raids between the two groups were becoming frequent and bloody, so she decided to undertake a peace-making mission. She asked the chief, her uncle (classificatory father), to assemble the people so she could appeal to them for gifts to present to the Shuswap to win them over to peace. She successfully persuaded the assembly to support her plan. Then, accompanied by another uncle, she entered the Shuswap camp at great risk. She presented her proposal of peace to the Shuswap, who accepted it along with her gifts. They gave her gifts in turn to present to her people when she returned home, thus sealing the peace.

Intelligent women with a facility for languages were sometimes asked to act as spokeswomen for their villages during negotiations with other groups.

Autonomy in the Political Sphere

Political autonomy is expressed in Plateau culture by sitting in council or assembly, speaking publicly, and voting (by consensus). According to consultants, access of the genders to these activities varied from one area to the next. The Columbia, Wenatchi, Chelan, and Entiat tribes, now all resident on the Colville Reservation, were members of the Columbia Confederacy, one of two confederacies in the Plateau Culture Area. Some women from these four groups said that women did not sit in assembly or council, but others emphatically contradicted this. One elder commented that the assembly consisted only of men when war was being discussed, since war was their province. They, after all, did the dying, she noted. The Wenatchi assembly in the past did consist of both genders, but consultants say that the Entiat and Chelan women were somewhat less politically active than women to the east. My interpretation of this is that women in all the tribes traditionally participated in the assembly, but this may have changed quickly in some areas in contact times. Since the Moses Columbia and Chelan tribes have produced a number of unusually distinguished female leaders in recent history and in contemporary times, including the famous Lucy Covington (Moses Columbia) and Shirley Palmer (Moses Columbia and Chelan), it seems reasonable to conclude that their political activism is a survival of the aboriginal period in which women had equal access to the political process.

In the other Colville Reservation tribes—the Methow, Southern Okanogan, Sanpoil, Nespelem, and probably the Lakes and Colville—both men and women spoke publicly and sat in the assembly. Again, consultants disagreed on details. Most said that though women were present at the assemblies they did not speak much, while others said women spoke freely. Sometimes a woman who did not enjoy speaking publicly had her husband present her opinion, which might differ from his own.

Only the Nez Perce definitely excluded women from council; but they also excluded most men, as councils were made up only of prominent warriors. Both genders, however, lobbied the council members as a right; consequently, all opinions were heard. The Nez Perce were far more involved in hostilities with Plains peoples than most Plateau tribes, and much of their political action must have been concerned with warfare. As war excludes most women, it is not unreasonable that women were excluded from council along with those men who were not active or successful warriors. It should be noted that women on the Nez Perce Reservation in Idaho are often elected to the tribal governing body today.

In those instances in which women had the right to speak in council but rarely did so, some inhibiting factor may have been operating. Perhaps the female consultants who insisted that women habitually spoke publicly in the past were married and living within their own natal communities, in contrast to politically reticent women who may have moved into their husbands' communities as adults. In other words, women living with affinal kin might feel inhibited about making public speeches. This possibility was discussed with consultants and rejected by them. After consideration, they decided that the factor of *age* was the source of reticence, and it applied to both genders. Only the elders of both genders made speeches in assembly. Young people did not presume to speak, as they lacked the necessary experience and oratorical skills. Consultants mentioned a number of contemporary politically active elders of both genders who never spoke publicly as young people.

In contrast to female public speaking, consultant opinion on the subject of voting was unanimous. Both genders voted, and husband and wife were independent in casting a vote in assembly. They did not always agree with each other on particular issues.

Before Plateau people were restricted to reservations, a few women participated in warfare on a voluntary basis, sometimes in defense. While under siege from the Assiniboine, a Flathead woman ran out of a besieged tent with a pistol and shot an attacker dead (Teit 1930:366). Southern Okanogan women and children retired behind barricades during raids on the village. If an enemy approached too closely, a woman "with much power" (spiritual) seized weapons and fought even if menstruating. Her guardian spirit protected her and made her strong. Under such circumstances, a woman could touch weapons and retain the enemy weapons she had captured (Walters 1938:80).

Traditions of warrior women were collected in 1980 on the Colville Reservation. Emily Peone, a granddaughter of the great Chief Moses of the Moses-Columbia, narrated:

> Women fought in battles; went out with war parties. My mother's father took his younger wife along. She dressed herself in her finest clothes so that if she died, she would be wearing her funeral clothes; they wouldn't have to dress her. Women used a club on enemies, and lances too. They took stuff along to dress wounds. They helped the wounded and rescued men in trouble. Chief Moses was always noticeable by his fine clothes in battle. So his sister-in-law saw him fall in the fighting. She galloped to him and chased away his attacker. Then she fixed his wound. These were brave women. The warriors on the other side would kill women.

The women who rode out with raiding parties were distinguished from other women only by their great physical courage: they had no unusual social status. Consultants did not recall where they obtained their weapons and shields, but they carried them. Since female combatants were as likely to be killed or captured as a male, they were prepared to fight. Most women saw their function as helping the wounded and rescuing men in danger, as in the narrative above. In the course of these activities, however, they did not hesitate to kill opposing warriors if the opportunity arose. A few women participated as warriors completely, as recorded by early missionaries in the area (Point 1967:158). Such full female warriors were not remembered on the Colville Reservation, but a female Nez Perce from Idaho participated in the war against the Euro-Americans. She was able to do so over the objections of her husband and two young children (Gidley 1979:90), indicating the extent of the autonomy that Plateau women exercised.

The factors relevant to gender status for the political sphere are abstracted in table 5. In the political sphere men and women have mostly complementary access to authority and identical access to power and autonomy.

THE RELIGIOUS SPHERE

Power in the Religious Sphere

Power in the traditional Plateau religion involved the use of sorcery, which may be defined as an antisocial application of spiritual power. The religious abilities given by guardian spirits to any shaman could be perverted to sorcerous uses. Consequently, all shamans were capable of sorcery; whether they practiced it or not depended very much on the person. Some shamans adamantly refused to use their religious ability in a destructive manner, no matter what the provocation. Others had a fearful reputation of using sorcery against other people, including children, for minor accidental offenses or for no obvious reason at all.

Since almost all people had guardian spirit ability of some kind in the past ("all oldtimers knew something"), they had influence on others through their particular talent. A woman endowed with hunting ability given by her guardian spirit, for instance, would inform a hunting party where animals might be found, and her advice was always followed by the Hunting Leader. In general, when anyone with a spiritual talent became well known for his or her ability, people in need of services sought that individual out, increasing his or her influence.

Authority in the Religious Sphere

Authority was inherent in the roles of shamans (healers) and prophets, the latter being a particular type of shaman. Prophets were able to make

TABLE 5

The Political Sphere: Traditional Culture

MEN	WOMEN
POWER	
superior economic skills equaled political influence (both genders)	
	wives, other female relatives advised chief
AUTHORITY	
assemblies made up of both genders	
chief, head political officer	possibly chief, head political officer in past
	sku'malt—judicial and advisory functions: "female chief"
subchief, herald, spokesman	
Hunting, fishing Leaders	Gathering Leaders
	chief's wife substituted as chief when husband away
only males became chiefs in most tribes	chief's widow or daughter nominated successor; in some tribes, she became temporary chief
	political roles: peacemaker, negotiator, spokespersons to other groups
AUTONOMY	
both genders spoke and voted in assembly	
a married couple's votes did not need to coincide	
warriors	

predictions, particularly of disastrous occurrences such as earthquakes. One prediction related to me in several anecdotes and credited to different individuals concerned the arrival of white people in the country, with a description of the peculiar kind of clothing they would wear (red flannel). The prophets were able to show someone what the red flannel looked like. Numerous female as well as male prophets existed, but the proportion of each cannot be ascertained at this late date.

The Salmon Chiefs, Food Gathering Leaders, and Hunting Leaders are discussed in the economic section because of their economic importance, but a crucial aspect of their roles involved the performance of religious rites. The rendering of these rituals endowed them with religious authority, which they retained for life.

Those with shamanic powers had the authority to interpret the visions of others during the Guardian Spirit Dance. Their healing abilities also gave them authority, since their advice was followed during the course of an illness.

Ray (1932:200) reports that Sanpoil and Nespelem male shamans outnumbered female shamans considerably and that this situation was general throughout the Plateau (Ray 1939:93). More men than women shamans occurred among the Wenatchi, according to consultants, but they were definitely equal in ability. Among the Methow, Nez Perce, Okanogan, and perhaps Lakes tribes, consultants report that male and female shamans occurred in equal numbers and were equal in ability.

Autonomy in the Religious Sphere

Religious autonomy was expressed in the traditional culture by the exercise of spiritual powers awarded by a guardian spirit. The search for guardian spirits was not always an autonomous act by a young person, who was often coerced by elders to undertake the quest for his or her own good. Youngsters sometimes balked. In later times some of them refused to undertake a quest altogether. Once a guardian spirit was acquired, however, the exercise of spiritual talents was autonomous.

Descriptions of the spirit quest are similar today to those recorded in the literature. Almost everyone of both genders acquired guardian spirits in the past in the Entiat, Chelan, Nez Perce, Wenatchi, Columbia, Okanogan, and Methow groups. No information was acquired on this point for the Lakes and Colville tribes. Sanpoil and Nespelem girls almost universally acquired spirit power in the past, despite a previous report stating that only 20 to 30 percent of these girls did so, compared to 100 percent of the boys (Ray 1932:182). Several individuals commented that all girls as well as boys were sent on explicit spirit quests.

It is possible to get by without a spirit, but having one does a lot for a person. Most people did get spirits in the past, boys and girls both. A person without a spirit is as good as a person with spirits, but it is better when you have one. (Nez Perce)

Boys and girls both found spirits. Women need one for gambling, digging, trade. Men need spirits to hunt, gamble, have courage, fix wounds. (Methow)

All boys and girls got spirits. They used to go up Badger Mountain and the spirits would talk to them. Then they became good camas diggers and hunters. My mother was ten or eleven when she got her spirit. (Wenatchi)

Girls had to have the chance to get a spirit since having one provided such great benefits. Everyone knew something in the old days. One could not be a very good hunter or camas digger without spiritual power, but could only get by. (Southern Okanogan)

These remarks are supported by the Flathead record that spirit power was as necessary for girls as for boys (Turney-High 1937:27).

Other spiritual talents were encouraged. Eating a meadowlark egg would endow a young child with oratorical skills. This political talent was seen as suitable for either gender and in fact was the power or one of the powers of a recently deceased female political leader.

A woman exercised her religious abilities ("power") completely independently of her husband and vice versa. If a woman was a shaman, her husband could neither influence her use of her spiritual abilities nor prevent her from using them.

A successful gambler was highly respected in Plateau culture and was awarded this ability by a guardian spirit. Men and women gamblers were equal in numbers and ability in traditional times; but they gambled separately, since the outcome of gambling contests could be skewed by menstruating women in their favor.

Religious factors regarding gender equality are summarized in table 6, which demonstrates that men and women had identical, not complementary, rights in the religious sphere. As religion was and is the most cherished part of Plateau culture, thus qualifying it as a central institution (Schlegel 1977b:18), the identical access of both men and women to this sphere is particularly significant in an evaluation of gender status.

TABLE 6

The Religious Sphere: Traditional Culture

MEN	WOMEN

POWER

sorcerers of both genders

both genders acquired guardian spirits

AUTHORITY

prophets of both genders

resource leaders (fishing, gathering, hunting)

in some tribes, shamans of both genders equal in number
unequal in others

shamans of both genders equal in power

AUTONOMY

exercise of spiritual gifts

children of both genders sent on spirit quests

independent use of spiritual ability

gamblers: equal in number and talent

CONCLUSIONS

It seems certain that gender equality did indeed exist in traditional Plateau culture (see tables 3 to 6). Some rights were balanced or complementary, while others were identical for both genders. Traditional Plateau culture illustrates that equality can occur when men and women do not have exactly the same rights. Significantly, complementary rights also allow for gender equality.

Many North American cultures are egalitarian in character and are generally characterized by complementarity between men and women (Klein and Ackerman 1995). Complementarity appears to prevail among the Iroquois, Tlingit, Navajo, and Ojibwa, as well as others. Additional characteristics of the gender system in North American tribes include the rarity of dominance of one spouse over the other and mutual respect between spouses (Albers 1989:137).

Gender equality is also found outside of North America, even in the generally male dominant area of New Guinea. A recent description of such a society on the island of Vanatinai off the coast of New Guinea finds that they are matrilineal and bilocal: a married couple takes turns living with each family (Lepowsky 1993:47). Maria Lepowsky believes that the existence of gender equality is derived from women's central position in the web of kinship, the ownership of land in this horticultural society, and control over the fruits of their labor. Along with men, they have access to prestige and influence as well as wealth (Lepowsky 1993:72). It is significant that gender equality can exist in other than foraging societies, for it can occur in an industrial society (see chapter 6).

Traditional plateau dwelling. Lucullus Virgil McWhorter Collection.

Sweat house frame. Lucullus Virgil McWhorter Collection.

Colville Indians, Okanogan, Washington, ca. 1910. The man on the left is Twit-mich or "Big Jim." Holding a blanket is Charley Leo, a rancher. On his left is Suzanne Leo, a relative (not his wife), who was a popular medicine woman. The identity of the two other men is unknown. Frank S. Matsura Collection.

Plateau weir or fish trap, Chiliwhist River, 1911. The weirs were designed to capture salmon (in this case, the fall run). Weirs were constructed of willow strips and bark lashings to form a net wall, held in place by log tripods. Frank S. Matsura Collection.

Chiliwhist Jim, ca. 1910. Chiliwhist Jim (La-ka-kin) was a Methow medicine man and prosperous rancher from the town of Malott, Washington. The pattern on his vest probably identified him as part of his unilinear descent group or extended family. Frank S. Matsura Collection.

Children on swings, ca. 1905. Children playing on swings by the roadside, with their schoolhouse in the background. Frank Fuller Avery Collection.

Indian girls, ca. 1905. Two Colville Reservation girls beside an apple tree.
Frank Fuller Avery Collection.

Nellie Friedlander and granddaughter Emily, 1914. There are many Friedlander descendants on the Colville Reservation today. Emily was one of the
most prominent: she was greatly respected and very knowledgeable about her
culture. She died recently at an advanced age. Frank Fuller Avery Collection.

Emily Friedlander Peone (left), Lucy Friedlander Covington, possibly George Friedlander, and unidentified child, 1914. Lucy Covington became one of the most prominent political leaders of her generation. She, among others, was instrumental in saving the reservation from termination. Frank Fuller Avery Collection.

Group of Colville Reservation women playing the stick game near Nespelem, Washington. The date is unknown but is probably about 1910, because the group is entirely composed of women. Soon after that date, men and women were intermixed on the teams. Lucullus Virgil McWhorter Collection.

CHAPTER 5

The Formation of the Reservation and the Effects of Forced Acculturation on Gender Status

This chapter describes the period when the people were confined to the reservation and farming became a major occupation. The traditional culture did not disappear because the people took up farming and were exposed to other portions of Euro-American culture. It persisted, but with an overlay of changes originating from outside.

PRE-RESERVATION HISTORY

Governor Isaac Stevens made plans to meet the Plateau Indian tribes at Walla Walla in 1855 with the intention of creating reservations for the indigenous people and then making the rest of the land available to white settlers. The year before the Walla Walla Council met, many of the Plateau chiefs assembled in the Grande Ronde Valley to devise a strategy to deal with his demands. They intended to mark the boundaries of the various tribes and ask Stevens to make the land inside these lines into reservations for their people. The consequence would be that no lands would be left for sale to the Euro-Americans, and Stevens's objective would fail (Anastasio 1972). Governor Stevens prevailed on some of the Plateau tribes to sign the treaties anyway (see chapter 1). A feeling of betrayal ensued, and wars soon followed the unfair treaties. The Colville, Lakes, Sanpoil, Nespelem,

Okanogan, and other Indians in northeast Washington did not attend the Walla Walla Council. Stevens intended to meet with them later and negotiate for their land, but the breakout of the Yakama War intervened. Consequently, these groups never agreed to sell land to the United States government, and the title to their lands was never extinguished by treaties (Bloodworth 1959:24–25).

This situation continued until 1862. In that year the superintendent of Indian affairs for Washington Territory pointed out that these tribes had signed no treaty and that the discovery of gold had made it mandatory to do so. In 1864 he recommended that an agent appointed for the tribes be located at Fort Colville. Fort Colville at this time was no longer a post of the Hudson's Bay Company, having become a military fort of the United States government. The commanding officer at Fort Colville had been acting as unofficial Indian agent before this time (Bloodworth 1959:28).

CREATION OF THE COLVILLE RESERVATION

In 1865 George Paige of the Indian Bureau was appointed as Indian agent and sent to Fort Colville. Paige observed the situation of the Colville and Okanogan Indians and visited all the tribes under his jurisdiction by 1868. Some Indians were farming in the Colville Valley, he noted, but most continued to follow their traditional annual round (Bloodworth 1959:28).

In 1867 C. W. King, the farmer in charge at Fort Colville after the death of Paige, reported to Brevet Colonel Ross, superintendent of Washington Territory, that the country was being rapidly settled by whites and crossed by miners, with unpleasant consequences. The Indians tilled the soil in season, but four-fifths of their support was still derived from the salmon fisheries. He complained to the colonel about the liquor trade with the Indians (Bloodworth 1959:30).

On April 9, 1872, President Grant created the Colville Indian Reservation by executive order, which included the nontreaty bands: the Methow, Okanogan, Sanpoil, Lakes, Colville, Kalispel, Spokan, Coeur d'Alene, and "scattering bands" (Rooney 1973; Royce 1899:856). The Spokan, Kalispel, and Coeur d'Alene were initially included on the Colville Reservation but were later given their own reservations (Bloodworth 1959:31; Royce 1899: 856). At this time the Colville Valley in Stevens County was counted as part of the Colville Reservation (Bloodworth

1959:34). John A. Simms was appointed the first special agent in July 1872 and served in that capacity until 1883 (Bloodworth 1959:33).

Three months later, by the executive order of July 2, 1872, the government changed the boundaries of the reservation and excluded the area east of the Columbia River occupied by the Colville, Spokan, and Pend d'Oreilles tribes (Rooney 1973) (see map 4). This is a very fertile valley, the only land really suitable for farming on the original reservation. The loss of the valley occurred through the machinations of W. P. Winans, who was the appointed "farmer in charge" to the Colville Reservation from 1869 to 1873. Winans took "the part of the settlers" and encouraged whites to settle the valley: he did not tell the Indians already farming, grazing, and foraging there that the land was part of the reservation. Consequently, the settlers encroached on Indian land without meeting any resistance or complaint (Winans n.d.).

The Indian commissioners in Washington, D.C., noted that Winans had reduced the reservation by fraudulent means. They further observed that the new reservation boundaries made farming impossible and cut the Indians off from their important fisheries on the Columbia and Spokane Rivers, including Kettle Falls. They complained that making the Indians go west of the Columbia River would either starve them or make them a perpetual burden on the government. By the time the deception was discovered, the executive order of July 2, 1872, removing the Colville Valley from the reservation, had been issued and the valley was so thickly occupied by white settlers that the government allowed matters to stand. It was said that Winans also illegally traded whiskey to the Indians and sold Indian goods in his charge, using the money for his own profit (Bloodworth 1959:36–38; Royce 1899:857).

When Winans was asked about these charges at a public meeting, he denied them and in turn accused John Simms, then superintendent of the Colville Reservation, of trying to "steal" the Colville Valley for the Indians. Winans was merely discharged from his post, while the superintendent of Washington Territory was removed from his position because he supported the Indians in this affair (Winans n.d.). Those Indians with farms already established in the Colville Valley were permitted to stay. Nevertheless, they were eventually forced to give up their farms and move onto the reservation because of intimidation and harassment by the settlers.

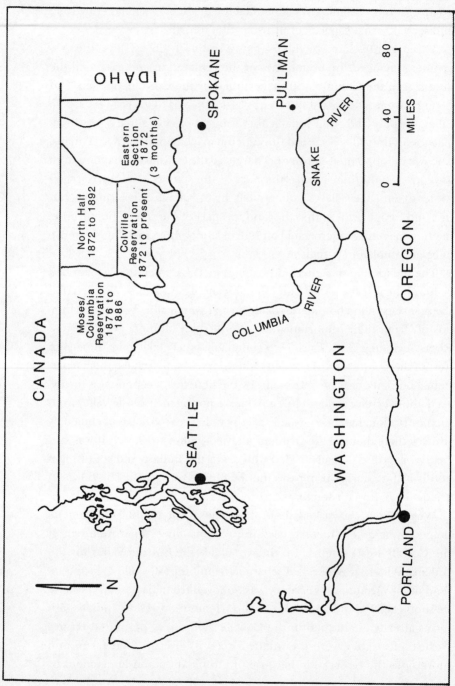

4. Boundaries of the Colville Indian Reservation from Its Inception to the Present. Adapted from Scott (1992:86) by R. E. Ackerman. Permission granted by author.

The western side of the new Colville Reservation acquired a new stretch of territory called the Columbia Reservation by an executive order of April 19, 1879. Chief Moses of the Columbia (Sinkiuse) was arrested on a charge of murdering miners in 1879 and sent to Washington, D.C. He was cleared of the murder charges, but while in Washington he pleaded for a reservation on the native land of his Columbia Confederacy tribes. Apparently he was persuasive (Ray 1960:788), since by executive orders of April 19, 1879, and March 6, 1880, two tracts of lands that included lands claimed by the Okanogan and Methow of the Columbia Confederacy were set aside as a reservation for Moses and his people (Bloodworth 1959:41–42; Royce 1899:910) (see map 4). This tract of land lasted only a little longer than the Colville Valley. In 1883 settlers claimed prior rights to part of this land. General Nelson Miles sent Moses and three other chiefs to Washington, D.C., where they signed the Moses Agreement, whereby the Indians of the Columbia Reservation would move onto the Colville Reservation or receive allotments of 640 acres for each head of family within the former reserve. Moses and the Columbia, Okanogan, and Methow moved to the reservation in 1884 (Bloodworth 1959:43; Royce 1899:910).

In June 1885 a remnant of the Nez Perce Wallowa band headed by Chief Joseph, which had been imprisoned in Oklahoma for several years, was placed on the Colville Reservation in Nespelem territory. Friction between that group and the Nez Perce (who numbered about 150) became endemic. The Nespelem resented that the Nez Perce were settled on their land without their consent (Bloodworth 1959:42). A few refugee Palus were adopted by and included in the Nez Perce band. Other Palus included the Colville Reservation in their annual round. Some finally settled there, having lost all their land in their home territory on the Snake and Palouse Rivers. Only twenty-five to thirty Palus remained in their home country by 1907 (Ray 1975).

Yenmooseetsa, the chief lieutenant of Chief Moses, was head of the Chelan. His grandson carried the same name and was also known as Long Jim. It took military intervention to force the Chelan and Entiat, two members of the Columbia Confederacy, to move to the reservation. The Entiat had joined the Chelan in their country only a few years before. When both groups were forcibly removed in 1890, a few allotments were allowed to some of the Chelan who remained on their original land. Cultus Bob and Long Jim were among those who remained (Ray 1975).

LAND PRESSURES

Other incidents demonstrated the unease and even turmoil on the reservation involving land. There was a whole series of cases dated 1883, which consisted of letters and telegrams to the commissioner of Indian affairs from settlers who had settled on land inside reservation boundaries. They begged for an exemption in their case. Some were ordered off, but some exceptions were made. For instance, the withdrawals of Indian lands requested for wagon roads and railroads were granted. Special Case 65 (1880) was devoted to mineral claims on the former Columbia Reservation. Certain citizens petitioned that mineral lands there be set aside by executive order, and the superintendent recommended in favor of this (National Archives n.d.: Special Cases 61–70). Exceptions were also made for the erection of church buildings on the Colville Reservation (National Archives n.d.: Special Case 102).

One case in Chelan County involved Long Jim and Cultus Bob, who had homesteaded land while the rest of the Chelan people had moved to the reservation. A white man, Enos Peaslee, had a dispute with Long Jim over his homestead. Peaslee received a letter dated December 2, 1890, from J. C. Lawrence, registrar of Chelan County. He notified Peaslee that his claim to land was in conflict with land claimed by Long Jim, an Indian who resided in his vicinity. A hearing was ordered to decide the correct status of the land in question (Peaslee n.d.).

Under the letterhead "Lake Chelan Lumber Company" Peaslee wrote the register office at Waterville, Washington, on January 6, 1891. He declared that he wished to reside on the land on which he had filed on July 14, 1890, but it was perilous to do so because Long Jim, a local Indian, was threatening him. Peaslee had not supposed that any Indian had a claim when he took the land; nor was the land office in Yakima aware of it. He cited threats made by Long Jim and Cultus Bob on the lives of several citizens and claimed that the local newspaper was inciting the Indians to violence. Peaslee engaged a lawyer to take the case (Peaslee n.d.). Another lawyer in Seattle that he consulted suggested that, while he could not defy the government in its support of Long Jim, he should hold on to the claim to make it clear that he left the land only under compulsion (Peaslee n.d.).

The acting agent of the Colville Reservation, Captain John Bubb, wrote Long Jim and informed him that he should not enter into negotiations with Peaslee about relinquishing his land. Peaslee in turn was advised by the registrar of Chelan County to write the commissioner of Indian affairs with his complaints. Other lawyers advised Peaslee to hold on to the land and not allow himself to be ejected by the Department of Interior; only the courts had to be obeyed (Peaslee n.d.).

Captain Bubb of the Colville Indian Agency attempted to remove the whites from the Chelan lands allotted to the Indians, according to the agreement of July 7, 1883. The secretary of the interior directed Bubb to notify the white claimants that the Indians had superior rights in this case. When Bubb tried to do so, A. W. La Cheppelle, another Euro-American with claims, filed a bill for injunction in U.S. Circuit Court. The court restrained Captain Bubb from removing the whites from the allotments of Long Jim and Cultus Bob and made the injunction perpetual. The entire matter was laid before the Department of Justice to institute an action of ejectment against La Cheppelle and others in possession of the lands allotted to these Indians under the Moses Agreement of July 7, 1883. The whites finally lost the case, and Cultus Bob and Long Jim retained their lands (Peaslee n.d.). This case was only one example of the turmoil on the reservation.

THE LOSS OF THE "NORTH HALF"

Hal J. Cole, the Indian agent, in his annual report of 1891 noted that the Colville Commission came and talked to the Indians about selling part of their reservation. This proposal came soon after the Dawes Act, also known as the General Allotment Act, was passed in the U.S. Senate in 1887. This law "gave" allotments of land to individual Indians. While the Dawes Act was well meant by those who believed that Indian allotments of land for farming would "civilize" the Indians, land speculators were significantly enthusiastic in their support. Some critics of the Dawes Act saw the objective of the law clearly as a means to seize Indian lands and open them to white settlement. This is what happened eventually. Despite the criticism, the act was passed. Each Indian was to receive 160 acres, and the unallotted land on all the reservations was to be opened to white settlement

(Debo 1970:300). The sorry results for the Sioux and other Indian tribes are narrated in Angie Debo's history (1970:304–15). Though allotments did not take place on the Colville Reservation until the early 1900s, the loss of the North Half of the reservation was a precursor.

In 1892 the proposed treaty negotiations for the land in the "North Half" of the reservation had the Indians selling 1,500,000 acres, or about half of the reservation, for $1,500,000, paid in five annual installments (Colville Indian Agency 1888–93). In his annual report that year Cole complained that, when the treaty was taken up by Congress, members of Congress questioned whether the Indians had any right to the land at all: the Indians were not given an opportunity to be heard. He pointed out that the incident had not increased the confidence of the Indians in the government, and he personally felt that he had been used. Cole further charged that white people were entering the not-yet-ceded portion of the reservation (the North Half) and seizing land before it was legally opened to white settlement. He was fearful that bloodshed might ensue (Colville Indian Agency 1888–93).

The Lakes and Okanogan tribes, however, wanted allotments to protect their land from whites. They had houses, farms, and cemeteries on their land and hoped that allotments would avert confiscation. Eighteen men and two officers in the police force kept order among the Indians and attempted to run down and eject white prospectors and trespassers who were on the reservation without authority (Colville Indian Agency 1888–93).

The North Half of the reservation was finally sold without consent of the Indians by the act of July 1, 1892. A total of 51,653 acres in the North Half was allotted to 660 Indians before it was thrown open to the public domain. The act was never ratified by Congress, however; consequently, the Indians never received the promised $1,500,000. The North Half was nevertheless opened to settlement by presidential proclamation on October 10, 1900. The affair was declared a farce by Cole, who greatly regretted taking part in the agreement. The Indians could not see how the agreement could be broken by the government while they were held to their side (Bloodworth 1959:44–46; Royce 1899:944).

The Indian allotments in the North Half did not last long. Many Indians were driven out or made so uncomfortable that they had to leave for safety's sake. This followed the same pattern as when white men had illegally taken possession of the lands on the Columbia Reservation and the Colville Valley that had been homesteaded by the Indians (Bloodworth 1959:44–46).

The diminished Colville Reservation or "South Half" was opened to mineral entry in 1898. Twelve thousand mining leases, many on reservation land, were issued in Ferry and Okanogan Counties. Instead of conducting mining operations, towns were built on placer mining claims and all kinds of businesses—except mining—were established. Saloons flourished illegally in the heart of the reservation. Most of the placer claims were fraudulent—the idea was to hold them for farming or fruit growing when the remaining reservation would be thrown open to white settlement as expected (Bloodworth 1959:46).

In 1905 the adult Indians of the Colville Reservation signed the McLaughlin Agreement, relinquishing all rights to the lands within the South Half. In return they received the promise of eighty-acre allotments to each Indian. The act of March 22, 1906, authorized the allotments for the Indians and the classifying of the remaining lands. By 1914, when the allotment rolls were closed, 2,505 Indians had been allotted 333,275 acres. The rest of the land in the South Half, totaling 422,144 acres, was opened to white settlement in 1916, with only timber and mineral lands being held back. The money from the sale of the "surplus" lands was supposed to be deposited for the benefit of the Colville Reservation Indians (Bloodworth 1959:46–47).

In the meantime another controversy came to light. After John McAdams Webster became superintendent at the Colville Indian Agency, he wrote a letter to the Department of Interior, U.S. Indian Service, dated February 6, 1905. He notified the department that he had discovered that A. M. Anderson, his predecessor, had taken over the guardianship of many Indian children who had property or moneys, and these assets were unaccounted for. The Wenatchi in particular felt that they had been swindled (Webster n.d.: Folder 4).

Details on how Anderson defrauded the Indians became public. He told women married to white men that they had lost their reservation status, but he could fix it with some money. He illegally rented Indian land to white men. There were many letters from Indians asking for protection from whites who ran cattle on their land, without result. Webster also reported that so-called placer claims were fraudulent, the purpose being to hold the land for agricultural purposes when the reservation was opened

(Webster n.d.: Folder 4). He noted in another report that miners were illegally swarming onto the reservation, hoping that in time they would be considered settlers or "old pioneers." The town of Keller was built this way and became a flourishing community (Webster n.d.: Folder 4). Indians were cheated out of their allotments. They were persuaded to sell them and never received the money. Anderson was active in this kind of deception (Webster n.d.: Folder 12).

ALLOTMENT PROBLEMS

The allotting of land was not a simple task. Special agents were appointed to complete it. One, Harry Humphrey, notified the commissioner of Indian affairs in Washington that 520 allotments would take eighteen months to complete. There was a great deal of political pressure to get the work done so whites could move in. Two assistants were hired to help Humphrey and hasten the work. One indignant letter from a would-be settler was very critical because land was being given to half-breeds and "blonds" (National Archives n.d.: Special Case 147). Inquiries were made about adoption into the tribe, so people could be eligible for land. Others claimed Indian inheritance but had only a small percentage of Indian blood. Another problem was the eligibility of Indian women married to white men to receive allotments (National Archives n.d.).

Even senators and congressmen wrote letters for their constituents, asking when the reservation would be open to settlement. On October 17, 1914, a rather sarcastic letter from members of the Spokane Chamber of Commerce was sent to the secretary of the interior, saying in regard to the reservation that they wanted to open up "good, agricultural lands in such a way that they can be utilized by several hundred families . . . the biggest work we are trying to do is to encourage the right type of agricultural development." They said there would be little agricultural development without a change of policy in classifying these lands. In an accompanying letter of the same date, they urged that the timber lands be cleared by homesteaders and opened up to agriculture: the Indians would be better off if "bone [sic] fide" settlers developed the land and served as good examples for the Indians. The Indian commissioner wrote back that he had no authority to dispose of timber lands (National Archives n.d.: Box 308).

Several letters were received regarding the case of Long Jim and Cultus Bob, saying that these Indians should be removed to the reservation because the settlers felt threatened by them. There was also a letter from a local minister, who wrote that the whole affair was being manipulated. The Indians in question, he said, were hard-working, dependable men, while those who hoped to replace them were of questionable character (National Archives n.d.: Special Cases 147).

Thirty-seven allotments had been made originally in connection with the Moses Agreement. In 1908 the Wapato Irrigation Company asked for the sale of some of these allotments for its irrigation project. The Indians did not want to sell all but only part of their land for the irrigation project, as they were interested in the water themselves. The Indian land was sold; but when the irrigation company was finally in business in 1911, it refused to deliver water to the Indian farms (National Archives n.d.: Special Case 147).

In the fall of 1913 the Colville Indian Agency moved from Fort Spokane to Nespelem (Gough 1990), where it is located today.

ADMINISTRATION OF THE RESERVATION

Accompanying these events was the daily running of the reservation, dealing with routine problems and some not so routine. Superintendent Simms, in a letter to the commissioner dated August 26, 1876, spoke well of the Catholic missionaries (he was Catholic himself). He observed that the school they ran was doing well but reiterated the need for a mill, a request he made constantly. In another letter dated 1876 he noted that the Indians had a very poor fishing season at all the fisheries, which he blamed on the large numbers of salmon caught at the mouth of the Columbia. Simms said that the Indians would need help with subsistence from the government because of the situation. He complained in a letter dated July 28, 1878, that there was a need for an agency farmer to teach the Indians farming methods so their farms would be successful. The only employees on the reservation at that time were the miller, blacksmith, physician, and interpreter. Most Indians were self-supporting. They picked up a few jobs, like cutting wood for the military in exchange for cash payments. Simms threatened at one point to resign because he could not get the support he needed for his projects to help the Indians (United States Federal Archives n.d.c: Box 35a).

In many of his letters, Simms showed himself to be a partisan of the Indians. He complained that he was forced to spend his time adjusting relations between the settlers who were moving in and the Indians. He protested that his employees were underpaid. A major problem that took up much time was the issue of cattle trespassing on Indian lands. Whites would sneak their cattle onto reservation lands without asking permission or paying fees (United States Federal Archives n.d.c: Box 35a).

Many Indians had to be defended from whites who squatted illegally on their land. Simms intervened on Chief Kamiakin's side when his homestead on Rock Lake was encroached on by whites. Simms had the whites ejected (Simms n.d.: Box 213). He said he found that the Indians adjusted to their situation and noted that many were intelligent and industrious, with successful farms. They were opposed to dissolving their tribal relations (Simms n.d.: Box 213).

School problems abounded. Children ran away from the boarding schools. Many had been coerced and taken from their families without consent and transported to the missionary schools. There were two overcrowded boarding schools on the reservation, at Colville and Tonasket. An "unrespectable woman" wanted to buy a farm near one of the schoolhouses, but this was prevented by the reservation administration. There were many allotment and homestead disputes to settle. When the Indian commissioners in Washington, D.C., asked at what point would the Indians become self-sufficient, Simms answered that they needed sufficient arable land, agricultural implements, and more schools (letter dated September 25, 1874; United States Federal Archives n.d.c: Box 35a).

By 1916 there were seven day schools on the reservation and two mission schools. Whites could attend them if they paid tuition. The day schools were small one-room structures that accommodated twenty-five to thirty students. The missions were educating one hundred children by 1916, including a kindergarten (Gough 1990).

Simms was notified by the Office of Indian Affairs that Indians were forbidden to leave the Colville Reservation without a special permit in writing from the Indian agent: "The interchange of visits between different parties or bands of Indians residing on reservations widely separated from each other is objectionable, especially in cases where the route for travel from one reserve to the other necessitates frequent contact with white settlements or mining districts." If such a permit were granted, the Indians were to have a guard of soldiers accompany them and remain with them as long as they were near white settlements (Simms n.d.: Box 213). I could not discover whether this policy was ever put in effect in the records I examined.

In a letter dated January 21, 1875, Simms complained that Indians were exploited at white stores. A flour mill near Spokane, 100 miles east of the reservation, charged Indians extra to grind their wheat. Simms argued again that a mill was needed on the reservation (Simms n.d.: Box 213).

One of the major problems throughout the history of the reservation consisted of squatters who occupied or tried to occupy Indian lands (letter dated April 30, 1889). The Indians were alarmed because whites were "swarming" into the territory. They took forcible possession of land and houses and drove the Indians away (Colville Indian Agency n.d.: Cage 2014).

Other major problems included illegal grazing and drunkenness, the latter often with lethal consequences (Colville Indian Agency n.d.: Cage 2014). Even when cattle belonging to whites were grazed legally, there were problems. One woman complained that a herd of cattle had knocked down her fences several times and destroyed her gardens. Thomas McCrosson, the agency farmer, wrote the cattle company on September 20, 1905, fining it $75.00 for damages and warning it to control its cattle or be ejected from the reservation. Many letters refer to similar problems (United States Federal Archives n.d.c: Box 331a).

In his annual report of 1888 to the commissioner of Indian affairs, Rickard D. Gwyder, the U.S. Indian agent, noted that a white farmer was hired that year to instruct the Indians in farming techniques. He further recorded that while Chief Skolaskin of the Sanpoil and Nespelem wanted to improve the lot of his people, he would not take anything from the government, though some of his people cultivated land. Skolaskin had a court and a private police force and was regarded as a prophet. The Okanogan under Chief Tonasket occupied the land between Osoyoos Lake and the Columbia River. They farmed and ranched and had a mill and school. They also had a Catholic chapel on the banks of the Okanogan River (Colville Indian Agency 1888–93). The loss of life was great at Nespelem due to epidemics of measles and scarlet fever. Gwyder recommended that there should be a hospital at Nespelem and also one among the Okanogan Indians (Colville Indian Agency 1888–93).

Other reports to the commissioner by various agents noted that the Indians were industrious, had good farms, and raised stock. Only Joseph's band was unsettled and dissatisfied (Colville Indian Agency 1888–93).

Cole urged that another physician be appointed to the reservation. Indians were dying at an alarming rate, though no epidemics broke out that year (Colville Indian Agency 1888–93). Cole reported that the Indian court tried five cases of drunkenness, three of adultery, seven of gambling, one of larceny, and one for plurality of wives. The "bigamist" was sentenced to sixty days in jail. Cole rejoiced that a great change in marriage relations had taken place in the previous two years, noting that adultery was punished with a jail term. He believed that in time adultery and bigamy would no longer be practiced on the reservation (Colville Indian Agency 1888–93).

In his annual report for 1893, Cole reported that a large majority of Indians were farming or cattle raising: only Joseph's band received subsistence from the government. The Nespelem raised more grain per capita than any other group on the Colville Reservation. They still refused to accept issues from the government, for they feared that Washington would then take their land. The Sanpoil still lived primarily by fishing and hunting, with some small-scale farming. He noted that everyone lost much stock the previous winter because the weather was very severe (Colville Indian Agency 1888–93). Despite the progress the Indians had made, Cole believed that intermarriage (with whites) and the heavy death rate would lead to extinction in a few generations. He noted that some Indians, like some whites, did well at farming and liked it; but others, like white men, preferred mining, and many liked the "wild and reckless life of a cowboy." He urged that some leeway should be allowed for these choices (Colville Indian Agency 1888–93).

The agency physician in a letter dated January 6, 1894, notified the acting U.S. Indian agent, Captain John Bubb, that smallpox had broken out in Seattle. He requested 2,000 fresh vaccine doses for the Indian population (United States Federal Archives n.d.c: Box 35a).

SOCIAL PRESSURES AND CULTURAL IMPACTS

It can be construed from the above narrative that life was hard psychologically as well as materially for the Indians. We do not hear from the Indians directly, but certain events reveal the stress. The life and career of Kolaskin (or Skolaskin) reflected the pressure of white incursion and how the culture was distorted under its influence.

Kolaskin started a cult of the general Prophet Dance type, which flourished among the Sanpoil, Spokan, and Southern Okanogan between 1870 and 1880. In his youth he had gained a guardian spirit—not a powerful one, but he was affable and well-liked (Ray 1936).

About the age of twenty, Kolaskin was taken ill. His body swelled and developed sores. His legs became flexed, and he could not straighten them. Herbal medicines and shaman's cures did not work. At the end of two years he lost consciousness, and people thought he had died. He was staying among the Spokan at the time because his parents were dead. While preparations were being made for burial, Kolaskin "came to life" and began to sing a song no one had ever heard. His pain was gone, and he declared that he had experienced a great revelation while he was dead. He began to preach that people must not drink, steal, or commit adultery and must pray to the new god before bed, on arising in the morning, and before meals. Every seventh day had to be devoted to praying and singing: no work could be done. No dancing or gambling could take place on Sunday. One should be friendly and kind to everyone. His listeners gave their allegiance to "the newly revealed god" and to Kolaskin as prophet and leader (Ray 1936).

Kolaskin made only a few converts among the Spokan before returning to the Sanpoil and taking up residence at Whitestone. He regained the ability to walk; but his knees were permanently flexed, so he walked in a stooped position with a hand on each knee. His success in gaining converts among the Sanpoil Indians was phenomenal, and he was hailed as a great messiah. Most Sanpoil were converted, and Kolaskin became chief at Whitestone. He married two women and later others; he had a total of at least five wives (Ray 1936).

Meetings were held once or twice on Sunday during which Kolaskin taught prayers and songs addressed to the deity Sweat Lodge. He repeated the story of his miraculous recovery, which eventually in the retelling became an instantaneous cure. He built a structure at Whitestone to hold the meetings. Then he received a second revelation: he saw a great flood coming in ten years. To avoid destruction, a sawmill was built near the church to produce lumber for making a boat. A male and female of every animal and bird would be included. All in the boat would be saved (Ray 1936). The lumber was cut, but the boat was never built.

In 1873 Kolaskin predicted that some kind of disaster was going to happen. A major earthquake did occur soon after, on November 22, 1873. It was preceded and followed by tremors until the following spring. This event enhanced his reputation and increased the number of his followers, including the Protestant Indians on the Spokane Indian Reservation.

Kolaskin had a jail built for those who failed to live up to his standards. This consisted of a pit covered with boards. Men and women were forced to spend some of their time doing his bidding, but ill-will started when he imprisoned people for minor offenses and allowed them only a starvation diet while in jail. He appointed policemen who acted as judges as to who should be imprisoned (Ray 1936).

The Indian Agency at Fort Spokane (where the Colville Indian Agency was located at the time) did not know what to do about the situation. In the meantime two of Kolaskin's prisoners escaped, and searchers were sent after them. One of the escapees was found. When the "policemen" started to tie him up to take him back, the uncle of the prisoner tried to intervene. He railed at Kolaskin and told him he was always making trouble. Kolaskin had him tied up too and taken to jail (Ray 1936). When another nephew heard about this, he got into a fight with Kolaskin's policeman, who shot him dead. When the policeman confessed, Kolaskin did nothing. Friends of the dead man took the body to Whitestone to be buried. Then they broke down the jail door and released the uncle and the other nephew. They decided to burn the jail, but they had no matches and so destroyed the cover of the pit (Ray 1936).

Because of this incident Kolaskin and the policeman were held in custody. The actual murderer was released after a hearing, but Kolaskin was sent to prison on McNeil Island for three years. After his return, he tried to disband his organization. He told the people that his teachings were wrong, but many stayed faithful to the new religion. Kolaskin remained chief during his lifetime and continued to be unfriendly toward whites. He advised the Sanpoil to accept nothing from the whites or they would lose their land. He successfully practiced as a traditional shaman after his return from jail. Kolaskin died in 1920. The cult he founded lasted until 1930 (Ray 1936).

FURTHER LAND LOSS AND CULTURAL PRESSURES

The Indians had to cope with the chaotic social climate of land disputes, cultural misunderstandings, and governmental pressure. For instance, Thomas McCrosson ("Additional Farmer") urged Superintendent Webster to remove Joe Moses as a judge of the Indian court because he had tried a shaman and found him not guilty (February 4, 1907). The charge was that the defendant attempted to cure a sick man and have a medicine dance. The other judge declared him guilty; but in the case of a tie, the defendant was let free. McCrosson complained that Joe Moses approved of these "superstitious practices" and wanted him removed (United States Federal Archives n.d.c: Box 331a). This was a prime example of the cultural misunderstandings and pressures that the Indians had to deal with. McCrosson further observed that the judges would not punish a friend or relative and were afraid to punish those with a bad reputation. They also set free a prisoner who promised to do better (United States Federal Archives n.d.c: Box 331a), which fits into traditional practice. The Indians believed that people could truly reform, and the society was small enough to judge if a person was sincere in doing so.

McCrosson also complained about two white miners who got drunk and tried to break into the house of an Indian woman while her husband was away. He asked if there was some way of getting rid of these people (United States Federal Archives n.d.c: Box 331a). There were many disturbances on the reservation, including fighting, knifings, and shootings. Children ran away from school, and it was McCrosson's job to find them and take them back. His duties included writing letters to the superintendent for the Indians. He also pressured a young man who had a wife and child on the Yakama Reservation not to live with another woman on the Colville Reservation because he was not "entitled" to do so (United States Federal Archives n.d.c: Box 331a). The man was "entitled" by Plateau Indian custom: by leaving his wife, he became divorced and free to remarry. This was not as callous as it sounds, for women could and did easily support themselves and their children. If reservation officials understood the custom of Indian divorce, they obviously did not approve of it.

McCrosson addressed a letter to "friend Joseph": he had heard that Joseph had been drinking hard along with his mother and cajoled him to better behavior. Apparently, he valued the young man enough to exhort him to avoid self-destruction (United States Federal Archives n.d.c: Box 331a).

It is evident that many employees of the reservation were ethnocentric; and it is equally evident that many of the same people tried to do their best, as they saw it, for the Indians in their charge. This is especially notice-able during the period just before and after the allotment period, when reservation officials were being inundated with letters from would-be set-tlers all over the country, asking for details on the available land, the amount of water available, and the nature of the soil (I. A. Knutsen to "The Indian Reservation Information Bureau," September 10, 1914). A private entrepreneur took it on himself to sell booklets regarding the sale of reser-vation lands and asked for pictures and information to fill it (F. B. Freeland to J. M. Johnson, Superintendent, October 16, 1914). The Northern Pacific Railway Company on February 27, 1915, asked for essentially the same information in order to distribute it to potential settlers in other parts of the country who would be using the railway line to travel to the reservation (United States Federal Archives n.d.c: Box 331a).

The reaction of reservation personnel to this bombardment was a strained, patient politeness, since the reservation was not yet open. At the same time, they were exerting themselves to find potential unallotted members of various bands that would be eligible for allotments, including Smohalla's band of Columbia River Indians; Soch-hoppy's band, also on the Columbia; Jim's band of Snake River Indians; a band of Palus living at the mouth of the Palouse River; and Black Wolf's band of Klickitat living on Rick Creek. The employees expressed anxiety when several Indian groups or families wanted to stay in their traditional homelands, regard-less of the problems they would face living outside of reservation bound-aries (United States Federal Archives n.d.c: Box 331a).

While allotment was going on, reservation officials were trying to deal with the smaller matters that make up people's lives. It was sensibly con-cluded to recognize Indian-custom divorce (separating and living apart) in at least one instance, but not Indian-custom marriage (living together); and officials erred in attempting to terminate or at least curtail Indian celebrations (powwows) as late as 1930 (United States Federal Archives n.d.c: letters).

Mourning Dove gives us a more intimate look into the lives of the peo-ple during this period. She was born about 1885 and died in 1936, before the revitalization of Plateau culture took place on the Colville Reservation. Due to Catholic missionary influence, she believed that a woman shaman's powers were never equal to those of an influential man and that women in Indian life were never up to standards equal to those of men (Mourning Dove 1990:35). Such beliefs were the result of social pressures emanating from Euro-American culture. In traditional Plateau culture, female shamans were as powerful as male shamans and women had equal status, as detailed above. Mourning Dove did not interpret parts of her culture correctly, though she was perceptive in other aspects. For instance, she believed that the whipman at least sometimes whipped children "for his own amusement" (Mourning Dove 1990:35). On the contrary, this was an important office appointed by the chief. The whipman in the past was the only disciplinarian in the tribe, for parents by custom never struck their children. This institution lingered on the Colville Reservation during the lifetime of elders living in the 1990s (Ackerman 1982) and continues on the Umatilla and Nez Perce Reservations today (Ackerman 1971).

Mourning Dove's father objected when her mother wanted her to go on a spirit quest. He said she should be like whites. While her parents were discussing this, her mother waved her hand at Mourning Dove, who was obliged to leave—clarifying that it was her mother who had the final say on the matter. Mourning Dove followed the traditional rituals in the hills (Mourning Dove 1990:44); but, as she commented later, the Jesuits won out and these cultural practices fell into disuse in her time. She failed in her spirit quest that time and several other times, because doubt had been planted. Her adopted grandmother finally gave Mourning Dove her spirit, which was the power of Eagle, and also gave her the leg bones and breast feathers of that bird (Mourning Dove 1990:45).

Mourning Dove's mother sent her out again on a quest so she could meet the Eagle spirit. Again her father objected, but her mother won out without much of a discussion. Mourning Dove climbed toward the bluffs where the eagles nested; she sat down near a nest and waited for the spirit to manifest itself, but it did not appear. She was sent out on other quests and finally saw a dog spirit but resisted it (Mourning Dove 1990:47–48), an outcome similar to that of several of my consultants' quests. She decided at that point to choose the Christian God.

By the time Mourning Dove was writing, other customs had changed. Now instead of the traditional marriage trade, the chief presided over an "important" marriage. He passed a pipe around the room and then gave a speech. This little observance married the couple. The husband removed the bride's "virgin cape" (Mourning Dove 1990:55—no doubt the puberty blanket that I found in my fieldwork, described below), and that completed the ceremony. Her description is much like Ray's (1932) description of marriage forms among the Sanpoil. Mourning Dove notes that the Colville marriageable girls always had a chaperone so they were not bothered by men. Ray (1932) also mentions this custom for the Sanpoil but doubts that it had much time depth, as it was incompatible with a foraging lifestyle. By the time I first worked on the Colville Reservation in 1978, elders did not mention the chief's ceremony, because most groups no longer had chiefs. They described the marriage trade and alternate marriage forms for the traditional period (Ackerman 1982). Perhaps the chief presiding over a marriage was an attempt to substitute for a priest. Mourning Dove (1990:52) does refer to elopement by some "romantic" couples as another form of marriage. She notes that a man never openly showed affection to his wife in public unless he meant to mock her (Mourning Dove 1990:58).

Mourning Dove (1990:147) reports that each tribe took its identity from the site of its winter villages. When the Colville tribe (her people) were forced to remove to the reservation, they had to move across the Columbia River from east to west, away from their native land, and go to much less fertile lands (Mourning Dove 1990:226).

The loss of the North Half of the reservation severely curtailed traditional Indian economic activities by limiting the hunting and gathering areas. The more barren portion of the reservation left to them (the "South Half") was not sufficient for these purposes. The allotments assigned to the Indians in 1905 provided each individual tribal member with eighty acres. The people thereafter necessarily restricted their residence to their allotments, thus destroying the spatial integrity of the traditional villages. When the unallotted land in the South Half of the reservation was opened to Euro-American settlement (Bloodworth 1959:46–47), that land was lost as well. Acculturation began in earnest.

The people tried to combine the newly introduced cultural elements with the traditional culture. Though the villages no longer existed spatially because people were living on their scattered allotments, the traditional political system still operated. People belonging to a former village continued to meet in assembly and vote for chiefs to serve as their judge and to represent them to white authorities. This did not change until 1938, when the chiefs and assemblies in each village were replaced by a reservation-wide tribal council representing all of the tribes together. In 1933 the construction of Grand Coulee Dam began; by 1941 the turbines had gone on line, destroying most of the fish runs on the reservation and much of the remaining traditional economy with it (see chapter 6 for Colville history from 1938 to the present).

The period described below is the time that my older consultants lived through in their youth, roughly 1900 to 1938, when economic, political, social, and religious changes continued to be forced on the people in an attempt to integrate them into Euro-American culture. While my description of the traditional culture in chapter 4 is derived partly from the experience of consultants and partly from the oral history learned in their youth from their elders, this section mostly applies to the cultural shifts directly experienced by individuals who were sixty years of age or older when I first interviewed them in 1979. All data in the following narrative not referenced are derived from my fieldwork.

I made no attempt to record all of the cultural modifications that took place on the reservation in this study, but I attempted to investigate as many issues as possible relevant to gender status. Cultural changes did not take place simultaneously in all locations. For instance, the menstrual taboos seemed to have lingered longer in some areas of the reservation than in others.

I have keyed the change in subsistence from foraging to small-scale farming to other modifications of the culture during this period. Such changes included the continued use of tipis or mat lodges in the summer but the use of log houses during the winter, the dilution of the power of chiefs, the undermining of the traditional religion by the missionaries, the discouragement of polygyny, and the disruption of extended families.

THE ECONOMIC SPHERE

Power in the Economic Sphere

As was the case in traditional culture, there appeared to be no power or informal influence in the economic sphere in the farming period of culture wielded by the Indians themselves. Economic activity was still undertaken at the initiative of the individual, and no one within the society was able to prevent another person from obtaining wild resources from the environment or from using allotments to farm or ranch. Economic and political power was used by Euro-Americans to inhibit Indian economic activities, however, if Euro-American obstruction is defined as illegitimate. If it is defined as legitimate, then Euro-Americans used authority to obstruct Indian economic activities.

Authority in the Economic Sphere

Since authority continued to find expression in the new economic gender roles in this period, each subsistence method is discussed in turn. Farming was now added to the traditional subsistence tasks of fishing, hunting, and gathering.

Gender Division of Labor

Fishing   Men continued to fish for salmon at the traditional locations available to them, while the women processed the catch in their accustomed manner. At sites like Kettle Falls, Washington, Indians and whites now fished together. Salmon Chiefs still functioned at the customary fishing spots, and fishing platforms and weirs remained in use.

Though fish were fairly plentiful during this period, the State of Washington began to regulate the activity. A Methow consultant stated that about 1920 state game wardens allowed fish weirs on the Okanogan River near Monse, Washington, to extend only halfway across the river, rendering them useless. When the Indians spanned the river with weirs anyway, the game warden had them destroyed. This harassment forced the Indians of the Okanogan area to give up weir and trap fishing entirely.

The fishing activities of the Carrier people of British Columbia, Canada, suffered similarly. The Canadian federal government eliminated the salmon weirs so that they would not compete with the owners of commercial canneries on the coast. Then debris falling into the Fraser Canyon from railroad construction in 1913 eliminated the salmon run entirely, destroying much of the Carrier economy (Hudson and Wilson 1986:444).

On the U.S. side of the border, fishing on the upper Columbia and its tributaries was curtailed when Grand Coulee Dam was built, since the dam blocked the salmon from reaching most of the area. Other dams built later on the Columbia and Snake Rivers terminated the fish runs almost completely. The loss of this resource in most areas, amounting to about one-third of the traditional diet, forced the Indians to pursue new economic patterns simply to survive.

The taboos on women in connection with weirs and fish traps began to disappear during this period. In fact, almost none of the elderly women who were interviewed had ever followed such taboos in their lifetimes, though all knew of them. In Yakama country, a consultant told me in 1980 that men capturing salmon with dipnets from fishing platforms were aided by girls aged fourteen to sixteen who hauled the fish from the platforms to the trucks. Menstrual taboos did not operate in this situation because women were prohibited from approaching weirs, not platforms, according to my consultant. Whether this was a traditional behavior or one that evolved later I was unable to learn.

Hunting   Men still hunted during this period but were limited by reservation conditions. The hunting of animals under the direction of a Hunting Leader continued, and groups of people dispersed into the uplands in the fall as usual to hunt. A hunting party in 1926, described by an elder who was sixteen at the time, consisted of five hunters in their prime: two older men and three younger and presumably less skilled men. Three women plus an older married couple accompanied this group to dry the meat and tend the camp.

Deer were scarce that year, but the hunting party was able to kill sixteen or eighteen animals. All families shared the meat. Four pack horses were needed to haul it home. The rules of butchering and dividing game were not known by everyone at the time of this hunt, so the leader sometimes had to intervene to direct the division of the carcass. For instance, the neck, head, and hide went to the hunter responsible for the kill, and other parts were set aside for older people (as described in chapter 4). If women did not accompany the hunters, a knowledgeable elder, as in earlier times, distributed the meat to the other men, who took their share home to their wives or mothers.

A man had the option to hunt alone in winter and summer. The meat procured during these seasons was kept within the family unless it chose to share the game with neighbors living nearby.

Hunting as well as fishing came to be regulated by the State of Washington. Native hunting and fishing subsistence patterns were considerably distorted by the new game laws. In 1926 a young man of sixteen (mentioned above) was jailed because he had killed a deer out of season. "They kept me in jail for thirty-three days, and even many whites felt that I should not have been jailed."

Gathering   The gathering of plants was also jeopardized during the farming period, although Euro-Americans were not generally interested in wild plants as such. Instead, the activities of farming and cattle-raising destroyed the natural habitat of wild crops in a number of areas, leading to a reduction of these resources. The flooding of bottomlands by Grand Coulee Dam further destroyed many square miles of prime wild plant areas, causing an additional decrease in availability of vegetal foods. Older women today bitterly mourn the loss of these gathering areas.

The First Foods Ceremony preceding general gathering persevered during this time, and the Gathering Leaders still conducted their office in the traditional manner. Women continued to cleanse themselves ritually before the first gathering of plants in the spring so the roots "would allow themselves to be found."

Women no longer made their own digging tools but hired a blacksmith to fashion the shafts out of metal. The women were able to pay a blacksmith cash through their earnings from various economic activities.

Farming   Farming was not a completely alien concept in the traditional culture. Some wild plant tending occurred in aboriginal times, so horticulture was a curiosity that many took up willingly. The Indians even experimented with Euro-American–style farming and ranching *before* they were forced onto reservations. For instance, Chief Kamiakin had a large herd of cattle before the Yakama War of 1855 started, and he was not unique. The interesting point, however, is that the Indians still pursued their native economic activities as well. After restriction to the reservation, they were pressured to take up farming exclusively, especially after allotments were made in 1905; but the people continued to practice the two economic patterns side by side as long as possible.

For their pre-reservation farming or ranching experiments, the Indians used any piece of land in their native area without regard to European-style concepts of land ownership. They learned the farming techniques from missionaries or early Euro-American settlers. Two elderly women in

1980 spoke appreciatively of white men who showed them how to irrigate their gardens when they were young.

Under reservation conditions, many of the people took to farming and ranching with enthusiasm. George H. Newman, an Indian agent for the Colville Reservation, commented that farming was the Indians' principal occupation and lauded their willingness to work their farms even when the crops were poor (Newman 1897:289).

The Allotment Act of 1887 introduced the principle of European-style land ownership to tribes in the United States (for the Plateau Indian style of land ownership, see Ackerman 1994). Allotments were not imposed on the Colville Reservation peoples until 1905, when 350 of 551 adult Indians on the Colville Reservation were persuaded to sign an agreement whereby they accepted allotments of eighty acres for themselves and for each of their children. As noted above, the "surplus" land on the already-reduced reservation, consisting of over half of the land in the South Half, was then withdrawn. Allotment was completed in 1914, and the withdrawn land was opened to Euro-American settlement in 1916 (Bloodworth 1959:46–47).

Most of the elders I interviewed experienced adversity from the consequences of allotment. Many eventually lost their allotment farms because of bad weather, inexperience in money management, or inability to get loans. One individual sold his allotment around 1930 to feed his horses after a bad winter, because he could not obtain a bank loan. Thus, additional erosion of Indian ownership occurred. A railroad built through the Okanogan Valley in the early twentieth century opened the territory further to Euro-American settlers, who bought the lost allotments.

Throughout these events, women grew gardens and enthusiastically planted corn, potatoes, squash, and watermelons—all exotic foods to them. One woman described a garden near Ephrata, Washington, where a communal garden was grown before allotments were made. Both genders cared for the garden and built a fence to protect the crops from the deer. When it was time for harvest, everyone collected the food and divided the produce.

Plows for farming were not available to the Indians at first, but the government later provided them along with mowing machines and hay rakes so that grain cultivation became possible. Ten to fifteen acres made up the average plot planted in wheat. Some of the wheat was sold to obtain luxury items like flour and coffee.

The new work was not strongly gender-typed, and farming involved the labor of both men and women. Many women plowed and pitched hay and helped the men to stack it. Consultants estimated that it took a month to plow and seed thirty acres of land for hay. Though the Indians copied the farming methods of their Euro-American neighbors, they ignored the Euro-American gender division of labor.

Cattle, hogs, chickens, and especially horses were among the animals that the Indians raised. Ranching was more important than farming, as good arable land for crops was rare in the South Half of the reservation. A herd of twenty-five cattle made a family self-sufficient. Horses also continued to be very important within the culture and remained an index of wealth.

Consultants say that in the period from 1900 to 1938 (the time of their youth), men hunted, fished, plowed, raised grain and hay, and cared for the livestock. Women gathered roots and berries, kept a garden, raised grain, plowed, baled and hauled hay, harnessed horses, cut wood, and added canning to their skills. Some women worked with the cattle and horses, and they all cooked for the harvest crews. Children were pressed to help with plowing—one child to each handle of the plow, gender being irrelevant. One boy was eleven when he started this task. Children had daily chores, which included cutting wood, getting water, sewing, cleaning house, and feeding chickens, plus getting training in the traditional subsistence tasks. They were allowed an hour a day for play. In more recent times, the women have happily taken up freezing meat and berries, acknowledging the greater ease of food preservation with this method. Women continued to be the managers of the family's resources during the farming period. Despite the new situation, women maintained their traditional role of owning and managing all foods and their distribution within and outside of the family and keeping surpluses for trading purposes.

Irrigation was provided by the government for a short period, enabling the Indians to raise wheat for market. Farming became profitable enough in the area to attract itinerant grain-threshing crews with equipment who followed the ripening of crops in the region. The reservation had a grange and a harvest festival during the years when my consultants were young, with Indian dancing as one of the features of the festival.

When irrigation was terminated by the government, many people were unable to raise wheat. They were forced to seek wage employment to provide an alternative source of income, though little steady employment was available in the immediate area. Many men and women left home for the Yakima Valley to work as migrant crop workers in the hopfields or the orchards. Building Grand Coulee Dam provided a few jobs for the men. When World War II started, many men enlisted in the armed services.

Consultants say that before wild resources were destroyed or regulated by the State of Washington, the Colville Reservation Indians were able to integrate the traditional and Euro-American economic modes without much trouble. For instance, Okanogan men began hunting in the Okanogan Valley in November. In May and June they built fish weirs. Hay and grain were raised by both genders, and the men and some women cared for livestock in between these activities. The women gathered, dried fish and meat, and tended their gardens and grain fields. Despite the multitude of tasks, one individual commented that there was plenty of time for everything. There were days free from labor, and he remembers the period wistfully, as a time of unhurried calm.

The traditional attitude of placing equal value on the work of both men and women persisted throughout this period. Resources continued to be distributed to the extended family as before, even though people were more spread out geographically.

Autonomy in the Economic Sphere

Autonomy in the economic sphere or any other sphere did not mean irresponsibility. Though people were autonomous, they had obligations to support their families, contribute to their communities, be generous with their neighbors, and share food with visitors. Even so, they had ample scope to express their individuality.

Fresh opportunities for trade became available in the new context and were pursued with the old enthusiasm. Prior to the building of Grand Coulee Dam and the destruction of many fishing sites, Euro-Americans as well as Indians went to Kettle Falls during the salmon fishing season. There the two ethnic groups exchanged goods and shared fellowship. One Nespelem consultant recalled that she not only met her Indian trading partners at Kettle Falls but sold fish and fish eggs to Euro-Americans as well. She and other Indian women also sold pies and breads to both groups, which provided them with cash. A rodeo called Salmon Days was a feature of Kettle Falls during the fishing season. Some people of both ethnic groups came not to fish but to buy and socialize. The gathering at Kettle Falls came to assume the character of a country fair, perhaps similar in spirit to the traditional Indian spring encampments.

In former times, new arrivals who appeared at the fishing grounds shared in the fish caught that day as a matter of custom. During this period, late arrivals purchased their fish for the day's meal if they arrived too late for the free distribution. By selling fish and other items, Indians of both genders obtained the cash required to purchase such commodities as coffee, flour, and cloth. Trading proceeded at other locations as well, with food continuing to be a female specialty. Women obtained paints and coastal crabs in exchange for their commodities, while men carried on trade in horses.

Rodeos became a favored pastime with the Indians as well as their white neighbors, reflecting their mutual enthusiasm for horses. Some famous rodeo cowboys have emerged from the Colville Reservation, and an Indian rodeo circuit continues to this day. Women as well as men were excellent riders, cultivating their traditional skills. Several women as young girls earned money as jockeys but gave up the sport when they became too heavy for racing.

The Colville people earned some money through wage labor. Young unmarried girls obtained employment in the homes of Euro-Americans to help with the housework and cooking. Women and men both became seasonal farm workers, picking hops, apples, and other crops for Euro-American farmers. Men obtained occasional employment with the government, cutting wood and freighting government goods.

Gambling continued to be a passion for both men and women. Sometime around the turn of the century, consultants say that gambling was no longer segregated by gender: the menstrual taboos had apparently lapsed by then. Women readily beat men at gambling as well as vice versa (Ray 1932:181). "Women are considered by the natives . . . to be better gamblers than men—that is, they bet more freely" (Ray 1932:159).

Both genders retained economic autonomy. Women learned to drive automobiles by watching others do it, because watching is the traditional way a skill is acquired in Plateau culture. One woman who learned to drive by observing her husband later drove a truck, loaded and unloaded hay from it, and changed the truck's tires. A male consultant said that women were sometimes better drivers than men. Thus, it was not only men who had mechanical aptitudes—women did too.

Sometimes women acquired a car as a gift from their father, but more often they bought one for themselves through money they earned. They usually paid for the car in a lump sum and bought horses in the same manner. In traditional times, women had always owned a few horses for transporting children and household goods.

Any item, large or small, bought by a woman could not be taken by her husband for any reason. He could not gamble it away or sell it. Husband and wife could use each other's property only with the other's permission. The woman often had more money than her husband.

During this period, women also owned cattle separately from their husbands, which provided a source of cash to buy cars. Women inherited cattle and other property or often bought cattle through wages or earnings through trade. Both genders cared for their own stock and milked their own cows.

A few horses came to be owned jointly by a married couple, though each owned animals separately as well. Joint ownership became an ideal due to Euro-American influence, but the idea did not really take hold. A female elder commented that she and her husband owned cattle in common but later mentioned that she sold them and kept the proceeds.

Young women dug separately and dried roots separately from their mothers-in-law, even if they lived in the same dwelling. Sometimes food was pooled for a particular meal, but the stores were kept apart so that the younger couple could move around independently during the annual round. Factors pertaining to gender status in the economic sphere during this period are outlined in table 7.

THE DOMESTIC SPHERE

Power in the Domestic Sphere

The traditional extended family, in which a group of grown siblings with their spouses and children lived with their parents and other elders, lapsed during the farming period. Though elderly parents might still reside with a married child, siblings and their families did not join such a group, because their major economic assets, their farms, were not in the same location once allotments were assigned. This resulted only superficially in a nuclear family situation, because the elements of the extended family still shared resources and met often for social purposes.

TABLE 7

The Economic Sphere: Farming Period

MEN	WOMEN
POWER	
none recalled by consultant	
AUTHORITY	
Salmon Chief, Hunting Leaders	Gathering Leaders
farming not strongly gender-typed	
livestock raising	kitchen gardening
	managers and/or owners of food
work equally valued	
AUTONOMY	
trade, traditional and new patterns	
rodeo riders	
horse jockeys	
employment	
gambling no longer segregated	
both drove and owned cars	

During the period of my consultants' recollections (about 1900 to 1938), the children always remained with the mother in case of divorce. The individual ownership of a piece of land in the form of allotments distorted much social behavior that before was taken for granted. Consultants note that the woman and children no longer returned to her extended family but now remained on the farm, their major economic asset, and worked it when the husband and father left. Often the farm included his allotment; but because land had been communally owned before allotments were made, the abandonment of land to a former spouse was taken casually. Further, the mother's custody of the children occurred despite any traditional claims the father's relatives might have had on the children. In this period most relatives had little interest in taking children in, since it was no longer practicable to support large extended families. Cash was in short supply, and food was no longer easily obtained from the environment. Thus, a divorced mother retained the children and land. This may be construed as an expression of power, but it also could be interpreted as the most practical solution in a new social context. Certainly, children eventually became a social and economic asset to the parent who raised them.

Compliance with the mandatory rule of the levirate or sororate lapsed in a few instances. This is interpreted here as an exertion of power.

Authority in the Domestic Sphere

In this period the custom of bride service, in which a newly married man worked for his in-laws for a year, continued in a few families. The groom was under the authority of his in-laws during this time. Some men continued to live with their wives' families for the rest of their lives instead of taking the wife and children to their family's household. Such decisions were based not only on economic circumstances but on social ones. If the in-laws had no other adult child to look after them, the son-in-law and the daughter did so, and his family had no objections to this arrangement.

In some extended households, the oldest woman (the mother-in-law or grandmother) continued to run the household as in the past and was unquestioned in her authority. As Mourning Dove commented, the grandmother "remained the supreme head of the family, ruling her husband, son, daughter-in-law, and children when they arrived. Her wisdom guided the household" (Mourning Dove 1990:61). The custom persisted of leaving the oldest grandchild of either gender to live with the grandparents while the parents worked outside of the home. In the farming period, in which grandparents and parents were more likely to reside in different households, children spoke as if they had been raised by their grandparents, so ubiquitous was their authority. The children were sent to their grandparents' house to be lectured when misbehaving and when they needed an unusual amount of comfort.

Physical punishment inflicted by the immediate family was avoided, as in the past. The whipman institution was still in effect throughout this period and in fact lasted until very recent times in some areas of the reservation. When the children were judged to need more than lecturing, the whipman was summoned by parents or grandparents to whip the children. He received gifts for this service. Since households were now scattered on allotments, he made frequent visits to the families that used his services and whipped the children for past and even future misbehavior. In the past, this man was appointed by the chief.

The resident grandmother's role was crucial. Even today many Colville residents believe that young mothers cannot care for or, more accurately, train and educate children properly since they do not have the experience. Grandmothers are thus allocated extensive authority over their grandchildren. As children grew past the infant stage, their grandfathers also had great influence and authority over them.

Women continued to exert their traditional managerial authority in domestic affairs in the farming period. They raised and gathered vegetal foods and preserved them by canning or drying and continued to process the meat and fish brought into the household. They also distributed the food as they saw fit, as women's traditional property rights to all foods were uncontested. They still retained the prerogative of trading extra supplies. Women often handled their husbands' cash as well as their own, extending their economic authority into a new dimension.

Since new kinds of property were now available, old rules of ownership were extended into new areas. In one interesting example occurring in the 1930s, a married couple raised grain separately and sold it separately. They then pooled their money, and the woman managed it. Farms were said to belong to a married couple jointly, which was a Euro-American concept urged on them by the government and missionaries. In the case of divorce, however, the farm was left to the woman for support of the children, as noted above. This appears to have evolved into a custom, for a consultant said that the chief occasionally had to enforce this rule.

Money derived from wages or trade always belonged to the person earning it. This principle made it possible for both men and women to buy horses or automobiles for their personal use. Each individual had the right to spend his or her money for personal clothing or use it for gambling. Very often the money was used to clothe the children, given to a needy relative, or used for other domestic purposes. The conversion of the society to a cash economy must have made this a necessity. Formerly, relatives could have been cared for more easily, since surplus food and skins were available in the environment.

When menstrual taboos were still in force, deer carcasses were slipped into the back of the tipi or mat lodge under the tipi cover, never through the front entrance, since women entered and left the lodge by that entrance. Women took care to avoid the back of the tipi or mat house completely for that reason. While butchering the deer, women avoided stepping over the head or blood of the kill as a safety precaution. Failure to observe these taboos could lead not only to damaging a man's hunting power but to fatal hemorrhaging during the woman's next menstrual period. Since women retired less often to the menstrual hut during the farming period, they had to avoid weapons such as guns at all times.

Autonomy in the Domestic Sphere

A custom that is not noted in the literature but was found during my recent fieldwork was practiced after puberty during this period. A young woman who had just attained puberty was publicly presented with a "puberty blanket" by one of her parents or grandparents. A Sanpoil consultant stated that the blanket was handed down within a family line and was a signal that the young woman was ready for "open flirtation." She used the blanket to wrap herself and her lover together when they were courting. I was told that, while this is no longer a custom, in the past it was perfectly acceptable behavior condoned by the entire community. The use of a courting blanket in the traditional culture was confirmed by a Southern Okanogan male.

Mourning Dove (1990:49) mentioned what may have been the same kind of blanket but called it the virgin cape. The cape indicated that she was unmarried, and she was supposed to wear it so men could not see her figure. This is very likely the puberty blanket that today's elders described to me. Mourning Dove was born in 1888 (Mourning Dove 1990:3), at a time when missionary influence was extremely strong on the Colville Indian Reservation, and the function of the "puberty blanket" as described to me would have been anathema to the missionaries and government agents of the early twentieth century. Now that their influence has decreased, the private knowledge of its real function has again surfaced.

Autonomy continued to be expressed in the independence of movement of both genders without regard to their spouses. If a woman decided to shop in town, she needed no clearance from her husband. If she left the area to collect berries, she may not even have left a note telling him where she was going or for how long. I knew a Nez Perce woman in Idaho in 1965 who decided to attend a baseball game and did so without leaving a note or arranging food for her husband's supper, as a Euro-American woman might have done. The custom of counseling young men to tolerate their wives' independence of movement continued during the farming period, suggesting that some men did indeed attempt to control their wives and also indicating that the attempt was futile. Men also were not required to inform their wives of their movements.

Some marriage patterns changed during this period. Missionaries considered arranged marriages a practice of "selling" daughters—which of course it was not—and consequently persuaded parents to let their children choose their own spouses. Thus, arranged marriages largely disappeared early in reservation times, eliminating the need for elopement, which was such a frequent practice in the past. Pressure was also exerted by Catholic missionaries to dissolve polygynous marriages, a step that produced painful situations in stable families. In one example recounted to me, missionaries intervened in a family of two sisters married to the same man. They attempted to persuade them that their situation was immoral and exhorted one of the women to leave. The demands they made were so insistent that the older sister did leave, reasoning that her children were grown but her younger sister's were not. After her departure, her husband attempted to find her to persuade her to return, but she was able to evade him. Chief Moses of the Columbia tribe experienced similar pressure to give up his "extra wives"; but his prominence enabled him to resist the demands, and he was finally left alone.

The missionaries also succeeded in convincing many people that non-Catholic marriages were not true marriages and would not be recognized by the church. The aboriginal "marriage trade" or ceremonial exchange of goods between two families was thus discouraged and became less frequent, though the practice occurs sporadically today on some Plateau reservations. The function of uniting two families through affinal ties, consequently, is attenuated in contemporary times.

First marriages contracted in the traditional manner (without Catholic ritual) continued and were often as unstable as before. Many people had a number of marriage partners before they settled down with one. Some people avoided Catholic marriages, because the church would not recognize the validity of the native pattern of divorce, which was signaled simply by taking up separate residence. The decision to marry and divorce remained an individual choice during this time, so long as traditional forms of marriage were followed.

Abortion and contraception were among the practices discouraged by the Catholic missionaries. Refraining from sexual relations to control fertility was encouraged but led to marital problems. The number of children per couple increased; but as the people became sedentary farmers at the same time, the immediate cause of the population increase is uncertain. No preference for boys or girls existed in the society at this time or in the past. Infants of either gender were equally welcomed.

Schooling was unavailable locally during the early years in the lifetime of living elders but was greatly coveted by some youngsters. For most, education was found only in boarding schools far away from home, located across the country or the state. Some of the boarding schools were run by the government, while others were mission schools. It was usually up to the child rather than the parents to decide whether he or she wanted to attend a school, but government agents often forced children to attend boarding schools, circumventing their autonomy.

Children continued to have the right to visit relatives in other communities for long periods, thus reinforcing consanguineal ties. When schools became common, however, and education was required, most children visited relatives only for the summer. Sometimes they stayed with relatives for as much as a year, attending school in that area. A long-term visit was often a child's idea; his or her decision was completely respected by the parents or grandparents, indicating the extensive autonomy that each individual enjoyed at any age in Plateau culture.

When divorce occurred during this period, the man still owned only his clothes, tools, and horses. The woman stayed on the farm, as noted above, and did not return to her parents as she might have done formerly. Land did not end up in women's hands completely, as might be expected, for it was redistributed to both genders through inheritance.

Since divorced women remained on the farms with their children and supported them there, support from the children's father was not expected—a situation similar to the past. As had not been the case in the past, however, children now suffered from divorce. Formerly, children remained with their father's or mother's extended family. If the parent remarried and left the home, the children simply remained with their grandparents and their parents' siblings. Ties were close, and the children's emotional as well as physical needs were met by the extended family or descent group. In the farming period, when nuclear households became more common, children often stayed with their mother's parents after her divorce and remarriage; but now they were without the mother's siblings and their spouses, who once would have served as surrogate parents to the child and would have contributed their economic services to the extended family. If the grandparents and parents were deceased, aunts and uncles who once would have routinely adopted orphans were now reluctant to take other children into their nuclear household. This led to the deprivation of these children, physically and emotionally. The children were often passed from one nuclear family to another or entered a boarding school run by the Jesuit missionaries. When a mother remarried after divorce, she often may have wanted to keep her children, but her husband was sometimes unwilling to take them for the same reasons that aunts and uncles were reluctant to have them: support in a cash economy was more difficult than in a foraging economy. The foundering of the extended family played a large role in the dilution of Plateau culture and in the frequency of juvenile delinquency today (Ackerman 1971:597). Factors in the domestic sphere are outlined in table 8.

THE POLITICAL SPHERE

Power in the Political Sphere

Examples of illegal or uninstitutionalized power in the Colville Reservation's political sphere seem as rare during this period as in traditional times. Chiefs' wives continued to advise their husbands informally on political matters. The question is, was this authority or power? Since the wives who gave advice publicly could be criticized by band members, their advising function must have been viewed as an expression of power. One may in fact infer that the wife's role as adviser was not institutionalized *because* criticism existed, and her advice could then be categorized as a use of influence or power.

A chief's widow was also influential, perhaps even crucial, in choosing a successor to the deceased. She always chose ("named") her son if she had one. Consultants' opinions were divided as to whether her preference

TABLE 8

The Domestic Sphere: Farming Period

MEN	WOMEN

POWER

	kept children after divorce
levirate and sororate sometimes ignored	

AUTHORITY

	oldest woman ran household
whipman punished children	
grandparents' authority over children	
	owned food
	managed money for self and husband
farm owned jointly in marriage	
labor's proceeds belonged to individual	

AUTONOMY

independent in decisions and movements	
	puberty blanket
marriage partners chosen by individual	
divorce initiated by either	
kept only horses and personal property after divorce	owned farm after divorce

made it mandatory for the council or assembly to affirm her choice, thus making her position one of authority; or if the assembly could ignore her choice and choose their own candidate, which would mean that the chief's wife was only exerting influence, an expression of power. Further, a chief's wife who was a good orator was said to be more likely to persuade the assembly to accept her preference, indicating the use of power rather than authority.

In one Southern Okanogan example, the chief's widow and daughter named the chief's successor (his son), who was accepted by the assembly. The tone of the conversation with the consultant suggested that private doubts existed regarding the son's suitability for the office. At least some members of the band felt the need for someone capable of meeting the

Euro-American pressures; but no one wished to make an issue of it, so the nomination stood and was accepted by the assembly. Band members theoretically had the right to suggest other candidates but chose not to do so in this case. Thus, the mother and daughter's role here seemed to be an exercise of power rather than authority, though the distinction in this example is perhaps not great. In at least three other tribes (the Sanpoil, Coeur d'Alene, and Columbia) the deceased chief's close female relatives also chose his successor.

Among the Southern Okanogan early in the twentieth century, a chief's widow and daughter nominated someone outside of the family because he had general ability and a good command of English. It was expected that he could better defend their interests against the Euro-Americans. This choice coincided with the refusal of the deceased chief's son to take the office.

Authority in the Political Sphere

Distance did not hinder communication in traditional times, and communication was even easier in this period. The various chiefs, while independent, consulted each other often on how best to protect their common interests. At the same time, all chiefs consulted their respective assemblies frequently. In 1912 and again in 1915 or 1916 several chiefs ventured a trip to Washington, D.C., in an effort to preserve their land rights. Since they had already lost the North Half of the reservation, they were painfully aware that they could lose it all. The allotment process in particular was blamed for alienating land, and the Indians hoped to dissuade federal officials from breaking up the reservation further. Since the stakes were so high and contact with the federal government was necessary, individuals contributed what cash they could to pay for the chiefs' train fare. Chiefs attempted to be well informed and effective, but their authority was constantly undermined by the federal government during this period.

Political decision-making in the farming period is illustrated in an incident that occurred in a Southern Okanogan group. A young man was arrested for killing a deer out of season (a case referred to above). After he was released on bond, the assembly was called together to discuss how to deal with the impending court case. Should they hire a lawyer or have the chief defend the young man in court himself? "The meeting went on all night. Some people felt a lawyer was necessary. Others felt that you needed a lawyer only if you had committed a crime . . . The vote was taken before breakfast . . . They decided the chief should make the decision. The chief decided to take the case to court himself because killing deer is not a crime . . . He was not able to get the young man off and he went to jail. They considered appealing to the Supreme Court, but couldn't raise the money."

The chief's function at any political assembly was to present both sides of the matter. If no consensus developed regarding the problem, then the chief made the final decision. In this example, the assembly (both genders) concluded that a lawyer was needed only if the defendant was guilty, so the chief's appearance in court on behalf of the defendant was judged to be adequate. In this instance, they lost the case.

Another serious political problem of the time was the loss of reservation allotments to white settlers. The social and political disruptions were severe enough to open the chiefs to criticism, largely unwarranted.

The band chiefs were appointed by the federal government to serve as judges in the farming period much as they had done traditionally; but now they consulted a white law book in addition to drawing on their own customs to reach a decision. The office of sku'malt or adviser disappeared among those tribes in which it existed, and its functions were exercised solely by the male chiefs. The chiefs dealt only with minor offenses in this period.

The Indian Reorganization Act

The above situation prevailed until 1934, when it was expected that the Indians would modify their political system according to the Indian Reorganization Act, also known as the Wheeler-Howard Act. The new law was a reaction to the misery experienced by Indians everywhere in the country due to the Dawes or Allotment Act of 1887. The intent of the Indian Reorganization Act was to end allotment, return unallotted lands to the tribal entities, and encourage tribal self-government.

The Departmental Orders of September 19, 1934, and November 5, 1935, temporarily withdrew further sales of undisposed lands on the Colville Reservation—818,000 acres. These were the lands that had not yet been sold to white settlers. They were held back in the expectation that the Colville Indians would organize under the Indian Reorganization Act and the undisposed lands would then be restored to the tribes. The Colville

Reservation members, however, rejected the Indian Reorganization Act in a vote on April 6, 1935. Consequently, the secretary of the interior retained the lands in withdrawal status (Bloodworth 1959:47). These events caused confusion and dissension among the Colville Reservation tribes.

The strongest opposition to political reorganization came from the Nespelem district and from older leaders and chiefs. Another partisan group on the reservation was called the Colville Indian Association, organized in 1930. This group had favored the Indian Reorganization Act, which in effect would have curtailed the influence of traditional leaders and chiefs. Its primary objective was to remove the influence of the Bureau of Indian Affairs, which was widely believed to be misusing tribal money; and its second aim was to protect the reservation's interests from off-reservation exploitation, particularly by the timber companies (Bloodworth 1959:48; Ross 1968:68). Later the association supported the move of the government toward termination of the reservation (described in the next chapter).

Another election was held in 1936, in which 24 percent of the eligible voters participated. The constitution they voted for contained provisions and grants of power that the government could not approve, so political reorganization was again thwarted. Three districts, however, favored the adoption of a constitution and so continued the efforts to reorganize. At a meeting in Nespelem in 1937, all nine delegates from Inchelium, Keller, and Omak voted in favor of having a constitution. Three out of four delegates from Nespelem voted against it (Bloodworth 1959:47).

On February 26, 1938, yet another election was held regarding the question of political reorganization. This time the new constitution was approved, with about 30 percent of the eligible voters participating. As a consequence, the Colville Business Council was formed to run tribal affairs, becoming the governing body of the Colville Confederated Tribes (Bloodworth 1959:49–50). The council has fourteen members from four voting districts. Each district has four council members except Keller, which has less population and consequently only two council members (Bloodworth 1959: 47–50).

Enrolled members living off the reservation may also participate in elections by voting absentee. Many of the tribal members did not live on the reservation due to a lack of available wage employment nearby, and these people were more inclined to vote for political reorganization. The members of the Colville Indian Association were in favor of reorganization because their interests were different from residential tribal members. They were younger people whose families had lost their allotments (Bloodworth 1959:48, 50).

A source of tension in the new arrangement was the disappearance of consensus democracy, which prevailed in native polities, and the establishment of majority-rule democracy, which was alien to Plateau culture. In the past, no one had been required to submit to majority decision. Someone who did not agree with the general consensus could leave the community. This was no longer possible in the reservation era, which led to considerable frustration (Ackerman 1978–95).

Village chiefs continued to be elected in some areas, but they no longer had authority unless they were elected to the Business Council. A number of village chiefs sat on the council in the early years; but inexorably, as the chiefs became older and died, the office of chief gradually disappeared. The only exception occurred among the Sanpoil in the Keller area, who continued to elect a chief, though he no longer had any authority.

The household of Chief Moses during this period saw that everyone in his group (the Columbia or Sinkiuse) had sufficient food and clothing. The chief's wives, led by the head wife, either bought or produced clothing as well as food for those who were short of supplies. One woman in the early years of the reservation who was inexperienced in the use of money spent all she had on pies and cakes, and the chief's family had to provide her with staples for the rest of the year. Even the cream that women learned to apply to their hands after digging for roots was provided by the chief's head wife as needed. Sufficient provisions had to be accumulated by the chief and his family to supply the entire community as necessary, and the chief's wives had to keep this factor in mind when collecting food.

Autonomy in the Political Sphere

Both men and women continued to participate in assemblies before the 1938 reorganization. Men were the primary orators, but at least a few women orated as well. Women had the right to speak in council or assembly; but apparently some preferred that men speak for them, according to some consultants. This is in contrast to their behavior in the past: Joset (n.d.), an early missionary, noted, "It is no rare occurrence to see a woman step in during council and severely upbraid the chief." The change may have occurred due to Catholic upbringing, since several consultants noted that the Catholic boarding school tried to teach girls to be subservient. The women's political behavior during the farming period also contrasts with the present, when women do speak easily, frequently, and forcefully in public.

All adults in the assembly participated in the discussion of a problem and tried to reach a consensus. The opinions of married couples were not necessarily the same; both might speak, taking opposite views of a matter. There is some testimony indicating that male and female blocs operated in political matters. It was recollected that, among the Nespelem, a chief's widow canvassed the women on their choice of a successor for her deceased husband. While the men discussed possible candidates among themselves, the women did so as well. Unfortunately, not much else was remembered regarding this incident.

During the 1930–38 period, women stepped into new leadership roles, ran for the Business Council, and won. The women seemed to be more resilient during this period than the men, who were demoralized by the loss of land and the disruption of the society that they were powerless to defend. Factors in the political sphere pertaining to gender status are outlined in table 9.

THE RELIGIOUS SPHERE

The Catholic missionaries were welcomed by the Indians, who became their converts and helped them to build churches. There are elders today who take pride in being fifth-generation Catholics. Many people practiced the traditional guardian spirit religion side by side with Catholicism, however, though some changes occurred in the traditional religion.

Power in the Religious Sphere

An apparently undiminished number of sorcerers of both genders continued to practice during this period. Children, for example, were still taught to avoid upsetting a shaman for their own safety. Some shamans were believed to have seized the power of a young or dying person through an antisocial use of their religious power.

Children were not as frequently sent on spirit quests to mountain tops and other isolated places during the youth of my consultants. Many refused out of fear, and others were dissuaded by the teachings of Jesuit mission-

TABLE 9
The Political Sphere: Farming Period

MEN	WOMEN
POWER	
	chief's wives advised chief
	chief's widow influential in having her nominee elected
good orator had more ability to influence others	
AUTHORITY	
chief	sku'malt office disappeared
assembly composed of both genders	
	chief's head wife in charge of dispensing goods
AUTONOMY	
participation in assemblies	
both genders had right to speak in assembly	
husband often presented wife's views for her in assembly	women spoke publicly less often; apparently a diminution of public role

aries. Concerned older relatives often gave their guardian spirit to a young-ster, sending the spirit to him or her in a dream, thereby endowing the youngster with religious power. Guardian spirits also could be inherited. A person who was dying could bequeath his or her guardian spirit to a descendant. The child or grandchild was given the medicine bag and taught the spirit song. Spirits were inherited from relatives of either gender: thus, a daughter could inherit a guardian spirit from her father, and a son could inherit one from his mother.

Authority in the Religious Sphere

Male and female shamans continued to have the same talents and the same quantity of power as before. I heard numerous anecdotes about Euro-American doctors who found themselves replaced by a shaman when they could not save a patient from dying. The Indian doctors, as they came to be called, often succeeded where the Euro-American doctors failed.

A Southern Okanogan consultant stated that he knew as many women doctors as men when he was young. During interviews, female shamans were more often mentioned than males for this period.

Ordinary people with religious power were common during this time, but no longer did almost 100 percent of the people of both genders secure some religious power. The influence of Christianity and the fear that must have always been associated with spirit quests discouraged the acquisition of spirits for at least a large minority of people.

Love medicine was much used during reservation times and in modern times, at least on the Nez Perce Reservation. Mourning Dove of the Colville Reservation in the early 1900s told in detail how she came to use love medicine and its effects on men. Through her experience, she came to understand that such power was to be used sparingly (Mourning Dove 1990:79–90).

Autonomy in the Religious Sphere

Some, and perhaps many, children sought a guardian spirit by means of a formal quest during this period. Spirits were also encountered fortuitously. When children were lost, a spirit was said to come to them and keep them warm until they were found. During this experience, the child acquired spiritual abilities ("powers").

Grandparents often deliberately placed children in situations where they might encounter spirits. Children were frequently sent on solitary errands in the dark to encourage a visitation. Grandparents often gave up their own guardian spirits to their grandchildren, sending them after the children during their solitary errands. One woman related:

> I was too scared to get a spirit. When we was living at Keller, I heard an owl. I didn't think anything of it at first. Then I heard another. Then the sun went down. I heard more and more owls coming towards me. I got up and ran back to my grandma's house. I told my mother about it, and mother said that I was dumb. I should have stayed and I would have gotten a spirit. I think my grandma left me out there deliberately so I could meet a spirit.

Those individuals who accepted a spirit visitation as a child often rejected it in adulthood due to missionary influence and thus never went through the process of dancing in the winter Guardian Spirit Dances.

TABLE 10
The Religious Sphere: Farming Period

MEN	WOMEN

POWER

sorcerers
guardian spirits

AUTHORITY

male and female shamans equal in numbers in many groups,
but not in others
male and female shamans equal in power

AUTONOMY

guardian spirit acquired by both genders in equal numbers
gamblers of both genders
gambling teams composed of both genders

Many in middle age bitterly regretted their rejection of a spirit in their youth.

The numbers of boys and girls sent on spirit quests were equal, at least among the Methow, Southern Okanogan, and Nespelem during this period. More male than female shamans occurred among the Nespelem, however.

The winning of stick games is a manifestation of spiritual power or ability. Consequently, they are discussed here. Stick games were not segregated according to gender during this period—men and women were intermixed on all teams. This probably occurred due to the lapse of menstrual taboos. My consultants did not recall an approximate year for the change. Factors in the religious sphere pertaining to gender equality in the farming period are outlined in table 10.

CONCLUSIONS

Gender equality, though discouraged by missionaries, persisted throughout the period of forced acculturation in all four social spheres (see tables 7 to 10). While the Colville people tried to follow the Euro-American ideals in gender roles by at least giving them lip service, the attempt to subordinate women to men was largely unsuccessful.

CHAPTER 6

Gender Status in Contemporary Colville Reservation Culture

The contemporary phase of Colville Reservation culture began in the 1938–39 period, as defined here: 1938 marks the beginning of the modern political structure on the reservation (as described in chapter 5), and 1939 marks the virtual end of the foraging economy caused by the construction of Grand Coulee Dam. Some foraging continues to the present, but it no longer can provide substantial support. This chapter describes the cultural adjustments made to these conditions, with emphasis on the effect they had on gender status. Unless noted otherwise, all cultural data were gathered in the field from consultants, mostly younger than the age of sixty.

GRAND COULEE DAM

The year after the Colville Confederated Tribes accepted their new constitution in 1938, a new problem arose. Ground was broken in 1933 to build Grand Coulee Dam, which by 1939–41 adversely affected the use of reservation lands by the Indians. The dam's principal proponent was Rufus Woods, the publisher of the *Wenatchee Daily World*. Woods first proposed the dam on July 18, 1918, with the purpose of providing irrigation for 1,029,000 acres of farming land in the Columbia Basin. Most of these lands were privately owned by white farmers, and the rest was owned by the government. From 1890 to 1910 rainfall was above normal in the Columbia Basin, encouraging agricultural development. When a drier climate returned, much of the land was abandoned, but a high percentage remained in private hands (Woods n.d.).

When the proposal was implemented, the dam was situated in the Columbia River Canyon near the head of the Grand Coulee. The Coulee was fifty-two miles long and one and one-half to five miles wide, with perpendicular walls rising nearly 1,000 feet (Woods n.d.). The building of the dam was an exciting event in the white community. The newspapers avidly quoted statistics regarding its size and printed articles about the people to be flooded out. The *Spokesman Review*, a Spokane, Washington, newspaper, noted on December 15, 1938, that the village of Gerome, founded about 1900, was to be flooded. The town of Peach was to be under 235 feet of water, Gifford under 90 feet, and several bridges would be flooded (Marsh 1918–66:154). A total of 12,500 acres of tribal and allotted lands would be affected by the inundation (Gough 1990).

The same *Spokesman Review* article noted that the water was to rise 1,310 feet above sea level in the canyon behind Grand Coulee Dam. Ten towns would be flooded, including Marcus and Kettle Falls, where the famous Indian fishery was located. If the line had been a little lower than the 1,310 level, these two towns would have been saved. Title to the lake bed cost ten million dollars (Marsh 1918–66:156).

On January 1, 1939, the *Spokesman Review* reported that the first towns covered by the rising water would be Peach and Keller (the latter an Indian community) on the Sanpoil River, which would be flooded by the summer of that year. In June 1941 Kettle Falls would disappear. The lake formed by the dam was expected to reach its final level by 1942. Eighteen thousand acres of the land in Ferry County to be covered by water consisted of Indian allotments. Inchelium, home of the large Indian subagency with school and hospital, would be moved four miles north to avoid the rising waters (Marsh 1918–66:158). The government bought portions of allotments for the right of way for the Grand Coulee Reservoir.

TERMINATION

The 818,000 acres not disposed of under the Dawes Act that were to be returned to the Colville Confederated Tribes were never subject to state taxes, and their acquisition by the tribes would prevent them from ever being taxable. Therefore, Okanogan and Ferry Counties opposed the restoration of the land unless the federal government paid them in lieu of taxes. The federal government refused to do so. Instead the Bureau of Indian Affairs, Congress, and federal, state, and county officials pressed the tribes to agree that the only way to get title to the 818,000 acres was for the tribes themselves to pay the estimated taxes. This agreement was reached on April 24, 1954. The tribes had to pay $40,000 per year total to Ferry and Okanogan Counties. This was an arrangement that no other tribe in the country had to accept. The disposition of moneys was later deemed unconstitutional, but in the meantime the tribes had paid out $680,000 to the counties (Colville Confederated Tribes 1972).

Public Law 772 was approved on July 24, 1956, which restored the 818,000 acres of undisposed lands dealt with by the Act of March 22, 1906 (34 Stat. 80) to tribal ownership. Section 5 of the Act of July 24, 1956, harbored a Trojan horse, however; it provided that the Business Council had to submit a termination plan within five years from the date of enactment of the act. The assets arising from this action were to be divided among tribal members (Bloodworth 1959:51; Colville Confederated Tribes 1972).

Other problems also arose. Public Law 280 was passed, which allowed the State of Washington to assume complete civil and criminal jurisdiction over the reservation. In opposition to this public law, Washington Territory's enabling act required the state to disclaim jurisdiction over all Indian lands before it would be admitted to statehood. Therefore, there was some question of the legality of the Colville Confederated Tribes' delegation of the responsibility for law and order of their members to an outsider, even though the council voted for it seven to six. Later Business Councils sought retrocession of this action for many years after. From 1965 to 1970 the tribes paid $86,986.90 to Okanogan County and $50,584.97 to Ferry County for maintenance of law and order. The exercise of the policing function by the counties was spotty at best. The Colville Confederated Tribes claimed that county police officials slighted their responsibilities to the reservation (Colville Confederated Tribes 1972). The tribes fought and finally won retrocession in the 1980s so they could retain their funds and reestablish their own police force (Ackerman 1978–95).

There was a controversy over water rights as well. Tribes have a superior and prior claim to use all waters that arise upon, traverse, or border their lands—this was decided in the Winters Doctrine Rights case of 1908. The State of Washington contended that the United States government held title to ownership of the bed and shores of the Okanogan River in trust for the future state—claiming that Washington Territory had the same legal status as an Indian tribe with regard to the federal-Indian trust relationship. The Colville Confederated Tribes asserted their claim to the bed and shorelands of those portions of the Okanogan River, Columbia River, and Lake Roosevelt Reservoir that border the boundaries of the reservation. In other cases elsewhere in the country, the courts had decided that the beds under the lakes and rivers did not belong to the states but to the Indians on whose land it was. The Washington Enabling Act of February 22, 1889, prevents any claim by the State of Washington. The Okanogan and Columbia Rivers play important roles in the lives of the tribes (Colville Confederated Tribes 1972). The reservation also won this case (Ackerman 1978–95).

Several groups favored the termination plan, including the Colville Commercial Club. The main reason why many groups did so was the fear of exploitation of reservation assets by the Bureau of Indian Affairs and outside business interests. If termination occurred, they reasoned that they could get rid of the Bureau of Indian Affairs and obtain the benefits from the sale of reservation resources. Adversaries of termination contended that those people who had sold their allotted land should not have a say on the reservation or have tribal rights. Only people who still had their land should have a say on withdrawal of federal trusteeship of the reservation. The Business Council came to a consensus that withdrawal of federal trusteeship was inevitable. It asked the Bureau of Indian Affairs to set up a withdrawal program and survey the physical assets and human resources of the tribe. Factions developed within the council as well as among other tribal members (Bloodworth 1959:52).

The depth of misinformation that the Indians harbored was not revealed until termination hearings were held by Congress. Hearings were held in Washington, D.C., on June 18 and August 13, 1965; in Spokane, Washington, on November 3, 1965; and in Nespelem, Washington, on November 4 and 5, 1965. In 1965 the Business Council voted 10–4 for termination. Representative Thomas Foley believed that the majority of the 4,600 tribal residents wanted termination. Seventy-five percent of tribal members lived off the reservation. There was 52 percent unemployment on it, with the average income being $2,500 to $3,100 per year. Stewart Udall, then secretary of the interior, testified that under the circumstances termination was unlikely to relieve the conditions of poverty. He anticipated a repeat of the Menominee Indian experience, with individuals in massive numbers turning to the state for welfare after termination. Senator Henry Jackson doubted that the views of tribal members had been truly sought on the subject of termination. He suggested a majority vote be obtained, and not just a majority of those who voted (U.S. Congress 1966).

Public opinion changed or was finally heard. New council members were elected who voted against termination. The government gave up its attempts to terminate the Colville Reservation in 1970 (Ackerman 1978–95). The consequences of that victory were positive for tribal members and their culture.

THE CONTEMPORARY ECONOMIC BACKGROUND

Despite legal and environmental problems caused by the building of Grand Coulee Dam, winning the termination battle in 1970 appeared to be a turning point. The tribal members are able to control at least a part of their destiny today. They participate in the modern industrial economy, though remnants of traditional economic patterns have survived to the present. The tribal government won the right to manage deer herds on the reservation, and under its management the herds have increased. Consequently, extended hunting by tribal members is possible.

Hunting today is fairly similar to hunting in the past. Extended families travel into the hills, where the men hunt the deer and the women butcher the meat. Each woman estimates the number of deer needed for her family that year, and the men kill that number. The meat may be dried on the spot or taken home for canning or freezing. After the women process the meat, they give part to the hunters (if they are not immediate family members) and part to older relatives who have not participated in the hunt. These practices are obviously traditionally derived. Hunting is necessarily a part-time occupation today, since both genders tend to be employed full-time. The Fourth of July holiday and other such free periods are used for hunting and other traditional subsistence pursuits.

Fishing for salmon is no longer economically significant in the area, since most of the local fishing sites have been destroyed by the dams on the Columbia River. For important reservation feasts, salmon are obtained from the Coastal Salish Indians and from the Yakama Indian Reservation through a network of consanguineal and affinal relatives. Individuals obtain their salmon through purchase or receive them as gifts through the kin network, often traveling across the state to get them. Salmon, along with certain roots, continues to be an emotionally evocative food.

Roots and berries maintain their position as highly esteemed foods. Younger women generally have their own digging sticks and know the botany and the techniques necessary for gathering. Because of employment, however, they no longer have the time to gather large supplies of wild foods even if they are available; so roots and berries are luxuries and feast foods today and no longer staples of the diet. Many women express regret that they are unable to provide wild plant foods for their families on a regular basis.

Employment opportunities have been extremely scarce on the reservation during almost all of its history. Only shortly before this study began in 1979 was employment easily available for a brief period. Thereafter, the recession of the 1980s again brought unemployment problems.

Due to the economic problems prevailing prior to the 1970s, large numbers of young people left the area to obtain employment, creating the situation in which almost as many Colville Indians resided off as on the reservation. Poverty was general and embittered some. Few went to college. I asked one consultant to discuss poverty before the reservation defeated termination. She said: "Ten years ago, Indians couldn't get a job because whites mostly had them. Also, we did not get good pay if we did have a job. It was hard. We did without a lot. There was little welfare. We had Indian foods and the elders gathered it . . . People had enough to eat ten years ago. They helped each other with food. We had schools here. Women were depended on, did the providing. Men picked apples for employment. Women were the mainstay of the family." People lived off the land the best they could during this period and gardened extensively to feed their families. It was women who held the families together, as many men (and women) were lost to alcoholism. Because women continued to be the mainstays of their kin economically, there was no question of gender inequality developing.

After the termination question was settled, the economy was rejuvenated, though there were occasional reverses. The reservation won control over its own forests and began earning an appreciable income from this source.

Independent Indian-owned companies, half of whose employees had to be Indian, logged 60 percent of the total timber cut every year. Lumbering provided not only a small per capita income for tribal members but also a capital sum for reservation development. A depression in lumber prices in 1986 hurt the fiscal health of the reservation, as it did in the rest of the state.

Prior to settlement of the termination problem, the tribal government had only 14 to 19 employees, whose work consisted of expediting termination. By 1979 to 1980, when data were first collected for this study, about 400 to 450 employees worked for the tribal government, 90 percent of them Indian. In addition, the tribal policy at this time was to hire any Indian high school or college student for the summer who asked for a job. They were fitted in somewhere, and the college students in particular had skills that were needed. An estimated 850 to 900 college and high school students were employed in the summer of 1979. The tribe planned to have trained tribal members replace the skilled 10 percent of non-Indian employees when the latter retired or resigned. The Bureau of Indian Affairs offices situated on the reservation also employed a large number of tribal members: 171 persons in 1980 (Colville Confederated Tribes n.d.:5). By 1985 the tribe employed 696 people, 315 of them male and 381 female (*Tribal Tribune* 11[2] [1985]:3).

With the increased prosperity of the 1970s, the tribal government made concerted efforts to upgrade housing, provide mortgages and loans, improve sewage lines and roads, and maintain other physical aspects of the reservation. It was also concerned with preservation of resources, including timber and grazing land. Outside experts were hired to give advice on such questions as the carrying capacity of range land. The tribal administration in 2002 was continuing all of these programs.

The level of education among Colville Indians is beginning to approximate that of the rest of Okanogan County, which is lower than average for the state of Washington but improving. The tribe pays one-third of the expenses of any tribal member of either gender and of any age who wants to attend trade school or college. The rest is paid from Bureau of Indian Affairs funds (one-third) and Pell Grant funds and other sources (one-third). The number of students did not decrease during the recession of the 1980s. Many graduates then and today hope to be employed by the tribe so that they may use their education but continue to reside on the reservation among their kin.

A decision was made in the early 1980s to allow molybdenum mining on reservation lands. The mining company spent $2,000,000 for social impact as well as physical impact studies in the area. Many public meetings with tribal members both on the reservation and in the large cities of the region preceded this decision. The company's representatives discussed problems (especially environmental and cultural ones) with tribal members. The need for new schools and roads was assessed. The mining company made plans to train Colville Reservation members as miners and construction workers without regard to gender and promised that tribal members would have priority in obtaining employment. Unfortunately, the drop in mineral prices canceled all the care and planning that went into the decision. Some people regretted the loss of the mine because of the obvious economic advantage it would have provided to individuals and the corporate tribe. Others feared that the social impact of the mine would have accelerated the loss of cultural heritage and adversely affected the pleasant rural environment.

Several reservation-owned industrial sites associated with lumbering exist on or near the reservation and employ tribal members. The Colville Indian Precision Pine Company is located at Omak and produces pine lumber for the manufacture of furniture and other items. The Inchelium Tribal Wood Treatment Plant makes wood products. Colville Forest Enterprises is situated at Nespelem. A private manufacturer has a site on the reservation (Colville Confederated Tribes n.d.:12).

Until 1984 the tribal administration was buying reservation land back from whites who wished to sell. Then the financial emergency struck. Fewer in-coming federal moneys and reduced timber prices added to the problem. The land buy-back was halted at that time but remains a long-term objective.

The tribe coped with the 1980s recession by having its employees work a four- instead of five-day week for a short period. In addition, 20 percent of the workforce was laid off, and the jobs of people who left voluntarily were not filled. In 1987 the unemployment rate on the reservation was about 60 percent, while the surrounding county's unemployment rate, one of the highest in the state of Washington that year, was 19 percent. The poverty rate on the reservation was estimated to be 30 percent at that time, and services such as mental health and speech pathology were cut back.

Despite this unpromising picture, the tribe set up an agency, the Colville Tribal Enterprise Corporation (CTEC), to start new industries for the reservation and find jobs for its tribal members. Even with economic problems, it was estimated that by the mid-1980s the tribal enterprises had become so profitable that they were able to spend $15,000,000 per year for goods and services, plus additional moneys in taxes to Okanogan and Ferry Counties. An official of the CTEC told me that the reservation is the largest economic entity in north-central Washington and forms the mainstay of five counties.

The tribe organized businesses in timber (a mill, logging, wood treatment plant), recreation (gambling, houseboating on Lake Roosevelt), retail (grocery stores on the reservation), construction, finance (providing credit to tribal members), and agriculture, with other enterprises planned. By fiscal 1992 the CTEC had made a net profit of $5.09 million; while unemployment is still higher than 50 percent (about a 10 percent decrease from the mid-1980s), optimism is general that the situation can be further improved (*Spokesman Review,* November 3, 1992; *Tribal Tribune* 18[10] [1992]:5). The modern economic situation on the Colville Reservation shows what an Indian reservation can do, even in hard times, provided it is given the autonomy to manage its own affairs.

Today the economy of the reservation is similar to that of Euro-American society in that the reservation staffs offices, manages forests and businesses, maintains roads, plans economic development, and administers health, education, and welfare offices. The reservation consequently is firmly situated in an industrial system. Nevertheless, the economy remains somewhat separate from the economy of the larger society. The tribe does its hiring by its own rules, based on its indigenous traditions and values. These traditional values are evident in the data presented below.

THE ECONOMIC SPHERE

Power in the Economic Sphere

Women maintain their reputation of being "take charge" people, as one consultant phrased it. A number of Colville individuals have described women in general as "having a lot to say" not only in the traditional and farming phases of the culture but in contemporary times too. While no opportunity arose to observe this kind of behavior within a young family in the contemporary culture, I observed an incident of female dominance occurring in the work place (an office) between an unrelated man and woman in 1979. Though the man was the woman's supervisor, the woman criticized him forthrightly and aggressively without anger or embarrassment, pointing out the man's lack of tact toward a third person. Since a similar situation among Euro-Americans is relatively rare, I interpret the incident to be due to a difference in culture and to be an exercise of power.

The perception of most reservation residents is that men and women employed by the tribe receive equal pay for equal work, a condition that I believe is an aspect of authority. Equal access to desirable jobs, however, is an aspect of power and is more uncertain in perception. Some women complain that most women's jobs are not as good as those of men. They recognize that female opportunities improve as women obtain more education, but one woman commented that the lack of a college education is no hindrance to a man's advancement. Conversely, some men complain, or report the complaints of other men, that women are given all of the good jobs.

In 1979, under the immediate supervision of the three top tribal administrators (who were male), four division heads existed, and only one of them was a woman. Women, however, did administer branches and offices in large numbers and ran programs with both men and women employees under their supervision. They also worked in the offices as typists, secretaries, and file clerks. Women appeared to have equal access to all levels of employment except for the very top positions at that time.

The prominence of men in 1979, holding three out of four top management jobs in the tribal administration, may have been due to acculturation processes. It may also be a reflection of the traditional value of men acting as spokesmen for the tribe and family. A third possibility is that men filled these positions because they frequently dealt with outsiders, who preferred to deal with men. The situation had changed by 1986.

In the financial emergency of 1986 on the reservation the four division heads were eliminated; the most important subdivisions within the four divisions were preserved and administered directly by the executive director, who was male. As of 1986 the administrative department had five male and five female administrators, the Comprehensive Planning Department had two male administrators, the Human Resource Development Department had three male administrators and twelve female administrators, and the Physical Resource Development Department had four male and one female administrators, making a total of fourteen males and eighteen females. With such a count, it seems that women have a fair share of administrative positions, assuring women equal access to economic power.

Since the tribal administration has had the autonomy to choose its own employees from 1974 on, today's hiring practices reflect reservation cultural traditions and not those of Euro-American society.

Authority in the Economic Sphere

In contemporary society newborn infants of either gender continue to be equally welcomed. No preference for either a male or a female is expressed by either expectant parent. Girls are raised in the expectation that they will be leaders, at least within their own families, and often within and outside the community.

The custom of distributing the "first foods" that a child captures or gathers is still occasionally practiced in the contemporary culture. Presently, meat from an animal killed by a young boy is given to his older relatives just as it was in the past, though sometimes a feast does not follow. The grandparent may simply distribute the meat to other elders. Sometimes, too, the meat may be frozen so that it can be taken later to a grandparent residing on another reservation. There a feast may be given in the boy's honor, or the meat may be distributed to other elders. Girls are still taught to dig roots by their grandmothers and mothers; their first independent gathering efforts are commemorated by a feast celebrating their achievement.

Additions have been made to the custom of celebrating a child's first economic achievements. When a child wins a prize at a powwow for the first time, at least some of the winnings are given to elders. Even the first loaf of bread baked by a girl is given to elders to "show respect."

Native vegetal foods are now in short supply due to the flooding of lands by Grand Coulee Dam and the occupation of traditional root-digging grounds by Euro-American farms and ranches. Wild carrots have almost disappeared, because cattle eat them. The cattle leave bitterroots alone, but even they are disappearing without known cause. One elder believes that wild crops are killed by the pesticides used on farmland. As an alternative, she tried to cultivate native roots in her garden but was unsuccessful, she speculated, because the soil was not suitable.

The traditional gender division of labor is somewhat obscured today. Formerly, if a young boy tried to dig roots, he would be stopped. Today men sometimes dig roots and pick berries. Women occasionally obtain a hunting license and hunt elk and deer. It is said that in Yakama country today women have begun to fish for salmon and men to dig roots. This crossing of traditional gender lines does not evoke the indignation that one might expect. Consultants smile indulgently when they relate these incidents; in contrast, they express unhappiness or even anger when speaking about the disappearance of wild foods.

Since employment and education are more accessible today than they were before 1970, families expect that both boys and girls will be employed when they are adults. The employment of both is judged equally important, and their work is equally valued. Young people of both genders are equally encouraged to seek vocational training, college training, and/or employment. They are also expected to participate equally in athletics.

Most of the people who are adults today lived in a milieu of poverty during their formative years and had little opportunity for employment on the reservation. Indians were poorer than poor whites thirty years ago, and their expectations were lower. This is supported by the demographic data collected for the 1970 United States census for Ferry and Okanogan Counties, where the reservation is located (Planning Support Group, BIA 1974:43–56, 169–82). The figures for Ferry County show that only 64 (or 35 percent) of 182 Indian males age twenty-five or over worked 50–52 weeks of the year. Of the 184 women age twenty-five or over, only 10 (or 5 percent) worked 27–39 weeks, and 17 (9 percent) worked 13 weeks or less. Of the Indian men, 36 percent were employed in agriculture, forestry, and fisheries, 25.4 percent in lumber and wood products, and 10 percent in public administration. The remaining 29 percent were scattered over several labor categories. The 27 female jobs were not analyzed by labor category.

In Okanogan County only 159 (38.7 percent) of the 411 Indian men age twenty-five or over held full-time jobs. Only 57 (12 percent) of the 474 women in the same category had full-time jobs; 196 women (41.4 percent) had no wage employment all year. Half of the employed Indian men in Okanogan County were working in agriculture, forestry, and fisheries. The median income for Indians fell in the range of $5,000 to $6,000 in 1970, while the median income for whites in the county was $10,000 to $12,000 per year for the same period.

In this situation older women, as the managers of households, continued to handle all of the meager resources of the family and coped with scarcity. They taught the children to "be tough" and survive despite poverty. When the reservation won the right to manage its own affairs in the 1970s, more employment became available, and people gladly grasped these opportunities.

The Colville Confederated Tribes were awarding college and vocational school scholarships to young people by at least 1966, a practice continued to the present. A fair number of men and women over age forty have also acquired college training today with the reservation's help. Before such assistance was available, a few people achieved higher education without outside aid. These individuals include business school graduates, college graduates, and a few with graduate degrees.

In June 1986 I was told that the tribe sponsored 71 people in higher education and 63 in vocational or other kinds of training. No breakdown by gender was available for these numbers: that factor was not important to the tribe.

In the public schools some differences between genders are noted. Reservation girls are reported to have higher grade point averages than reservation boys and also have higher educational aspirations. Girls aspire to higher-status occupations as well and appear to utilize job information more readily than boys. Female students involve elders more readily in their educational programs (Brod and Brod 1981:23, 30, 71).

Indian public school students report their parents' occupations as follows: 10 percent of fathers and 12 percent of mothers are professionals; 7 percent of fathers are administrators and managers, while 4 percent of the mothers hold a similar position (Brod and Brod 1981:27). Thus, at the higher levels of employment, Indian males and females are found with similar frequency.

In 1979–80 women were often employed in positions that would have been viewed by Euro-Americans as suitable only for males, such as directing parking and organizing camp locations during the Fourth of July tribal celebrations. Others managed their ranches and handled their own cattle, which is true to the present day. Women also worked beside men in blue-collar occupations. When the advent of mining was expected on the reservation, women were being trained along with men as miners. In the timber industry in 1979 women sorted poles, scaled trees, used chainsaws, and ran heavy equipment. At the tribal pole and post plant in December

1979 two women raised trees in the greenhouse, four sorted poles in the yard, one drove a D-3 caterpillar tractor, one served as night watch, and thirteen worked in the woods. Women are accepted in these jobs by male colleagues. One administrator who had worked both for Euro-American corporations and for the reservation said that women with the right training could get any kind of job on the reservation. He commented that this was not true of the Euro-American corporations for which he had worked. Some women filled positions in offices, beauty shops, and stores, which are categorized as female work by Euro-Americans. Reservation men also work in offices and stores.

The tribe employed 601 men and 620 women in August 1979. At that time men earned an average of $5.42 per hour and women earned $4.56 per hour, a difference of $0.86. This differential is skewed by the fact that the top three administrators during that time were men, however, who made three times more than the average male. According to my consultant, if these three positions were eliminated from consideration, salaries would be equal for both genders.

The overall average salaries would also be higher if only year-round employees were considered, according to consultants. While there were about 1,221 tribal employees in August 1979, as noted above, about 850 of these were summer employees (mostly high school and college students) who earned only $2.95 per hour that summer, thus depressing the average wage per hour.

Those individuals of both genders who hold management positions appear to have no problems supervising either male or female employees. A male consultant notes: "Women administrators have no problem. Most men around here are trained by women anyway; a mother or grandmother. If you can't deal with a woman in a people position, you can't deal with people."

A few men resisted the authority of women managers, but on investigation these cases of resistance appeared to be based on personality or policy differences rather than on problems of gender status. Employees of both genders do not hesitate to approach their female supervisors with problems and do not question their authority. Women administrators in tribal offices are generally judged to be very effective by individuals of both genders.

The two women on the Colville Business Council in 1979, Lucy Covington and Shirley Palmer, were reputed to be among the most influential and effective individuals on the reservation and in fact were also influential in non-Indian national politics and national intertribal politics at the time. I observed that they inspired great respect in their colleagues on the council and in the community.

The chief judge of the Colville Confederated Tribes in 1986 was a woman who had been the chief judge for four years at that time. She was one of five lawyers on the reservation. The qualifications she needed for the position were to be a tribal member and to have a law degree. There were two female associate judges in 1986, who were not required to have law degrees, but tribal membership was required. All of these positions were obtained through application. Gender is not a factor in becoming a judge. The sitting chief judge in 1986 was preceded in her position by another female lawyer, whose predecessor was male.

My consultant noted that Indian women judges were not uncommon. She pointed out that in the Plateau area a woman who was the Coeur d'Alene chief judge retired after a twenty-year career. Another woman was the chief judge on the Warm Springs Reservation. In 1986 the chief judge on the Yakama Reservation was male, but he had five female associates. The chief judge for the Nez Perce was a female. On the Northwest Coast the chief judge of the Quinault was a woman, and there were two women judges among the Makah. The Squamish had a female judge in 1986, while the Tulalip and Puyallup judges were male. Female judges occur among the Shoshone Bannock, Blackfeet, Northern Cheyenne, and tribes in Oklahoma and Michigan. The equal access of both genders to this position in many North American tribes is not a recent phenomenon, according to my consultant, but has existed since the beginning of tribal court systems. Certainly, equal access to judgeships appears to be emphatically present in the Plateau area.

Individuals of both genders commented that women are generally more efficient and reliable as workers than men. One male Euro-American consultant admired the speed and skill displayed by a group of Colville women who built a road on the reservation. He noted that women generally are more industrious and more thorough about completing a task and keep an eight-hour day more conscientiously than men.

This modern opinion is reminiscent of the phrase "men don't work," which encapsulates the emic or Indian women's perception of the male economic role in the traditional culture. Of course men "worked" in the past, by providing fish and animal flesh; and their defense of the community was risky "work," which was generally applauded. Apparently, however, these activities were not regarded as "work." Male activities occurred in strenuous spurts with leisurely periods in between, whereas women more often were continuously occupied with tasks on a daily basis. In my opinion, the traditional economic role of Colville women better prepared them for the eight-hour day and five- to six-day work week required of workers in an industrial society. The traditional pattern did not prepare men for this. Accentuating this difference is the lack of a "moral imperative" for Colville Reservation men to earn money for its own sake, which equals power and prestige in Euro-American society.

The traditional Indian male pattern of intermittent work may account for the observation that women in many North American tribes acculturate more readily to modern society than men do (Maynard 1979; McElroy 1979). It is argued that this differential acculturation among the Oglala Sioux occurs because women are able to continue their homemaker roles in contemporary times and thus experience less cultural disruption than men. In contrast, men are completely deprived of their former roles as warriors and hunters (Maynard 1979:12–13). This explanation cannot apply to the Plateau tribes of the Colville Reservation, because little continuity has occurred in women's roles either. Though child-bearing and child-rearing continue, all else is changed. Office employment is as different from gathering and preserving wild foods as lumbering is different from hunting. What remains from the past is the ethic that women do what they must to support the family and even provide the major share of support if needed, as they did in the traditional culture. Women's better adjustment in contemporary times may be due to their being accustomed to sustained rather than strenuous intermittent work. It would be interesting to see if other North American tribes had conceptions on the nature of male and female work similar to those in the Plateau and to correlate those conceptions with the differential acculturation of the sexes.

Autonomy in the Economic Sphere

One of the expressions of economic autonomy in contemporary Plateau culture is the independent decision to seek employment. If the following discussion seems concentrated on women, it is because the surrounding society expects men to work and disparages those who do not or even cannot. For many women in Euro-American society, however, seeking employ-ment is still considered by some a matter of choice not necessity; but who makes the choice and with whose assent are necessary questions to ask for both Colville and Euro-American groups.

Colville women today expect to be employed unless they have a good reason to stay at home; and husbands expect, not demand, that their wives will work. Colville women have worked outside the home for generations. When gathering was curtailed by circumstances, they farmed their land (see chapter 5). When employment became the only option to support the family in modern times, the decision to seek a job was made by the woman herself. I found the independence of women in making this deci-sion striking, but it is a natural outgrowth of the traditional culture in my opinion. The universal perception of both sexes is that the majority of women, perhaps 90 percent, are employed. Only the presence of pre-school children in the home and the absence of child-care services pre-vent women from seeking employment outside the home.

The validity of the perception that 90 percent of the reservation women work outside the home is supported by a 1979 Colville Reservation survey which shows that 81.8 percent of the women were employed at that time (Colville Confederated Tribes 1979). Furthermore, some employment (such as providing child-care services) may not have been reported in such data. During the workday, the young women I saw caring for their own preschool children were also caring for an employed woman's children. A young woman without children who had no employable skills would also care for other people's children to earn income. I noted during fieldwork only one young mother who cared for her own preschool children exclu-sively, though other examples were mentioned during interviews. While a day-care center flourishes in Nespelem, the number of children it can accommodate is limited. It was reported that, when employment was more easily obtained, some women hired high school girls during the summer to care for their children so the mothers could work for that period. These work strategies were undoubtedly necessitated by the low income earned by many Indians, making two incomes desirable (at this time most Euro-American women were still staying home). It is far more likely, however, that Colville women expect to be employed, just as they expected to spend their lives gathering plant foods in the past. Employment outside the home is simply something that women do.

I had an interesting conversation with a woman in 1979, who was about age thirty-five at the time. She was emphatic in saying that there is nothing women cannot do, and she could not understand why white women were pushing for equal rights. She was sure that she could always get her way in white society. This woman had been raised to be a leader and was unaware that most white women were raised to be disempowered.

Older women today still sell and trade, both to whites and to Indians of other reservations. Money derived from selling handicrafts is kept as individual property by both genders. Women do beadwork, for which they earn great respect; they tan hides, make baskets, and fill them with dried huckleberries and other foods for trade. Men make leather articles and clothing items for sale, such as feather bustles for powwows. Some men have taken up beading and are highly respected for their skill. One of the foremost Plateau beadwork artists today is male. As in the past, autonomy can be expressed beyond one's gender status, so that no talent is denied.

Ortner and Whitehead (1981:8) claim that women are defined everywhere in relational terms to men (e.g., as wife, mother, sister). This does not occur on the Colville Reservation. People are identified by their descent clan names, and at least some elders use European-style married names with some awkwardness when referring to other individuals. The factors affecting gender status in the economic sphere are shown in table 11.

THE DOMESTIC SPHERE

Power in the Domestic Sphere

Power as uninstitutionalized control or informal influence appears more often in contemporary Plateau culture compared to the traditional period, or it may be that power is simply more visible. Many of the traits presented below may have existed in the past, since they have no counterparts in Euro-American society.

Consultants say that a woman's duty is to protect her husband's image and dignity outside of the family. This is an ideal among the Nez Perce of Idaho too. A few women belittle their husbands publicly, but this is not generally approved. Women are considered responsible for the emotional success of their marriage just as Euro-American women are; but the Colville women are responsible because they are powerful, while the

TABLE 11

The Economic Spheres: Contemporary Culture

MEN   WOMEN

POWER

influence exerted by both genders

access to high management jobs by both genders

men outnumber women in   women outnumber men in
management positions in 1979   management positions in 1986

AUTHORITY

first economic achievements of youths ceremonially recognized

equally encouraged in training and employment

work equally valued

educational goals equally important

jobs less gender-typed than in Euro-American society

equal pay for equal work

authority equally effective in management jobs

women's work seen generally as
more efficient

AUTONOMY

decision to work autonomous

82–90% of women work (1979)

trade: proceeds owned individually

Euro-American women are responsible because they are powerless and must accommodate. Colville women decide whether a marriage is worth the effort, and Euro-American women make the effort because the alternative to remaining married may not be acceptable.

A male elder said appreciatively of women in the past: "Men had three duties: to provide, to defend, and to propagate. Women had uncountable duties. They were the backbone of everything. Everything depended on them."

The same perception and appreciation of women's strength is general today. Many people of both genders perceive women as actually dominant in many ways. They have strong personalities and strength of character and provide psychological support for the family. One male commented that men are not threatened by such women: they prefer to marry a woman of strength to depend on. Another male noted that during a recent bout of unemployment his wife had worked and kept the family fed. Without her they would have starved, he said. He appeared unthreatened by the episode and appreciative of her competence. This illustrates, in my opinion, that not even a myth of male dominance exists in Colville culture.

A woman noted that, although men seek support and concurrence from their wives, she did not see the male role as therefore weak or indecisive. Men depend on their wives without embarrassment, for wives are in the same category as mothers and grandmothers: all effective and strong-minded individuals. Women, however, do not normally seek concurrence from their men. If something a woman does disturbs her husband, he says nothing or uses nonverbal methods to inform her of his dissatisfaction.

Despite the influence that Colville women wield and the concurrence sought from them by their husbands, history indicates that Plateau men are not correspondingly weak. Their ancestors in the recent past displayed all of the usual male aggressiveness in war against the Plains Indians (Anastasio 1972:194). In later times the U.S. Army viewed the fighting ability of Plateau tribes with apprehension and respect (Alvord 1857:11).

A tendency for men and women to socialize separately in same-gender groups reinforces gender differentiation on the reservation. Clusters of female relatives sit together at celebrations and powwows, while sons-in-law and husbands sit on the periphery of such groups or socialize with other men in the general vicinity. Young couples of courting age socialize separately and openly without embarrassment. Individual men and women who are not courting speak together in a relaxed and unself-conscious manner, but such couples finish their conversation and drift apart.

One woman confirmed my observations that the genders tend to socialize separately and believed this occurred because in the past men and women were often separated geographically by their different economic duties. Today "the man is around the house a lot," a situation that was not formerly common. Despite the new situation, the genders tend to operate separately as individuals or in same-gender groups.

One female consultant, a social worker, believes that men tend to be emotionally dependent on women today because of acculturation problems. Previously they were reverent toward women because of their motherhood role, but now that has developed into emotional dependence—a recent phenomenon, in her opinion. I did not investigate this factor in the field, but a number of women in their thirties noted that women make the final decision in almost everything: finances, children, place of residence, and household affairs, all aspects of their managerial role. If a man wishes to move to take a job elsewhere, for instance, the woman may veto the move due to ties to relatives or other reasons. This may even cause a permanent separation. Acculturation may have increased men's dependence because of the simple fact that they no longer range the country looking for resources but are more often or even entirely within the traditional female milieu, the household.

Divorce is an arena where power struggles are rife. Many people come to recognize, particularly after a first divorce, that they may marry several times before they find a lifelong spouse. The marital troubles that may develop upset them, yet both genders react with far more aplomb than Euro-Americans in the same situation.

The cause of this self-assurance lies in the social structure. Both men and women receive emotional support from their nonunilinear descent groups when they have marital problems. In the past, as noted above, each often moved in with his or her descent group after a divorce. This is still true today, resulting in a system in which divorce makes less emotional and economic impact on an individual than in the larger society. A Colville person's first emotional commitment is not to the spouse but to the consanguineal extended family or the nonunilinear descent group. Material goods are still shared among its members, such as a car, food, and cash. Sometimes members of the descent group, especially a mother, view a happy marriage as a threat to family unity and try to cause dissension between the couple out of disapproval or jealousy. One man's parents accepted his marriage, but some of his other relatives did not. A long time may ensue before a new spouse is accepted by consanguineal relatives, especially if the spouse is not the first.

The Colville people are far less concerned with property than Euro-Americans, a factor that makes divorce easier. As one woman said, "When a white woman divorces, she is worried about property, like my two white friends who recently got divorced. When I decided to divorce, I had the right to keep the house and the furniture, but I took my clothes in a paper bag, my kids, and myself. I felt it was best to simply leave. If I kept all that stuff, I would remember my ex-husband too much. By leaving all this, I was protecting my emotional, mental, and physical self." Thus, Colville women more readily abandon material goods in order to expedite the dissolution of a marriage. This woman knew she could always return to her extended family, who would help her out until she could accumulate material goods again. While these social supports indicate the extent of an individual's autonomy, they also provide individuals with a great deal of power in marital relationships.

Power is also indicated when a man returns frequently to visit his ex-wife on the pretext of visiting his children. If his ex-wife has a new husband or partner, he sometimes attempts to disrupt the relationship by making the new husband jealous. I noted this pattern on the Nez Perce Reservation as well.

The custom of a woman using violence against her husband's lover persisted at least until 1980 and perhaps beyond, as it did on the Nez Perce Reservation (Ackerman 1971:601). One consultant says that she prefers to abstain from beating her rival: "That is too easy. I like to make it unpredictable so that the woman is always on guard and uneasy. I am always friendly to my ex's girlfriend. I could beat her . . . , but I prefer to be unpredictable." I interpret this intimidation as a form of power.

Before marriage, men ask for dates only when the women indicate that they are willing. A woman pointed out:

Women put pressure on men to ask for dates. Indian women have control of sex; they are in control—period. Indian women look for a man, whereas among whites, men look for a woman. This is not regarded as bad; it is accepted that women control the situation. Women hint about marriage or moving in. If men were to make the suggestion, they would put themselves at the woman's mercy, so they don't do it. Thus, it is up to the women to make the suggestion . . . It is presumption for a man to ask . . . She sets the tone of a relationship.

Sometimes when a woman puts pressure on a man to ask her out she has to warn other women to stay away from him so that he has no alternative. This is usual behavior and acceptable to both genders.

Some of the characteristics cited above are included in Euro-American gender role models, but many of the attributes of each gender are reversed. Euro-American women are perceived as being less aggressive in romantic situations and more emotionally dependent on men than vice versa. This reversal of gender role content between Colville and Euro-American cultures causes a few problems for some reservation individuals who perceive Euro-American and Colville gender roles to be the same when they are not. For instance, they learn that women are "supposed" to be passive and submissive. They may learn to imitate Euro-American gender roles as presented in school or as seen on television. Since the content of Euro-American gender roles is incompatible with the Colville socialization of the genders, in which women are supposed to manage households, money, and people, confusion in behavior results. Some men try to dominate women, and some women try to be submissive; but this causes severe conflict within the individual as well as marital disharmony. The cultural contradictions in the two gender role systems presented to them are mostly unperceived. In contrast, the majority of Colville men and women experience no confusion in their gender role models, because they ignore or are unaware of Euro-American patterns, as exemplified by their bewilderment regarding the reasons for the feminist movement in Euro-American society.

Euro-American–Indian marriages might be expected to cause some confusion in gender roles, but this is not always so. Most of these marriages are very successful despite the difference in gender-role expectations. Indian women married to white men do not seem to be less effective as leaders and managers than their counterparts who marry Indian men. The Euro-American husbands of Colville women, however, most often grew up near the Indian community and probably accept the difference in gender roles without question or confusion. Even men raised in non-Indian communities seem to welcome their Indian wives' managerial skills.

In two out of three cases known to me of Colville men married to Euro-American women, the outcome was unhappier. The men attempted domination of their wives in the stereotypic Euro-American manner, learned from their contact with Euro-Americans on the job or through television; and these two marriages ended in divorce, suggesting that Euro-American women may not be as submissive as they are expected to be. The third marriage is successful and has lasted over a decade.

It is the Colville wife's responsibility to pay the family's bills, no matter what the source of income, thus retaining her traditional managerial role. It is said that this custom prevails on all of the (Plateau) reservations. As a consequence, older men often find themselves helpless in looking after family finances if their wives become seriously ill. Younger men have more competence in this matter, but even they say that women are more economically astute as a rule.

Because of the women's central role in household management and control over the finances, they have great influence on their husbands' decisions, including which jobs they should take. I noted that men performed tasks set for them by their wives promptly, without discussion. When a disagreement arose between husband and wife, one consultant noted that the wife would sometimes criticize her husband, who by custom received her remarks without comment. He was required to wait a full day to "get his ducks in line" and then give her his counterargument, which she in her turn had to take without comment. Presumably some kind of accommodation followed.

Money leads to power and prestige in the larger society, and a Euro-American male is threatened by a wife who earns a higher salary than he does (Gould 1976:116). These concepts are alien to Colville Reservation society. A woman's higher salary does not endow her with more power or extra influence within the home, just as a man's higher salary gives him no extra influence or power over her. A large income does not earn prestige in the community; a low income does not diminish prestige in the community. If a woman is at home and is unemployed, she has as much influence as if she were employed. A social worker pointed out: "Money is not a source of discontent. A woman's larger salary is not grounds for fighting. That's why Indians seem to squander their money: they don't care about it. I have never heard in my work couples complaining because the wife earns say ten percent more than her husband or that he doesn't make enough. Having enough money might be a problem, but the source of it is not a problem."

These observations were indirectly confirmed by a person who lived and worked away from the reservation for many years. He commented that in his tribal office building everyone knows how much everyone else earns: the only ones who fret about this public knowledge are the non-Indian employees, whose status in Euro-American culture is affected by the amount of money they earn. Such status concepts are not held by the Colville people. Their concepts of power and prestige do not equate with income level. Prestige is still earned the old-fashioned way: by being generous, wise, and temperate in judgment. Such a person becomes influential and is sought out for advice.

The source of income also has no effect on relative power or influence between spouses. Some men do not work and are totally supported by their wives. This is socially acceptable, especially for older men. It is said that since "men did not work" in the old culture, it does not seem strange for men not to work in the new one. Younger men who are not employed are expected by their wives to be helpful at home, however, and look after older children. No prestige is lost in this situation.

Some men feel strongly that housework is exclusively a female responsibility even if a woman is employed outside of the home. This is understandable if it is recalled that men were not often present in the home in the past. Consultants say that fewer than half of the husbands help their wives with housework, but younger men help more often than older men. Some wives press their husbands into giving help, and some men willingly perform household tasks without discussion. Men generally refuse to care for very young children, however, though I have seen them play with babies. Even when the father is at home, the mother must obtain child-care help elsewhere for the baby if she needs to leave for the evening. This custom was current on the Nez Perce Reservation during my fieldwork in 1965.

The custody of the children after divorce is uninstitutionalized today and therefore subject to the use of power. While most children remain with the mother, child support is not given indefinitely by the father in most cases, as in the surrounding society. Consequently, employment becomes necessary for a woman after divorce if she has not been working before. The women recognize that even if they remarry they need economic independence. Several once-divorced women commented that they would never again depend wholly on a husband for income as they did when their children were small.

The frequency with which men obtain custody of children, even infants, is said to be increasing, as it is in Euro-American society. Fathers are faced with the same problems as working mothers: they must obtain good child-care help while they work. If this problem is solved, placing children with fathers is reported to be a viable option.

Marriages continue to take place in which the woman is several years older than the man, a practice occurring in the past. These marriages are not infrequent, and their chances of success appear to be as great as those of marriages in which the ages of the couple are similar. If one of the spouses is notably older than the other, the older spouse usually influences the younger. Only one contemporary marriage in which the man is considerably older than the woman came to my notice, though the opposite situation seems common enough.

Consultants say that Sanpoil and Southern Okanogan women dominate men, while Nez Perce and Columbia men dominate women. These nuances were not perceptible to me as an outside observer.

Violence

Two forms of violence are discussed here: spouse beating or battering and rape. Both are noted in the literature (Mandelbaum 1938:116; Ray 1932:146).

Domestic Violence or Battering   Spouse battering, particularly of wives but occasionally of husbands, is a problem of some concern in modern Colville Reservation society, as it is among Euro Americans. Although battering occurred in the traditional past, it could not be kept secret as it often is in Euro-American society. Battering was immediately apparent because of the small size of the communities and residence among relatives. The assailant was prevented from going too far by his relatives and later counseled by them to solve problems another way. If the wife was quite young, her parents often persuaded her to leave her husband and return home. A persistent batterer might be punished by the chief. In one case a generation ago a chief judged a man guilty of this habitual conduct and had him tied up outside the village and left there. He was only allowed to go free when he expressed contrition. His descendants, however, are said to exhibit a similar tendency to violence. John Ross (1996:25) similarly notes that a pregnant woman who gossiped or watched the movements of her neighbors was likely to pass this "busybody" trait on to her unborn child.

A conference held in Okanogan, Washington, on the subject of domestic violence (February 6, 1980) explored the problem in both Indian and Euro-American families. The lecturers noted that domestic violence occurs occasionally in 60 percent of Euro-American families and repeatedly in 30 percent of them. No statistics were known for Indian families.

Professionals have reached no consensus on the root cause of battering. One theory indicates that low female status in Euro-American society is caused by socializing men for domination and women for subordination.

One young Indian man from the audience indignantly disagreed with the assessment that women had subordinate status. He declared that his mother was a woman and was not inferior to him. An Indian woman from the audience commented that women in white (Euro-American) society were not equal to men, but this was not true on the reservations.

The Euro-American professional opinion at the conference was that the cause of domestic violence lay in the personality of the batterer. They pointed out that some men when upset quarrel or get ulcers but do not strike their wives. The batterers, however, are used to a pattern of violence and must be taught a new method of dealing with their frustrations. Some of the members of the Indian audience whom I talked to later believe that the cause of battering lies in the woman's behavior, particularly when she refuses to have sexual relations with her husband. This occurs, they said, due to Catholic influence. When the missionaries first came, they prohibited the practice of birth control and approved of sexual denial within marriage. This caused and still causes much marital discord.

No frequency of wife battering was known for Indian families, but the Indian audience expressed great concern about its occurrence on the reservation. One woman said that she had tolerated beatings several times before she left her husband. Another was struck only once, motivating her to abandon the marriage immediately. This gives us a range of tolerance for battering by Colville women. Colville women in a battering situation have more options than Euro-American women in that their relatives readily support them emotionally and willingly take them into their households. The option of support from relatives, emotional and otherwise, is not always available to Euro-American women.

Some Colville individuals of both genders believe that the battered Colville women that they know tolerate the beatings, and in that sense the violence is self-imposed. The battered women believe that such incidents improve communication afterward. I have observed that Plateau groups are not as verbose as Euro-Americans, but the same belief in "better communication" for Euro-American couples after battering incidents was noted at the conference. Social work professionals see battering as an attempt by the husband to control the wife; this may be as true for Colville Reservation society as it is for Euro-American society.

According to gossip, which I was unable to verify, some men are battered by their wives on the Colville Reservation. The female batterers are not necessarily large individuals. Battering by either husband or wife is still condemned by this society.

Why do the strong Colville women tolerate battering at all? The answer is that only some do and only for a while. There are differences between individuals, after all. Some women are somewhat shy, and some not as assertive as others. As Schlegel (1990:23) remarks, "Variability exists within cultures as well as between them." I never met an intimidated woman over the age of thirty-five, however, and I believe that the battering tolerated by some women is a matter of their inexperience in conjugal relations. The overwhelming number of women I interviewed and met were assertive and acutely alert to their and their children's best self-interest.

Rape   A recent incident of sexual harassment occurred at one of the Indian celebrations I attended. The offender was seized by a group of older women and taken to a tent. He was treated much the same way as rapists were treated in the past (see chapter 4). Even while the man's humiliation was in progress, everyone at the powwow knew about it, adding public shame to his punishment.

Authority in the Domestic Sphere

A very small number of older women say that men are the leaders within the family and spokesmen for them, though women continue to run the household. Ideally, men are supposed to be the spokesmen; but Ross (1986:280), the early fur trader, noted that women and men shared equally in leadership within the family. Some older women today, however, were greatly influenced in their youth by the Jesuit missionaries, who tried to institute Christian subordination of the women to men among reservation tribes (Raufer 1966:26). Certainly, no subordination is customary among women today; nor did it occur in traditional society. A very few women of the group aged sixty or older, who grew up during the farming period, may speak as if men ruled their lives; but despite their words, they behave very much like their ancestors and descendants in exerting power, authority, and autonomy.

The contrast in behavior between women educated within the Catholic boarding schools and those raised at home was noted several times by consultants. In one case a granddaughter emphatically disapproved of her grandmother's boarding-school education, saying that it endangered the family's welfare. Women educated in the boarding schools were said to be more submissive and sometimes not as decisive as even devout Catholic women raised at home by parents or grandparents. The opinion was that such Catholic training in submission adversely affected the Colville woman's role in her domestic and other societal functions.

In another example, a woman intended to submit to her husband's decision that she should not work outside the home; but when finances became tight, she sought a job without consulting him first. He made no comments concerning her employment once she had made the decision.

Despite the existence of women's authority, a few "deferential" practices occur. Women wait on men at home during meals and do small tasks for them. Women fetched horses for their husbands a generation ago, apparently part of the division of labor. I noted an older woman step aside for her husband so he could precede her out the door at a recent powwow. This may not be an example of deference, however, but a practice left over from the past, when a hunter always preceded a group in order to kill game that might appear unexpectedly.

"Deference" is an elusive and imprecise method of evaluating gender status, since it makes judgments on what people are thinking. Comparing the rights of men and women seems to me to be a far more solid method of judging gender status than the small courtesies that men and women extend to each other. For instance, men opening doors for women in Euro-American culture is "deference" behavior but certainly has little or nothing to do with the actual status of the genders in that society.

The Colville Indian extended family continues to operate as a network. A household today still includes more than the nuclear family, at least emotionally. Often grandparents live close by and participate in family affairs, even if they do not actually live under the same roof with daughters or sons. Siblings and cousins live in the same neighborhood, and all the relatives are found together in one house after work or in their spare time. Many individuals are raised by the grandmother and/or an older sister while the parents are employed. Family elders, including uncles and aunts, still exercise authority and serve as resources for advice and economic support when family problems arise. Parents continue to be equally authoritative in the lives of their children, just as they were in the past.

Two consultants describe having "mentors," who supplement the functions of family elders. A man has a male mentor, while a woman has a female mentor. These individuals are not necessarily related or even of the same tribe, though a person of a "compatible tribe" is chosen. The mentors are part of the emotional support system, sometimes arranged by a parent. Only elders with good judgment and character are chosen. One man asked his friend to be a mentor to his son. The rationale is that a father or grandfather may be too close to a problem to give good advice, and the son (or daughter) should have an additional resource for guidance. This is said to be a very common practice.

Indeed, the mentor system does appear in the literature. It is called *tiwi'akt* (secret advice) in the Nez Perce language. Tiwi'akt is a custom where an adolescent male is sent to a respected older man who advises him "secretly" to respect elders and, I suspect, counsels him on how to have a good marriage. Girls, too, are included in this custom. They are advised to avoid having too many husbands and to select a good man and settle down. The advisers were given gifts by the young person's parents for their services (Thomas 1970:18–20).

Sometimes older persons may take youngsters under their wings if they are orphaned or need emotional support for other reasons. An elder said that it is easier to give advice to other people's children than to one's own grandchildren because he could be more objective. A young man with marital problems might seek advice from a female elder, not his mentor, if he has a problem understanding his wife.

The importance of both men and women on the Colville Reservation is indicated by the fact that children can inherit reservation membership from either parent, probably a result of the bilateral kinship system. This is not true on some North American reservations, where only the father's status confers tribal membership on the child.

When the original allotments were made, both men and women received them whether they were married or not. Some of the land in the North Half of the reservation was allotted to reservation tribal members as well as the South Half, which constitutes the contemporary reservation. Two other categories of allotments were made at this time, one in the Wenatchi area and the other on lands adjacent to the reservation.

As an additional measure of gender status, I examined the Numerical Allotment Schedule in the Bureau of Indian Affairs offices for the Colville

TABLE 12

Original Distribution of Allotments by Gender

	SOUTH HALF	NORTH HALF	WATERVILLE ALLOTMENTS WENATACHI HOMESTEADS	H&C ALLOTMENTS COLVILLE AND SPOKANE RESERVATIONS
Men	1135	320	48	30
Women	1147	275	16	41
Unknown	193	28	18	3

Confederated Tribes to discover if men and women owned equal quantities of land when the first allotments were made and if equal numbers of men and women own land today. I determined the gender of each allottee in the record by first names. The total numbers of land parcels belonging to each gender were then counted in both periods, the time of the first allotments and the present (see table 12). In the records of the first allotments I was unable to determine the gender of some individuals because they were designated by Indian names. At least for the South Half of the reservation, the distribution of land allotments appeared to be fairly equal between men and women; but it is unlikely that this datum is significant, since all individuals were supposed to be allotted, regardless of gender.

The original allotments were redistributed to heirs in the course of time. Land distributions according to gender were examined for the year 1986. Most individuals on the Numerical Allotment Schedule had several land tracts listed in their names. Though individuals might own many parcels of land and were thus listed several times, their names were counted each time they appeared, resulting in a rough measure of land ownership. The sizes of the land tracts could not be determined from this record and were said to vary, so the method of determining the amount of land each gender holds may be flawed. Still, it was the only method available to document ownership of land by gender. The gender of some of the owners of land tracts in this period could not be determined because of the use of unisex names like Dana, Merle, Leslie, Robin, and Tracy. These were placed in a separate category (see table 13).

Considering only the South Half, which makes up the modern reservation, the land tracts allotted to individuals total 16,243, while the total number of land tracts listed is 18,134. The tribe itself owns the land represented

TABLE 13

Distribution of Land Tracts by Gender (1986)

	SOUTH HALF	NORTH HALF
Men	7322	1472
Women	8778	1818
Unknown	143	23

by the difference between those two numbers. Women own 9 percent more tracts of individually owned land than men (1,456 more tracts). Colville tribal members on and off the reservation of all ages (since all ages inherit land), number 3,304 males and 3,483 females. There are 179 more females, a 3 percent surplus. It would seem that women inherit somewhat more land than men, though it is hard to judge because of the difference in size of the tracts. Even the 143 tracts of land belonging to individuals with unisex names would not even out the seeming lead of females in owning land. Consultants' perceptions are that land is inherited equally by men and women, however, which may indeed be true.

Since each individual held property separately from his or her spouse in the traditional culture, it was of interest to learn if the holding of property today (particularly allotments) followed the traditional pattern or was influenced by Euro-American culture. I found that allotment land inherited from one's family is kept in the individual recipient's name and is not shared with a spouse. This is predictable in light of the recent discovery that the extended families are really nonunilinear descent groups (Ackerman 1994), whose claims to "family" property would be far more important than the spouse's. Only three of the couples interviewed held allotment property in common and did so only for the tax advantages in holding property jointly. Other land and property accumulated by an individual before marriage remains with that individual after divorce. Property acquired during a marriage is divided equally in case of divorce.

Reservation members express a great deal of anxiety regarding the inheritance of allotment property; they desire that such land be inherited by their children, not by their spouses, thus retaining the land in the same blood lines. They fear that if the husband inherits allotment property from his wife and then dies without a will, his wife's allotment land might be distributed not only to their common children but to his children from a previous marriage, at the same time disinheriting any of her children from a previous marriage. Such a situation is abhorrent due to the nature of nonunilinear descent groups, which resemble clans, and pains are taken to prevent this situation from developing.

Married couples have joint or separate checking accounts: there appears to be no pattern. Two couples over age sixty keep separate bank accounts, while two other couples of similar age had joint property and joint bank accounts. Thus, age does not seem to be a predictor for how financial assets are held. No correlation was found between the way such assets are held and tribe of origin: two couples from the same tribe handled their assets differently. Furthermore, holding assets separately does not seem to be a symptom of imminent marital dissolution.

Younger couples tend to hold financial assets separately, particularly if they are not legally married (but are considered to be so by Indian custom). One individual noted that in a first marriage everything is held jointly, except for inherited allotments, and in a second marriage everything is held separately. This is partly to protect the wife's interests in case of divorce. A house and car go to the wife with children, even if the amount of other property is negligible, echoing the situation in the farming period (see chapter 5). Usually one of the cars is in the wife's name anyway, so it legally belongs to her.

If a married couple has joint bank accounts, a woman might keep a savings account in her name, as women are believed to save more effectively than men. One individual related that he and his wife have a method in which they use his paycheck first and then hers to cover their expenses. Any surplus is saved.

When bank accounts are held separately, a husband and wife usually contribute equally to clothes, food, and furniture. Other arrangements are described. In one family the husband takes care of the house payments and utilities, while the wife pays for food and has the children's teeth straightened. Each saves separately. The purchase of large items is a joint decision by the couple, although only one of them might pay for it. The man might pay all of the taxes. Skills may determine who buys certain things. A man in one family shopped for food because he was better at it, while his wife chose his clothes. No particular division of responsibility is institutionalized, but an attempt is made to equalize the burden.

Even when real estate is held jointly, cars and other property are held separately. Many women own their own vehicles, while the husbands own theirs (often a pickup truck). Some couples have easy access to their spouse's vehicle, but others must seek permission to use them. One consultant said that permission is only sensible, so the spouse is not deprived of transportation; another said that permission is needed because it is a matter of exclusive rights. An outsider cannot borrow a man's pickup truck by seeking permission from his wife: she has no say in the matter. Women who own a car obtain credit for it themselves and make the payments out of their own salaries or wages.

Some of these economic arrangements are reminiscent of traditional practices when spouses owned property separately, something that is harder to do today. The new economic arrangements are not overly important to the people of the Colville Reservation, except for allotment lands, but are described here to point up the differences from Euro-American domestic arrangements.

Autonomy in the Domestic Sphere

Autonomy is expressed by the retention of some money from each paycheck for one's own personal use. This behavior is institutionalized and also occurred on the Nez Perce Reservation in 1965. The custom began in the farming period when food was still directly available from the environment, so the occasional cash windfall was used to buy luxuries for oneself or presents for the spouse and children. Today, even though money is scarce and food and other necessities must be bought, the right to keep a small sum for personal use continues to be recognized. The use of the money is completely autonomous. There is no need to negotiate with anyone about how it will be used.

Sometimes personal funds are used to help extended family members in need. If this is insufficient, an individual who keeps joint bank accounts with his or her spouse draws on it to give to relatives without objection from the spouse. Even an unemployed woman has the right to help her relatives financially. Fourth or fifth cousins, who are the equivalent of siblings, also have a right to ask for and receive assistance. This practice of assisting relatives is derived from the traditional obligation to one's affinal and consanguineal kin.

Today large amounts of money withdrawn from a joint account require, if not a joint decision, at least a notification of the spouse so that money does not run short before the next paycheck. In traditional times food was easy to obtain, and sharing was definitely easier; but needs are great today, and few individuals refuse assistance to relatives. Sometimes those in need move in with kin for a short time or indefinitely, according to the situation. Such services as transportation are freely given.

A few married couples discuss the problems that might arise if a wife with small children decides to seek employment, but most do not do this. The woman herself is the one who chooses to find work or stay home. The husband says nothing if he disapproves, for he has no right to influence her decision. On the contrary, most men would not think of opposing the wife's decision: they are not socialized that way. The choice, they recognize, belongs solely to the woman. Thus, women neither need nor seek their husbands' compliance or permission to seek employment; and, in turn, those men who prefer not to be employed need not clear that option with their wives.

Young employed women today are like their mothers and grandmothers who worked on their farms and elsewhere. A few women started a contracting company in the Coulee Dam area (*Tribal Tribune* 11[10] [1985]:8); others sell cars; and still others serve in the army (*Tribal Tribune* 12[5] [1986]:14, 15). Many pick apples in season. The older generation of women plowed their land or worked as migrant workers, midwives, cooks, waitresses, and restaurant managers. Some went to Seattle to work in the aircraft factories during World War II. One elderly woman who was one of those who took the Catholic submission of women somewhat seriously nevertheless sought employment despite her husband's disapproval. Her husband accepted her behavior quietly, notwithstanding his Catholic rearing. She said, "My husband never wanted me to work. My daughter was ready for college and wanted to go into nursing. I wanted to work to get her through school, but my husband said no. So I took the bus to Boeing—we were living in Tacoma at the time—and got a job there. My husband didn't say anything. I worked from then on. He didn't mind anymore."

The organization of the extended family or nonunilinear descent group is crucial in nurturing the autonomy of individuals. The individual receives the uncritical affection and support of all relatives. Solidarity begins in childhood. During a celebration I saw children of both genders look after the younger ones and play with them. A boy of about six walked a toddler around very responsibly. Children played near their relatives in small, quiet groups. In one group I estimated that the mother had direct contact with the children perhaps only 10 percent of the time, since the children were occupied with other adult relatives and each other. Adult relatives greeted very young children with delight, forging bonds that last throughout life. Thus, the extended family or nonunilinear descent group, in my view, forms the basis for the considerable autonomy that Plateau individuals enjoy. In the vicissitudes of life, the extended family gives unwavering support and forms a haven for the individual that marriage cannot rival in this culture. An adult's emotional life is therefore not confined to a spouse alone. A few women had no hesitation in saying that they were closer to their fathers than to their husbands. Such an unquestioning emotional support system bolsters autonomy for the individual.

Marriage

No definite rule of residence after marriage is pervasive. Examples of both matrilocal and patrilocal marriages were observed. A young couple may live near either set of parents if economic opportunity is available in the vicinity. Neolocal residence appears to be common but is misleading, for relatives usually live nearby, and intense interaction is frequent.

Today most people choose their own marriage partners. Some families attempt to arrange marriages in the traditional manner, but the young people refuse to accept the arrangements. Family and peer approval or disapproval, however, does have some influence. Young people are encouraged to marry other Indians and are taken to Indian celebrations for the opportunity to meet other young people.

The usual marital pattern for most older people consists of one or two short-term marriages in their youth followed by one that lasts indefinitely. A large minority of people never settle down to one spouse, however, even though they choose their own marriage partners.

The same pattern is evident today among younger people. The usual marital history may include a legal (i.e., Euro-American) marriage the first time, perhaps followed by a legal divorce. A series of trial marriages (Indian custom marriages) then follows, often ending with a permanent and legal marriage. Some couples who have lived together for many years may never marry legally, so that they do not feel confined. These patterns are analogous to the past, when remarriage and divorce were easy and were an expression of personal autonomy.

A federal law in 1954 forced Indian tribes to relinquish their marriage customs and make their marriages conform to Euro-American laws to make them "legal." This has succeeded in illegitimatizing a fair number of children whose parents live in a union that would have been recognized as legal traditionally. Fortunately, Colville tribal rules do not exclude children of such unions from tribal membership and benefits.

The traditional incest rules are meticulously followed in most cases. Stories of second-, third-, or fourth-cousin marriages in the larger society and an occasional lapse in Indian society appall most Indian observers. They regard a couple with the same grandparents as scandalous and are convinced that genetic flaws appear in the children of such marriages.

Independence of movement in marriage is still characteristic of both genders. A woman may notify her husband that she is leaving town but does not ask permission, even implicitly. The same is true for men.

Divorce

Divorce continues to be autonomous for both genders in contemporary culture. Dissolving a marriage or liaison is still relatively easy for women because most are prepared to support children by themselves if necessary. A number of men willingly provide for their children after divorce; but this is a Euro-American rather than a Plateau pattern, since "support" was never a problem in the past, as noted previously. A female elder expressed scorn for a young woman who was seeking support for their children from an ex-husband, and another considered it inappropriate to seek such support. Unfortunately for autonomy, the greater difficulty in providing for children today as compared to the past is not widely recognized. Women cannot take their children along when they go to work as in the past and now must find child-care services as well as employment.

Nevertheless, female self-reliance persists. Assisting in this attitude is the indifference toward material objects, as described above, so unlike the aftermath of divorce in the Euro-American community. Of course, the difference in attitudes between the two cultures is explicable in that Euro-American women often do not have ready means to support themselves and their children and do not have an extended family to turn to for assistance.

A few Colville women are beginning to question their attitude of extreme self-reliance. They concede that—while it is considered shameful for women to ask for support and they themselves are working presently—times have changed, and children have certain rights. Food is no longer around for the gathering. Therefore, these few women press their ex-husbands for support. While present Colville divorce patterns are similar to those in the past, continuing the old custom largely unchanged, the contemporary economic situation may modify autonomy in divorce in the future.

The cause of most divorces and separations is still the involvement of one spouse with someone else or physical mistreatment. Nonsupport is never mentioned as a cause.

One may speculate that in the past and present married Colville couples did not and do not need extensive and intensive emotional support from each other: they have the extended family for that. The personality development and emotional support ideally present in Euro-American marriages appear to be largely absent from Colville marriages, thus making divorce a matter of *relative* unimportance. At least in the early years of a marriage, one person may be much like another, distinguished perhaps by good looks or economic skills. Spouses, then, may tend to be somewhat interchangeable. A couple does not need to be a "good match" as in Euro-American culture. Instead the Plateau system allows room for individuality, making the individual and the extended family basic social units. This is in contrast to Euro-American society, where married couples are the basic social unit and individuality is obscured by the necessity for unity. Such speculation perhaps exaggerates the situation, but the data seem to lead in this direction. Factors relevant to gender status in the domestic sphere are shown in table 14.

THE POLITICAL SPHERE

Power in the Political Sphere

There is still no class system today on the Colville Reservation. Some people earn more money than others, and some are unemployed, but this does not create class distinctions. Respect and influence are still accorded

TABLE 14

The Domestic Sphere: Contemporary Culture

MEN	WOMEN
POWER	
	psychological source of strength for family
women protect husband's public image	men seek women's concurrence
	take initiative in dating, marriage
	more economically astute
larger income does not lead to power	
equal power when either unemployed	
more than 1/2 do not do housework	
some instances of child custody after divorce	custody of children after divorce usual
some men batter wives	easy divorce a recourse, some women batter husbands
rape	women punish rapists
AUTHORITY	
spokesmen for families	run household (important institution)
receive deference from wives	
equal authority over children	
reservation membership inherited from either parent	
allotments inherited about equally; women may have somewhat more land	
financial assets held jointly or separately	
AUTONOMY	
small amount of money kept for personal use	
use joint moneys to assist relatives	
autonomous in making decision to work	
marriage partners chosen by individual	
independent in movements	
divorce no economic handicap	
	some problems appearing in support of children

to the person who is generous, kind, and helpful to others. Thus, the poor qualify for respect. Respect is also given to one who has overcome life obstacles such as alcoholism. One way to describe such a person is that he or she is serious, meaning not a person without humor but one who is conscientious in working hard and whose life goals are centered in care of family and community.

Both men and women exert political influence today. They speak publicly at meetings and have equal access to council members to discuss problems. As in the past, women's opinions are taken as seriously as men's in all political arenas. Youth is said to be somewhat more of a disadvantage than gender in political matters, though not as much as in the past.

A few individuals perceive women as having less political power now than in the past, while some young people who are unaware of part of their history see women as having no political power but believe they are in the process of acquiring it. Most consultants state that political power depends on the personality and character of the individual and that gender is irrelevant.

Women as well as men are seen as natural leaders in any context, including politics. According to consultants of both genders, women more naturally and readily perceive what is right and wrong in the political arena and are less susceptible to political pressure than men.

Authority in the Political Sphere

In the past, authority was vested in the chief. The chiefs and their functions are gone today except for the Sanpoil people based around Keller, Washington. A descendant of the Sanpoil chief serves as a liaison between his people and the Colville Business Council, informing the council of his people's concerns and informing his own people about reservation affairs. No authority remains in the role, but respect lingers. Consultants say that individuals descended from chiefs in other groups have not expressed interest in continuing a chief's role under modern conditions, and the role has lapsed in all other tribes.

Aboriginal villages and tribes, too, have largely disappeared, along with most of their functions. At least the descendants of some of the village groups and tribes continue to function in a ceremonial and social sense. Tribal picnics are held, and symbols of tribal and family affiliation are worn during the celebrations and dances. Tribal identity is no longer acquired from the area where one resides, however, because people of most tribes are scattered over all of the reservation. Many young people know which tribes they are descended from, but others seem uncertain. Some younger individuals recognize themselves as descendants of at least four villages and/or tribes and recite all four names when asked for tribal identity, instead of identifying with just their place of residence, as they would have done in the past. This varied inheritance appears to be of minor importance to them. The overriding identification for many young people is being a Colville Indian, not of Kettle Falls but of the Colville Confederated Tribes.

This identification is reinforced during the powwows and frequent gatherings at the community centers. The reservation-wide events serve to integrate the entire community. Indian dance contests take place within age groups and between age groups. It is impressive to see small, solemn four-year old girls quietly taking their place next to seventy-year-old great-grandmothers to compete for the title of best dancer. The children are not patronized but are taken seriously and thus learn to take themselves seriously. Whatever their other functions may be, the powwows seem to be a socializing, integrating force. These celebrations not only reinforce reservation-wide identity, but—as they include celebrants from other Plateau reservations, many of them close relatives of Colville Reservation people—they become a pan-Plateau vehicle, creating a union of reservations.

Colville Reservation identity is important in relation to Euro-American society. Young men wear T-shirts proudly proclaiming their reservation identity. While many local white people have intermarried with the Colville and accept the cultural differences, others do not understand why the tribal members do not behave exactly like Euro-Americans, since they now live in houses, wear Euro-American clothes, and go to college. Thus, the support and sympathy of other reservation residents with a common identity is helpful in the face of misunderstanding by outsiders.

The fourteen members of the Colville Business Council include both males and females, who have equal authority over tribal affairs. Their position is a full-time job, which includes council meetings and committee meetings on and off the reservation.

Nonunilinear descent groups, with historical distinguished chiefs as their founding ancestor, traditionally form a source for future political leaders, even in contemporary times. The descent groups train both their sons and daughters for leadership and encourage them to take on these roles as adults. Other people in the community also regard these families as sources for potential political leaders. Some but not all of the council members in 1979 and 1980 were descendants of historical Plateau chiefs. Members of nonchiefly families may also aspire to and achieve the same leadership positions; but they must learn on their own, a task that is considered difficult. Political office is said to be available today to anyone on the reservation who is interested and ambitious and has the "right kind of personality."

Women are reported to have no limitations in reaching for leadership positions. Consultants note that a number of women always sat on the tribal council from its inception in 1938. Records show that nine men and five women were on the council from 1964 to 1967. In 1968 eight men and six women sat on the council. In 1970 ten men and four women made up the council (Business Council Records n.d.).

In 1979, when this study was begun, only two out of fourteen council members were women, but they were unusually influential because of their role in successfully fighting termination. Both were descended from the most able chiefs in recent Plateau history, but they earned their offices through the exercise of influence (power), persuading people to fight termination. One of these women was Shirley Palmer, first elected to the Business Council in 1959, descendant of Chief Moses on her mother's side and the influential Wapato family on her father's side. She served on the council for twenty-eight years. During her tenure, she engaged in many important battles, including winning back jurisdiction over law enforcement (retrocession) for the tribe from the local counties. The most important battle she engaged in, along with three others on the council at the time, was termination. They organized the fight against termination when many individuals were intimidated by the federal government's determination to force it on them (Strong 1988).

The other very important woman on the council was Lucy Covington, a descendant of both Chief Moses and Chief Kamiakin. She was the granddaughter of Moses and had been raised in his family by Mary Moses, one of his wives. Mrs. Covington was steeped in Indian tradition, learning the principles of leadership through example and precept. She was especially prominent in the fight against termination, motivated by her belief that if Indians do not have land they do not have anything (Odyssey Productions 1978). By 1970 the termination battle had been won, and the two women continued to serve on the Colville Business Council (thereby exercising authority). Mrs. Covington served until she died, and Mrs. Palmer served until she retired in 1987.

While the two women shared authority with other council members, they had much influence (power) on the reservation and with the federal government—an influence that is not implicit in the offices they held. They were good decision makers and adamant in their principles, according to consultants. Decisions were not made that were contrary to their wishes: their concurrence was sought. I noted that, while they did not speak more frequently than the men in council, their opinions were always solicited and their advice invariably taken. I witnessed Mrs. Covington boldly challenging a federal official who was visiting the council, while the men of the council remained dignified and reserved. Consultants commented that these two women voted as the people wanted and were not swayed from what they perceived to be right. Consequently, their influence was extensive. Each served as the chairperson of the Tribal Business Council in different years.

In 1985 eleven women and nineteen men competed for seven council positions (*Tribal Tribune* 11[3] [1985]:11; half the positions come up for election every year). Two women, one an incumbent, were elected. In 1986 four women and eight men sat on the council. At least three of the female council members had grown children and grandchildren, indicating their relative freedom from family responsibility.

Many women run for election but do not win office. Consultants of both genders state that women are not handicapped by their gender in the political sphere. They say they would more readily vote for a qualified woman than a similarly qualified man, but fewer qualified women run for office. The pool of women is smaller than it could be because young women with small children are not willing to leave them with others frequently, and extensive travel is required in the council position. This situation has arisen only since 1970, when the end of the termination movement brought greater autonomy to the reservation. The necessary travel and overtime work now required of council members results in a crucial problem for women, perceived by both genders. In the 1960s, with termination anticipated, less time was required for the work, and keeping abreast of developments was easier. This is no longer true. Even with the work being full-time and well-paid, relatively few young women feel able to serve on the council. Many of these same women say that they would willingly consider running for council when their children are older. One noted, "I have been asked to run for the council, but I don't want to until my children are older. Even the job I have takes me traveling too much. It is a strain on me and my children."

These circumstances reduce the number of talented women available as candidates. Thus, while the gender of a candidate is not relevant in winning office today according to consultants of both genders, and personality and talent are the criteria that count, the social structure is changing enough to hinder many women who would otherwise be suitable to serve on the council.

Several consultants noted that women do not need to be on the council to have their concerns addressed. They point out that many capable women have priorities other than political participation. Males on the council seek advice from their wives, mothers, grandmothers, and others; and since "women run things on the reservation, anyway," as one male consultant remarked, their advice is routinely solicited on political matters. Consultants pointed out that formerly wives advised the chiefs openly, without anyone thinking it unusual. Women consequently continue to be intimately involved in the political process, say consultants, and their lack of equal presence on the council is not as significant as it would be in Euro-American society. Indeed no woman I spoke to feels that she is politically impotent because of her gender. Despite the structural inequality developing in the realm of political authority, women feel themselves to be ideologically equal.

If the Colville Reservation only had to deal with other Indians, then the relatively few women on the council would not be serious. In negotiations with Euro-American officials, however, the relative lack of women on the council could be a limitation. A young man said:

> Women are not interested in being on the council, and that's why there are not more women there. They are not discouraged from running. They are not interested in spending the time. Women sometimes are given more of a chance than men [to win office]. This is because women do a better job and are more authoritative. They have a stronger spirit. They are not scared to say what they feel, and the tribe needs more of that. Men are less willing to take somebody on than a woman. Men are more quiet, conservative.

A woman noted: "Women are more active in politics than men. They may never speak up, but they know a lot of what is going on. Caring for young children holds them back. My sister wanted to run for office, but was concerned about the amount of travel involved in the job. She has a small child and no husband."

Other consultants made similar comments regarding the position of women in politics and the strength they displayed. This was confirmed by incidents observed during tribal council meetings, in which the few women on the council appeared to be the pivot around whom decisions were made.

The presence of women on the Business Council of the Colville Confederated tribes is not unique in the Plateau. While doing other kinds of research on the Coeur d'Alene Reservation in 1987, I asked about female status there out of curiosity. I was told by a middle-aged male that women had equal status among the Coeur d'Alene people. He said that women were on the original council that organized the tribal government and have been on every tribal council since, except two. He noted that in an election that took place just prior to our conversation, 65 percent of the voters were women.

Council women on the Colville Tribal Council are usually assigned to the Enrollment Committee or to the Health, Education, and Welfare Committee. The affairs they deal with are seen to be female concerns, though men also sit on these committees. Welfare concerns are considered extremely important, not having the inferior status they have in Euro-American culture. The two committees are seen as insuring the future of the reservation and its people. Women also serve on the council committees dealing with leases and timber sales, activities usually associated with males in Euro-American culture. Thus, gender stereotypes, while present, do not have the same meaning in Colville and Euro-American societies.

Both men and women are active on boards and other decision-making bodies on the reservation. Boards include the Crisis Center (for suicide prevention), the Paschal Sherman School (a boarding school for older children), health boards, a day-care center, and the Indian Cultural Heritage Board. Social service programs are viewed as being extremely important since they are instruments for preserving the culture and improving the community.

One of the functions of the traditional chief was to orate: "give speeches" at gatherings and funerals. With the disappearance of the chief's role, other people are invited to perform this function. A council member or an elder may be asked. Formerly only men orated at these events, but today women do so as well on a regular basis. They orate because many of the knowledgeable older men have died, "so it is up to the women." The female ceremonial speakers today include a chief's daughter and a chief's widow. A knowledge of religion and traditions is needed for this extemporaneous oration.

A group of women served as tribal representatives when they met the Euro-American male Omak Stampede officials for the August 1979 rodeo. A great deal of public disagreement arose between the two groups regarding arrangements, but the women without hesitation forcefully pressed their side of the argument. This would not be unusual in Euro-American culture today, but it was in 1979.

Autonomy in the Political Sphere

Autonomy in the political sphere today involves speaking publicly and voting independently. Women were observed to speak publicly at least as often as men at public meetings. In 1979 women took successful political action by organizing a day-care center in the town of Inchelium and lobbying the council for funds to support it. The equal political activity of both genders today supports the testimony of those elders who say that men and women both spoke publicly on political issues in the past. The evidence suggests that the public participation of both men and women today is an inheritance from their traditions.

Spouses vote independently of one another. They never inform each other or anyone else regarding the way they cast their vote before or after an election. A couple married for many years may guess how the other votes, but the matter is never discussed. One woman said: "Husband and wife vote independently. I *know* I always vote differently from my husband." Another said: "I don't even know how my husband voted when my sister ran for office. This is the general tendency. We don't question each other on how we will vote."

This independence in voting is taken so seriously that one male, aged about thirty, was incredulous when I told him that a Euro-American couple would likely influence each other before an election and vote the same way. Such a possibility is considered absurd, if not scandalous, in Colville

TABLE 15

The Political Sphere: Contemporary Culture

MEN	WOMEN

POWER

access to political influence

age an advantage to either gender

both genders acceptable as leaders

AUTHORITY

Sanpoil chief

members of tribal council

chairperson of either gender

women with young children somewhat handicapped on council

orate on ceremonial occasions

active on boards

tribal representatives for rodeo
arrangement

AUTONOMY

both genders speak publicly in equal frequency

married couples vote independently, do not know how spouse votes

Indian culture. Factors relevant to gender status in the political sphere are
shown in table 15.

THE RELIGIOUS SPHERE

Several religions exist on the reservation today, including the traditional
Guardian Spirit religion, the Catholic Church, the Seven Drums religion
(a Sahaptian variant of the Guardian Spirit religion), the Methodists, the
Native American Church, which uses peyote in its rituals, and the Indian
Shaker Church. One person may adhere to two or more of these religions
at the same time, usually without ambivalence. The opinion of several consultants was that God can be interpreted many ways, and they disregard
claims of any one religion being the only true one.

The Catholic Church has a strong presence but may be losing adherents among young people. In recent years prayers and the catechism are

recited in Indian languages. The priests now tolerate the "Chinook" dances, the modern version of the Guardian Spirit Dance, in the community without criticism. The Methodists are present but as of 1980 appeared not to be greatly influential.

Some elders continue to practice the traditional Guardian Spirit religion, and many of the youth have sought to become practitioners of it. A return to the traditional religion is seen by some as an answer to the social problems besetting the reservation, such as alcoholism and a very high suicide rate. Sweat-bathing is returning as a religious ritual among some young people of both genders. Men and women continue to use separate bath houses.

The Seven Drums religion is associated with the Nez Perce and the Moses Columbia but is highly respected by other groups. The Seven Drums practitioners are often asked to perform their rituals at reservation affairs. The Native American Church is somewhat controversial because of its use of peyote but has made a few local converts.

The Indian Shaker Church began among the Coastal Salish and has made converts among the Plateau reservations, including the Colville Reservation. It is a vital religion that combines elements of the Guardian Spirit religion with Christianity and has a powerful emotional attraction for its adherents. It, too, attempts to address alcoholism and other social ills through its teachings, and it has had success in coping with these social problems.

Power in the Religious Sphere

Much of the Guardian Spirit religion has survived and may be undergoing a revival. I collected few data on the subject, as people were understandably reluctant to discuss it. It was said, however, that guardian spirits continue to be very important today in the lives of people.

The community still includes shamans of both genders who operate as sorcerers. Sorcerers have the ability to kill people through the use of their power, which they use for real or imagined slights. If sorcerers use their power for evil purposes too often, however, the power will turn on them and destroy them.

Women are said to be the backbone of the Catholic Church. They run the programs, raise money, decorate the altar, and keep the building clean, although they do not usher.

Authority in the Religious Sphere

Women are as deeply involved as men in the Guardian Spirit religion and in fact are said to dominate it. Consultants note that many elders and younger people have guardian spirits and have a variety of spiritual powers conferred on them. These include a knowledge of healing or love medicine, the ability to predict the sex of an unborn child, and the power to foresee that a woman is pregnant before she herself is aware of it. One elderly woman who denied being a healer despite delivering many babies successfully and curing the sick said:

> If there's anything, I can almost sense it, that something is gonna happen. Now if anybody that's pregnant, you know, after they're beginning to fill out, I can tell them what they have, and I have never missed. I had a lady down here who says, "Well, they tole me that you can tell people when they're pregnant, what they're gonna have." And I says, "Well, maybe I can, I don't know." "I wish you'd tell me what I'm gonna have." I says, "Well, you walk in, I'll tell you." So I tole her she was gonna have a girl. "Oh, no," she says, "I've already got three!" "Well," I says, "I'm sorry, but you're gonna have another girl." Then along about three weeks, she did get her girl.

The Guardian Spirit Dances, often referred to as Chinook dances today, continue to be held; but I did not obtain further information on them. Part of the reason for the relatively covert practice of the Guardian Spirit religion is that it was often criticized and suppressed by governmental and Christian authorities in the past.

Both men and women serve as healers, called "Indian doctors," but women healers were said to outnumber men in the town of Nespelem as of 1980. One consultant knew of only male shamans in the Inchelium district; but since they were her relatives, she was more likely to be aware only of these individuals. It is doubtful that the overall ratio of men to women healers has changed significantly.

Many of today's elderly healers, both women and men, began taking patients when they were in their early twenties. For women, that meant they were often wives and mothers with young children. One female elder recalled that her oldest child was two years old when she first "danced," that is, experienced her spirit for the first time at a Guardian Spirit ceremony. She denied that being a healer was incompatible with the role of wife and mother of small children. Living in extended families, other women would supervise children when their mother went into trance. Plateau healers were not marginal individuals, as they are in some cultures. They performed and still perform a highly valued function for their society.

I was told that prophets who could predict future events still exist. One female prophet follows the traditional Guardian Spirit religion and Catholicism simultaneously. It is said that she finds it difficult to reconcile the two religions.

Some resentment against the Catholic Church has arisen among younger people because the church prohibited the use of Indian languages in the recent past, leading to their disuse today. The priests discouraged the use of native languages so that acculturation to Euro-American culture would be facilitated. This error is acknowledged by many priests today, who are more flexible on cultural matters than they used to be. They also concede the existence of the concept of a Creator God in the traditional Plateau religion.

Ushering in the Catholic Church is considered men's work. Only men read the gospels, a situation that caused much discussion in 1979. Despite men's authoritative functions within the church, people perceive women as being its main support. A number of Colville women have become nuns, but the names of only two priests from the entire Plateau were recalled.

Consultants note that women are very active in the Native American Church or peyote religion. I was unable to collect data on this religion.

A Nez Perce woman who served as Gathering Leader for her people in 1979 remarked that this was a traditional role with religious functions. Her greatest concern was to guard against cultural contamination of the rituals.

I was generously allowed to observe the Sunday services and curing ceremonies of the Indian Shaker Church on the Colville Reservation. As noted above, this religion represents a blend of elements of the Guardian Spirit religion and Christianity. It arose due to the ban of the Guardian Spirit religion by the superintendent of Indian affairs of Washington Territory in 1871, who was particularly opposed to shamanistic curing (Gunther 1949:41). The Indian Shaker religion arose to fill the gap, combining Christianity with elements of the traditional religion (Amoss 1990:636). It was an indigenous movement that began among the Coast Salish of Washington in 1881 (Gunther 1949:37–38) and spread to many of the Indian tribes of the Northwest. The Colville Reservation represents an eastern extension of this distribution. While the Indian Shaker religion has some resemblance to the traditional Guardian Spirit religion in that possession occurs during the ceremonies, a Shaker becomes possessed with the spirit of God instead of a guardian spirit, according to a Shaker consultant (also see Amoss 1990:636, 638–39).

The life history of a contemporary Shaker woman recounts her spiritual struggle in attempting to rationalize seemingly conflicting religious precepts. She received a Catholic education as a child but was steeped in Indian culture. In young womanhood she was possessed by an Indian spirit and became ill with spiritual sickness, the usual occurrence until a Guardian Spirit Dance cures such a person. She resisted the spirit because the missionaries had taught her that possession was evil, and she feared it. Her struggle and illness continued for some time. Finally her father pointed out that in religion there is "not only one way." She came to accept that her Indian spirit was another manifestation of God. She then welcomed her spirit, a powerful one, and became a healer in the traditional manner. The attraction of Christianity remained, however, and after a series of personal crises she was able to integrate the two religions philosophically as an adherent of the Indian Shaker Church.

The members of the Indian Shaker Church included more women than men at the ceremonies I witnessed in 1979. The minister, assistant ministers, and several other functionaries were women. During one ceremony, seven men and thirteen women participated, while one man, a visitor, watched. People who were ill were seated in chairs in the middle of the church and were cured by others. All healers were women at one point in the ceremony, but a few men began curing later. Thus, women are prominent in this branch of the Shaker Church.

Autonomy in the Religious Sphere

Autonomy today is expressed by the personal choice of a religion. A large number of people follow several religious beliefs without experiencing internal conflict. One woman who was brought up Catholic and attends those services also attends Methodist services, gets healed by a Shaker, prays during a Seven Drums ritual, and has at least one guardian spirit. The characteristic autonomy of the Plateau individual has found new scope in the religious sphere, though not always without criticism by others.

Religion continues to be of paramount interest to the individual, regardless of the form it takes. One consultant commented that religion is more private than sex and is the key to the culture. A middle-aged Coeur d'Alene said that it was "the great mystery of life" and was a constant source of contemplation for him. Reflecting this interest in religion, a conference on the reservation discussing the Indian Freedom of Religion Act (a law passed by Congress on August 11, 1978) attracted several hundred tribal members of all ages. People as young as thirteen were present, and both genders appeared to be there in approximately equal numbers.

Catholic parishioners assume a characteristic Plateau autonomy in their relationship to the church. Some have disagreed vociferously with priests. A generation ago a priest refused to allow a couple who had separated to attend church with their new spouses, whom they had married according to Indian custom. When they were ordered out of the church, they retorted that they were there to pray to God, not to the priests, and intended to stay. Many people supported their side of the argument with the priest.

Though many individuals have a guardian spirit today, others regret that they do not. Many elders acquired a spirit in their youth but later rejected it due to missionary influence. Most young people today wish to follow the old religion, but not all have relatives who can guide them in a spirit quest.

Apparently at least some children are sent on explicit spirit quests today. Spirits are also acquired in other contexts—for instance, while performing a solitary task, while alone on a walk, or even when in the company of others. As during the farming period, elders prepare their children or grandchildren for a spirit encounter by sending them on errands after dark. Often the children become lost; the spirits seek them out and guide them home.

Skill in the stick games was considered to be the gift of a guardian spirit in traditional times (Ray 1932:155) and is still viewed this way in the present. Today gamblers travel from one Indian celebration to the next and are welcomed everywhere. A few people who still make their living exclusively by gambling are much admired.

The game appears to be little changed from the past (see Ray 1932: 155–59 for a description of the stick game), except that cash instead of goods is wagered and men and women are intermixed in all games. Formerly, men played only with men as partners and opponents, and women played only with women. The mixing of the genders in today's stick games is due to the lapse of menstrual taboos, making separation no longer

TABLE 16

Distribution of Men and Women in Seven Stick Games

| | TEAM A | | TEAM B | |
GAME	MEN	WOMEN	MEN	WOMEN
1	4	3	7	2
2	4	3	3	7
3	6	4	5	6
4	3	3	5	6
5	8	4	3	3
6	1	5	2	10
7	5	4	6	3
Totals	31	26	31	37

necessary. Women in the past never beat poles and drums when they played: today they do both.

During the stick game tournament on July 5, 1979, women were chosen to conceal the bones as often as men. One game was composed of Canadians on one side (probably Lakes or Northern Okanogan) and Colville Reservation members on the other. People changed sides when a game was over, however. One of the pointmen in this game was a very intense, solemn young man, perhaps under twenty years of age, but the players opposing him were relaxed and happy. One man sang his gambling song, joyously waving his arms, and others sang and made gestures calling on their spirits to confuse the pointman's spirit while he concentrated on making a winning choice. The players were not age-stratified: the teams included all ages. A very successful eleven-year-old boy hid the bones and confounded the players on the other side. People placed bets with individuals on the opposing side even after the formal betting was closed. One woman about thirty was self-assured and authoritative in this side-betting. I saw more pointmen than pointwomen on this date, but I was told later that the gender of the pointers was about equal in frequency most of the time.

On July 7, 1979, the stick game tournament was in full swing, and seven games were going simultaneously. At 9:00 P.M. I counted the number of male and female participants in each game. I considered as participants only those who were seated or kneeling at the poles, although others who were standing were sometimes chosen to hide the bones. Still other indi-

TABLE 17

The Religious Sphere: Contemporary Culture

MEN	WOMEN

POWER

sorcerers of both genders

guardian spirits

run Catholic Church programs

AUTHORITY

Indian doctors or shamans

prophets

Gathering Leader

read gospels, usher in Catholic Church | minister, deacon, elder in Indian Shaker Church

AUTONOMY

equal interest and participation in religions

gamblers

viduals were on their feet and placed bets while they watched. I found that the participation of men and women was roughly equal on this date: a total of 62 men and 63 women were on the stick-game teams (see table 16).

At the July 4 celebration of 1984, nine teams played in the stick-game tournament. The teams were named for their leaders, four men and five women. A team headed by a woman took first place in the tournament that year (*Tribal Tribune* 10[7] [1984]:7). Factors in the comparative status of men and women in the religious sphere are outlined in table 17.

CONCLUSIONS

Gender equality has persisted into contemporary times (see tables 11 to 17). Instead of having complementary rights, however, the genders seem to have a greater number of identical rights today than in previous periods, as discussed in the following chapter.

Comparisons, Commentaries, and Conclusions

THE COLVILLE RESERVATION

The equal access of men and women to all social spheres in Colville Reservation culture during all three periods described appears to be conclusive. Gender equality does indeed exist in Colville Reservation culture. It is a necessary component in the culture found not only in the foraging past but in the industrial present, with an interesting and perhaps significant difference. In the foraging and early reservation periods men and women exercised mostly balanced, complementary rights. In the present they have mostly identical rights in every aspect of culture. This suggests that access to identical rights is the only way to have equal rights in an industrial society.

The issue of complementary rights as an index to gender equality has been debated among anthropologists who specialize in gender. The consensus is that these kinds of rights are indeed a measure of gender equality. A recent book argues just that point for North American native cultures (Klein and Ackerman 1995).

One might then suggest that Euro-American women had complementary rights in the past and that their movement for identical rights today is misguided. Did Euro-American women really exercise complementary rights in their society in the past, however, similar to those of Colville Reservation women? Euro-American women on farms certainly raised chickens independently in the past to earn some income, but could they support a family on that sum? Further, did they have access to public arenas even thirty years ago? They might voice political opinions to their husbands or fathers, but how many approached the mayor? These women may have had the *legal* right to question or dispute the mayor, but that was not the *custom*, and customs are the subject of this book. In the recent past Euro-American women did not seek offices in any great number, for they would never even win nomination. Today women still are not equally represented in holding office.

I am not arguing here that the Plateau people, because they practiced gender equality in the past and do so today, are living in perfect harmony— they are too human for that. The Colville do not have an ideal world for either men or women; it is just different from Euro-American society and in many ways quite admirable on its own terms. The Colville people simply live by different rules.

Because of the cultural similarity among Plateau tribes due to inter-marriage and cultural exchange, it is likely that gender equality existed among all the Plateau groups in the past, as Ray (1939:24) states. Gender equality is also likely to be present among all Plateau Indians today, since intermarriage and cultural exchange among reservations are persevering traits (Ackerman 1994). The contemporary existence of gender equality was confirmed in conversations with members of other reservations and Canadian reserves in Washington, Idaho, Oregon, and British Columbia. Male dominance does not even appear to be a male fantasy in the culture, for most men easily and readily assert that men and women are equal.

Thus, gender equality on the Colville Reservation is an indigenous trait, a legacy from the past, not derived from Euro-American culture. It is an authentically Plateau social form, indicating not only the persistence of gender equality but the persistence of traditional Plateau culture itself. While it is true that the culture has changed, little of this change has been voluntary. Many cultural forms were lost or attenuated through force (e.g., the native languages, shamanism, the traditional political system, and polygyny); and changes in subsistence were forced through expropriation or destruction of lands and resources. One may speculate that voluntary culture change might have occurred only in the acquisition of Euro-American technology. Today's high rate of suicide and other social problems are reactions to the misery experienced when the traditional support systems are forcibly disorganized and the replacements offered are unsatisfactory or lacking altogether. The contemporary Colville people are now keenly aware of the dangers inherent in too much change for no reason. Thus, they keep what they can of their way of life, and the preservation of gender equality in the present day is included in that context.

How has gender equality been preserved on the Colville Reservation when female status has been debased in many parts of the country and in the world by colonialism and capitalism (see, e.g., Boserup 1970:53, 60; Bossen 1975:600; Leacock 1978:247)? Rayna Reiter (1975:14) notes that colonial powers are able to reduce women's status "when essentially parallel forms of organization between women and men are subsumed into one, and that one is male. Leadership roles and activities formerly associated with men are legitimated, while those associated with women are devaluated or obliterated." When missionaries and government administrators exerted their influence on the Colville Reservation, the office of sku'malt, the female judge who was equal in status to a chief, disappeared. They were not successful, however, in ranking men and women, in giving superior value to men's work, probably because women's work was too important. Using traditional subsistence methods, women provided not only subsistence in all periods but comfort and some luxuries in earlier periods. The only constraint on obtaining these goods was labor. In the past, if effort was exerted, one lived well. Women as well as men provided essential labor in the economy, and it was not labor easily controlled by anyone other than the person exerting the effort. I see women's prominence in economic activities as one of the causes of the persistence of gender equality in the Plateau.

This may not be the whole answer, however. It seems to me that gender systems change readily and rapidly when the economic way of life is disturbed. We certainly see it in Patricia Draper's (1975) account of the !Kung when they changed from foraging to farming. Ester Boserup (1970) narrated the plight of women farmers all over the world when their circumstances changed. Capitalism is often pointed out as the culprit in the debasement of women's status (e.g., Bossen 1975; Leacock 1978). Albers (1989:140) notes that women in the northern Plains tribes of North America lost status in contact times when their societies became dependent on the fur trade for European markets. The labor process was dominated by men, while the women of these groups became processors of buffalo meat and hides. The distribution of these goods was controlled by the men, who were consequently able to accumulate wealth and prestige (Albers 1989: 142), leading to inequality between men and women.

The situation was different in the Plateau. Instead of becoming dependent on the fur trade, the Plateau people hunted just enough furs to obtain guns and other desired goods and then turned to their subsistence activities for daily sustenance. Wealth as defined by the native economy was not disruptive of the culture or gender statuses; it was wealth to be used and distributed. Vibert (1997:146) noted that individuals did not generally accumulate wealth. It was generosity that was the social ideal, a trait lasting into the present. Thus, wealth derived through the fur trade did not accumulate; it was given away to relatives and others.

The fur traders tried to persuade the Plateau Indians to hunt but failed. The Indians were impervious to persuasion. This was quite frustrating for the European fur traders, who ended up hunting for most of their own furs. They complained bitterly about the indolence of the Indians (Vibert 1997:120, 122, 144). Consequently, the Plateau people avoided being fully integrated into the capitalist system.

One of the factors preventing the Plateau people from being fully integrated into the fur-hunting effort was the prevalence of epidemic diseases during this period. Too many men were ill or had died for many to hunt for anything other than their own food. It is possible that these diseases may have been a factor that prevented integration into the capitalistic system, as happened on the northern Plains.

When the Plateau people lost their land and control over their food resources and were restricted to reservations, another attempt was made to integrate them into the capitalistic system by teaching them to farm. While this was very successful at first, it became only indifferently successful in the long run, because the best land for farming was taken by settlers and other impediments for integration developed. Consequently, as time progressed, the Colville Reservation people became poor compared to their white neighbors and poor compared to their traditional economy. Children were taught to be "tough" by their mothers and grandmothers, to endure poverty. Survival came to depend very much on women's gathering of native foods, subsistence gardening, and above all their managerial skills in organizing all resources brought into the household by family members.

Women's economic activities were critical to survival in the early reservation years, especially as the men were prevented from hunting and fishing in quantity due to control by the State of Washington. I believe it was because of their key role in survival that Plateau women never lost egalitarian status in their own society.

Status reduction also did not affect the Tlingit after contact (Etienne and Leacock 1980:20). Women were strong and respected in the past, and they are respected and strong in the present. They control the purse strings in both periods (Klein 1976:173). Tlingit women work in jobs that do not bring in as much income as the men's fishing, but the work is steady and year-round, unlike that of the men. Because the women work with Euro-Americans, they get political experience, which translates into political office (Klein 1976:175).

Paiute women also have retained their high precontact status (Knack 1995:156). Women interfaced between their communities and the Euro-Americans because they had the opportunity to be employed, while the men's labor was not as readily used by whites (Knack 1986:97, 1995:156).

Retention of equal status has not always occurred. Apparently the status of women has been up, then down, and up again among the Seneca (Bilharz 1995:112), indicating that gender status can be variable, depending on circumstances. In contact times the Seneca depended on trade goods with the Europeans, forcing men to be mobile. This undercut the balance between men and women, making men's work more important (Etienne and Leacock 1980:12), which led to inequality. In modern times Seneca women expanded their political and economic roles, leading to the reestablishment of equality (Bilharz 1995:111–12).

Gender status on the Colville Reservation can be compared to a rubber band. It was stretched by outside forces trying to make women subservient; but when the pressure was released, gender status took its original shape, as did most of the culture. The existence of a tradition like gender equality may be explained another way. Because many Indian customs were forbidden by missionaries and government agents in the youth of elders of the 1980s, some of these prohibitions are still taken seriously by a small minority of elders (e.g., the uneasiness of some individuals who believe in Catholicism and the traditional religion simultaneously). Another alien imperative, the subservience of women, was taught by the Jesuit missionaries (as noted in chapter 6). Some older women raised in the Catholic boarding schools in their youth learned the lesson of subservience to a certain extent and today behave or at least speak accordingly, very unlike their mothers, daughters, and granddaughters. These older women have somewhat different ideals than their ancestors or descendants. They have been more conservative in the number of marriages contracted during their lives and live in nuclear families ideologically, insisting that their elders live with them instead of the reverse. These individuals represent a possibility that never became actualized: a possibility that Colville culture could have been changed permanently in the direction that the missionaries were urging— female subservience. The missionaries did not have enough time to solidify the culture changes they engineered before the influx of settlers reduced their influence, and the necessity of women being effective economic agents also interfered with their goal.

Instead of that particular evolution taking on shape and permanence, a resurgence of many once-forbidden Colville traditions is occurring today. While the menstrual taboo and traditional political forms are gone for good and the native economy is only a shadow of the original, the traditional religion is undergoing a revival, and marriage and divorce customs have come to correspond with the traditional types. How has this happened?

I believe that, perhaps due to extensive and wide intermarriage within the Plateau, some formerly prohibited customs such as traditional gambling, the quest for spirit power, and traditional divorce (defined as taking up separate residence) were reintroduced to families who had discarded them because of Euro-American pressure. This process of reintroducing cultural traditions to individual families can be compared to a huge gene pool consisting of traditional cultural behaviors covering the entire Plateau, where traditions once lost to the general population were nurtured in certain localities and through intermarriage were reintroduced into areas where they had previously been eliminated. Gender equality has been one of the Plateau traditions that were somewhat attenuated in one generation but that returned in force thereafter.

I believe the factor of cultural persistence is underrated. In North America, despite much pressure for acculturation, observers speak of the survival of cultural "remnants." Nancy Lurie (1971:418–23) argues that Indian communities represent more than remnants. Indian societies reinterpret desirable traits of Euro-American culture for adoption, while rejecting others. They retain many characteristics of their traditional cultures, which include at least the following traits:

1. decisions made by consensus;
2. high value placed on oratory as a means of reaching agreement;
3. humor as a means of social control or enjoyment;
4. institutionalized sharing as a means for community survival;
5. no emotional commitment to personal property;
6. an indirect style in attempting to control bad behavior in others;
7. respect for others;
8. withdrawal from tense situations;
9. respect for another's autonomy, even when a person persists in a disastrous course;
10. the ready adoption of cultural items that enhance the culture (such as horses, sheep raising, tape-recorders, outboard motors, and a preference for employment that is intense and of short duration).

These ten items represent at least some core values of North American tribes that are different from the Euro-American culture that surrounds them (Lurie 1971:444–48). The Plateau culture shares all the characteristics listed above and, along with other Indian communities, is involved in "the social and cultural reintegration of Indian institutions within the context of contemporary industrial society" (Leacock 1971:12).

Gender equality is also persistent. Colville women are noted as independent by the surrounding Euro-American population, but outsiders may be unaware of the extent of that independence. So perhaps Colville gender egalitarianism also survives because it is invisible to outsiders, who at this stage of Euro-American culture probably would not care in any case. With part of the larger society trying to win equal rights for women, the existence of gender equality on the Colville Reservation might even be applauded.

Of all the possible explanations for the survival of gender equality, however, the importance of women in the physical survival of their families and societies is, I believe, the most important. Men recognize and honor women for this quality, making gender equality a necessary component of the culture.

COMPARISONS OF COLVILLE AND EURO-AMERICAN CULTURES

Colville and Euro-American cultures are converging in the practice of gender relations in some respects. Many of the modern economic arrangements that Colville couples make are similar to the ones that Euro-Americans are evolving, like separate bank accounts and separate property. This independent ownership was not common among Euro-Americans in 1979 when I began fieldwork on this subject but is more common today. The evolving resemblance suggests that the exercise of gender equality or the desire for it results in similar economic rules among Euro-American and Colville couples. These similar rules may be the only economic arrangements feasible for a gender-egalitarian society at an industrial stage of socioeconomic integration.

Even the Colville marriages and the Euro-American couples who "live together" are similar, suggesting that a more autonomous relationship is evolving among Euro-American couples. The assumptions or mind-sets of Euro-American and Colville couples are probably quite different, however, and the social circumstances certainly are. For instance, there are no extended families to support Euro-American individuals if such a relationship dissolves.

The Euro-American marital form and gender system are not very old. Each gender arrangement is functional in a particular society. The Euro-American arrangement serves a capitalistic system well and in fact arose to serve it. The Colville marriage in the past was also functional, giving people the autonomy needed to exploit the wild resources of their environment. The Colville do not have the marital intimacy found among Euro-Americans if they are fortunate. They have the extended family for that.

The term "power" is often used ambiguously to describe some interactions between men and women and between groups in Euro-American culture and elsewhere. Power implies influence as well as force (see chapter 2), but influence is considerably more common. Influence looks weak compared to force (legitimate and illegitimate), because even the poor in Euro-American society have some influence and therefore power. Even women in societies where they have few rights have access to influence (e.g., Chinese culture; Wolf 1974). This suggests that influence is easier to come by than authority. The Colville material indicates that what women need to become equal with men is authority, not power. Thus, references to women with power (e.g. Oboler 1985:286)—that is, influence—mean very little. Influence can be exhausting to use: even an old-boy network wears out the central nervous system after a while. Many Euro-American women have used power outside of the family; but they must persuade, cajole, manipulate, and organize threats, all of which takes effort. Authority is much more effective. With authority, one is able to order a project done and get results without all the tiring preliminaries. So when women have authority, as in Colville culture, it is a far more significant element in judging women's status, I believe, than access to power or influence alone.

Power is judged to exist in situations of domestic violence and rape, especially when males are the aggressors. Since Colville women have the means and tradition to leave a situation where beatings occur (unlike many Euro-American women), they remain on the scene for their own motives, not because they are helpless. If the situation persists, most women leave the marriage.

The punishment visited on rapists and other sexual offenders by groups of Plateau women has been described above. The question of why rape occurs at all in a society in which men and women are equal is answered by Julia Schwendinger and Herman Schwendinger (1983:82). They point out that American men, who are autonomous (and who also have authority and power), are "assaulted, robbed, murdered, and even raped"—rape therefore has little to do with one's status. This is such a telling point that it suggests that the act of rape by itself might well be irrelevant to a consideration of gender status. Instead one should examine what happens after a rape within a particular society. Is the victim supported and protected? Is the criminal punished and deterred from further crime?

Children are connected to women. In Euro-American culture this is frequently a disadvantage, because it often seems that raising children is no one's business but the mother's: if she is poor, the child is poor. The family does not have the endorsement, support, and approval of society in general and is left to fend on its own. In contrast, having and rearing children in Plateau culture is highly honored. A child born "out of wedlock" does not suffer poverty any more often than any other child because the extended family or nonunilinear descent group still offers support and services to mother and child, and the tribal government keeps the welfare of all mothers and children foremost in its deliberations. They see children

as the bridge to the future. Although the marrying dance is no longer performed and the puberty blanket is no longer used, these customs insured
that the next generation would be born with the social approval of the
community. All children were and are valued. Consequently women do
not have to be "princesses" or be upper-class to be valued. Being a woman
was and is important enough in Plateau culture.

THEORETICAL IMPLICATIONS

Since the "status of women" was an important theoretical consideration
when I began this research in 1979, some anthropological colleagues may
believe that the work is dated and that the anthropology of gender has
gone beyond this point. While this is true to a certain extent, the question
of "women's equal status" was never settled; it was argued without any clo-
sure. The anthropological debate of the 1970s and 1980s regarding the
possibility that gender equality might have occurred in human culture
somewhere in space and time never quite ended. The prevailing view of
the time was that male dominance was more or less universal: that is, it
occurred in all cultures and across all periods. Variation in the scope of
dominance was recognized within different cultures (Morgen 1989:2),
without essentially softening the universal male dominance perspective.
Today the status of women is no longer the prevailing topic it once was: the
focus is now on studying the actual lives of women within cultures and making comparisons between cultures (Morgen 1989:6). Still, the debate over
whether gender equality exists or existed somewhere or not continues to
surface (Duley and Edwards 1986:39). No real consensus has developed,
partly because there are no standards to evaluate the status of men and
women and scholars use different criteria (e.g., di Leonardo 1991:17).
Thus, an interest persists in finding a methodology for analyzing gender
status. Such a methodology is proposed in chapter 2. It was devised for this
study to evaluate the Plateau material and found to be useful when applied
to the Yup'ik Eskimo gender system, a system that may not be entirely egalitarian (Ackerman 1990).

The issue of gender status has motivated a great deal of writing, with
mixed results. Some investigators argue, based on their field research, that
certain societies practice gender equality (e.g., Appell 1988; Bacdayan 1977;
Draper 1975; Klein and Ackerman 1995; Leacock 1978; Lepowsky 1990;

Schlegel 1977a). Others, on a theoretical basis, contend that men are universally dominant and that gender equality has never existed in any society, past or present (e.g., Chodorow 1974; Divale and Harris 1976; Rosaldo 1974:3, 7, 1980:393). Marla Powers (1986:6–7) questions the proposition of universal male dominance based on the data she gathered on Oglala women, while Harriet Whitehead (1981:86) maintains that gender asymmetry is the norm everywhere in North America, with men being valued over women. It is apparent that the question is still of absorbing interest (Sanday 1990:4). The controversy regarding the question of universal male dominance is far from settled (Duley and Edwards 1986:26). Further studies of gender status such as this one are needed to reach an informed consensus on the issue.

During field research I attempted to address as many theoretical problems on gender as possible, trying to find facts to support or refute various anthropological hypotheses. While my primary purpose here is a factual ethnographic description of gender equality in one group, I believe that this study can contribute to some of the debate on women's roles in the anthropological literature.

The extensive economic rights that Colville women possessed in their traditional culture support Ernestine Friedl's (1975:8–9) and Peggy Sanday's (1974:194) theory that women's control of their own property and control over the products of their labor lead to high female status or equality. The persistence of gender equality today on the Colville Reservation can be attributed to the important and necessary economic role that women perform on the reservation. Schlegel (1977b:34) proposes the theory that ideology plays a part in gender equality as well. Ideology may have a role in preserving gender equality once it is present but is unlikely to be a cause of it. Nevertheless, ideology influences the Colville economy today. For instance, it never seems to occur to the members of the Colville tribal administration to pay women a lower salary for equal work, even though they are aware of the Euro-American model. One council member when asked about this said that everyone realizes women need the money to support their families, so they do not reduce women's pay. Thus, the ideology of gender equality has made possible women's continued access to opportunity, though I believe that the economic role is crucial. The Colville have achieved that elusive goal of Euro-American women without fuss or debate: equal pay for equal work. Consequently, ideology bolsters the gender equality found on the Colville Reservation today.

The theory of universal male dominance was addressed in my fieldwork. One purpose of the Colville description is to portray gender equality on the Colville Reservation sufficiently well so that no one can deny the existence of gender equality somewhere in the world. Though other societies with gender equality have been described in convincing detail (Bacdayan 1977; Draper 1975; Lepowsky 1993; Schlegel 1977a), many anthropologists continue to deny the existence of gender equality and declare that societies everywhere are male dominated (Cucchiari 1981:31; Divale and Harris 1976; Ortner 1974:70; Rosaldo 1980:393–94). Refutations of universal male dominance (Schlegel 1977b:16) seem not to make an impression on holders of the universal male dominance theory. I hope that this study will contribute to the demise of the notion of universal male dominance and that the human being will be recognized as a far more flexible organism than the partisans of universal male dominance acknowledge.

In looking for explanations for the assumed universal subordination of women in all cultures, Michelle Rosaldo (1974:8) postulates that the division of the genders into public and domestic spheres is a possible cause of male dominance. She argues that, since women are necessarily confined to the domestic sphere to care for offspring, they are excluded from the public roles that bring prestige. Rosaldo is suggesting two things: first, the separation of the domestic and public spheres is universal cross-culturally; and second, the care of children is the cause of female subordination in that it keeps women confined to the home area. This view is not supported by evidence from traditional and contemporary Colville culture.

In the traditional period the Colville Reservation culture did not appear to be divided into strict public and domestic spheres. The household (domestic sphere) was an important and even central institution in the society and flexible in its operation. It had permeable boundaries. Older children and sisters-in-law cared for younger children when mothers were especially busy. More often mothers were able to take their children with them when they performed economic and other tasks. Their children were present when women visited other villages or traveled for trading purposes and even when they went into warfare/trading situations, as on the Plains. As in the case of the !Kung women (Draper 1975:90), childrearing did not circumscribe the mobility of Colville women in the traditional phase of their culture. Thus, the idea that children restrict women's work depends on the organization of work and the social structure that supports that work. The Colville public/domestic dichotomy appears to have been insubstantial and even nonexistent in traditional times in the domestic and economic spheres.

The traditional religious and political spheres appear to have coincided not only with the village but with regional boundaries well outside the domestic sphere. Women could have religious reputations that extended beyond their villages, and the political acumen of a few women was sought for problems occurring between villages and tribes. The presence of children was not likely to have inhibited the exercise of these functions, since children traveled everywhere with their relatives. Thus, a division into public and private arenas seems not to have occurred in the religious and political spheres in the Plateau area in traditional times.

Today Colville women at political and social gatherings still are relatively free from the care of children (even infants) at least some of the time. Infants in cradleboards are handed around to women in turn. I myself have cared briefly for infants at public gatherings. Older children are trained to play in quiet groups in the vicinity of their mother and rarely bother her directly. The "care of children," while a given in all societies, is given in varying styles: if society requires the presence of women in public roles, behaviors and institutions evolve to accomplish that objective. In the Colville case, children are not excluded from large public gatherings and are taught behaviors that make it easy to have them there.

In the political arenas today, however, where women cannot take children (such as council meetings and Washington, D.C.), women are inhibited in gaining access not by being considered unsuitable candidates for office but by having no satisfactory methods to raise their small children conscientiously at the same time. Many suitable women with young children thus choose not to run for office as council members. It can be seen that the domestic-public dichotomy present in Euro-American culture has insinuated itself into contemporary Colville culture in at least the political sphere. Rosaldo's (1974:8) postulate that universal male dominance occurs because all cultures are divided into public and domestic spheres, however, does not hold for at least traditional Colville culture. In contemporary Colville culture women are not inferior to men in overall status even though public and domestic spheres may exist. (The modern Colville household still has permeable boundaries.) Rosaldo may be right in that the division of culture into public and domestic spheres inhibits women from taking part in public activities that extensively interfere with child-care, but other cultural factors have to develop to make women inferior to men in a particular society. Henrietta Moore (1988:23) does not see the public/domestic dichotomy as occurring universally in human cultures, and di Leonardo (1991:16) has demoted the idea from a universal explanation to a research tool.

Rosaldo (1974:17) argues that in any culture where women have power and influence they always have less than that of the men of their own age and class. This concept used by Rosaldo and others is so indefinite that it is hard to ascertain its meaning. It has been shown that Colville Reservation women have equal influence (and authority) with men, however, and Rosaldo's theory is not supported by the evidence presented in this study.

Rosaldo (1974:19) further postulates that male activities are considered by both genders to be more important than those of women in any culture. Highly valued male social roles include the public distribution of meat, whereas the economic product of women's work through gathering is not distributed, leading to the higher importance placed on men's activities. Rosaldo's belief in the differential value of work by gender definitely is not borne out by the Colville evidence. It has been demonstrated through *unanimous* testimony of consultants that the work and activities of women and men are equally valued by both genders.

Friedl (1975:8–9) also states that the right to distribute valued goods extradomestically is the key enabling the individual to acquire power and prestige in all societies. Along with Rosaldo, she believes in the universality of male dominance and says it arises from the frequency with which men have the right to distribute goods outside of the household. While Friedl (1975:13) refers mostly to the distribution of meat by men to other men (see chapter 4 above), I have also shown that both Colville genders trade extensively, distributing goods outside of the household to other groups, with women having a monopoly on the valuable food trade. The Colville evidence seems to support Friedl's concept of "power" arising from extradomestic distribution but does not support her postulate that it is men who mostly have that privilege. Furthermore, her suggestion that power arises from extradomestic distribution is not precise enough. The distribution may be an effect of high status, not a cause of it. One would have to look to the economic power that women wield for the cause of high status.

If political influence is to be obtained through the distribution of meat, as Friedl (1975:21) postulates, Colville Reservation women and not men alone would have had political influence due to its distribution. As noted above, Colville women distributed all kinds of food (including dried meat, which they owned) when food ran short for some families in the winter. Neither women nor men, however, earned political influence through food distribution but through economic and social skills.

According to Rosaldo (1974:29), men in all societies have an identity apart from their domestic units, while women "are given a social role and definition by virtue either of their age or of their relationship to men." This appears to be a reading of Euro-American gender roles: it is not substantiated by the Colville Reservation evidence. Colville men and women both have individual public identities. Their individual achievements or failures do not reflect on the spouse at all. Even today women are identified by both married name and the name of their descent group. They are socially embedded in extended families or nonunilineal descent groups, a common situation cross-culturally, while Euro-American adults are embedded in a marriage relationship that is conceived as being somewhat isolated from the rest of society, "private," a "refuge." The Euro-American marriage carries much more freight than the Colville marriage, being almost the only form of social intimacy available with other adults within the society, so it is hard for Euro-Americans to perceive that marriage is not a similar form of identity in other cultures as well. This is illustrated by the differing reactions to divorce by the Colville Indians and Euro-Americans. Divorce is very hard among Euro-Americans for at least one partner because emotional security, economic security, self-identity, social definition, and social intimacy are all lost in one stroke. None of these things are lost in Colville Reservation divorces, except social intimacy with one person, the spouse. Social intimacies with consanguineal relatives continue to be available to the individual regardless of marital status, for the identity and security of the individual lies with his or her nonunilineal descent group.

William Divale and Marvin Harris (1976:523) associate male dominance with polygyny. While it is true that many polygynous societies are male dominant, many others are not (Clignet and Sween 1981). It is likely that the determinants of polygyny have to do with economic and other arrangements, not gender supremacy. Men will think twice about offending their wives in some polygynous societies (Hoffer 1974:177; Mandelbaum 1938:

117), while monogamy does not necessarily confer high status or equality on women—else why the feminist movements in Europe and the United States? The Colville Reservation evidence demonstrates that polygyny minimally is not a universal indicator of male dominance.

Divale and Harris (1976:524) doubt that "headwomanship" occurs in any culture at all, while headmanship is common. I have noted the "woman of great authority" in the Plateau (see chapter 4) and even women serving as the chief political officer of the group. Female band leaders have also been noted among the Washo (Friedl 1975:36) and the San (Lee 1979:344), while female chiefs have occurred among the Kpa Mende (Hoffer 1974), the Bemba (Friedl 1975:120), and others (Lebeuf 1963).

Sanday (1974:198) states that women attain high status in the public domain when a balanced division of labor exists. That is, if each gender produces about 50 percent of subsistence and other goods for the society, the women are likely to have high status. If they produce much less or much more than 50 percent of the goods, their status is lower than that of men. The Plateau data show that women may produce up to 70 percent of the food supply in the Southern Plateau (Hunn 1981:132); but perhaps significantly, both the Nez Perce and the Colville people believe that women produced only about half or slightly over half of the food supply in traditional times. So while the 50 percent subsistence factor may have relevance for high female status as Sanday suggests, production of 70 percent of the food supply does not seem to preclude the existence of high female status. Other factors may be more predictive of women's status than the percent of goods they produce in the society.

The existence of the levirate is seen as an index of female inferiority by a few scholars (Meillassoux 1981:153; Whyte 1978:76). The sororate and levirate both occurred in traditional Plateau culture. Claude Meillassoux (1981:153) defines a sororate as an "institution by which an unsatisfactory wife is replaced by one of her classificatory sisters." A deceased wife is indeed unsatisfactory, and the sororate operated in the Plateau only when a married woman died. The purpose of the sororate in the Plateau was exactly that of the levirate: to replace the deceased spouse with another spouse and parent and to preserve an affinal link between two descent groups. If the sororate provided a service to the bereaved husband, then, in the same way the levirate provided a service to the bereaved wife. They were completely analogous situations in the Plateau and perhaps elsewhere.

These institutions, in my view, are not evidence for gender stratification within a society. Neither behavior is an index of subscrvience in the Plateau unless it is subservience to the two descent groups that wished to retain affinal ties.

Lamphere (1977:619–21) argues that marriage in any form is so constraining an institution that gender inequality automatically ensues, for a husband claims the products of his wife's labor, and the woman retains no control over decisions involving marriage and sexuality. The data from the Colville Reservation do not support any of the theorized constraints of marriage postulated by Lamphere. Not only were the traditional Colville woman's economic products her own, but a case might be made that she laid claim to the products of her husband's labor, since he could not take food without her permission, even though he produced part of it himself. The Colville data on marriage and sex speak for themselves.

Women are theorized to be inferior panculturally due to their childbearing, lactating, and enculturating functions. Inferiority is believed to occur because these processes are natural, not cultural (Chodorow 1974:45; Ortner 1974:73–75). Di Leonardo (1991:16) sees Chodorow's theory as ahistorical and overly universalizing, while Moore (1988:20) views it as a culture-bound concept. While I did not inquire specifically into the existence of "natural" and "cultural" categories on the Colville Reservation, I was told that Colville women are honored for their childbearing functions by men, who honor not only their own mothers and grandmothers but all women. The Colville women's enculturating functions earn them a position of authority within the extended family in their old age, and they are able to exert influence within the community as well. At any age women are not considered inferior within Plateau culture because of their natural functions but are honored and receive economic and domestic rewards for exercising these functions, plus consideration from the community at large. Colville men do not devalue women either publicly or privately: they respect and confide in them. As a female ethnographer, I found testimony from men easily accessible on all subjects once I had overcome my own cultural conditioning.

Contrast this attitude with the medieval European view of women. Christian belief in the past was that women threatened the purity of men's souls. To nullify their attraction, women's bodies were declared to be "a vessel of filth, . . . the production of children is not a joyful and rewarding experience, but a degradation" (Rogers 1973:89). The cultural chasm between the two communities on the subject of women and their maternal function requires no further comment.

Early missionaries were fond of commenting on how degraded Plateau women were because of the work they had to do (Drury 1958:137), even comparing them to slaves (McKee n.d., vol. 2:408). Their comments, of course, reflected their middle-class European heritage. They failed to understand that Colville women were working not only to support their families but to acquire surpluses that they owned and manipulated themselves. Thus, their hard work was amply rewarded. The arrangement whereby women owned the products of their labor motivated them to produce surpluses, thereby providing a failsafe for the society in time of scarcity or other crisis. The prejudice of equating hard work with low status infects some anthropologists too, as in the reference to women's work as "drudge work," applied without exception cross-culturally (Divale and Harris 1976:524).

The phrases "high status" and "low status" describing women's roles are imprecise (Friedl 1975; Sanday 1974). Some investigators may point to one cultural trait as proof of "high status" for women while someone else may point to another culture trait as evidence proving that women have "low status" in the same culture. The methodology that I have used based on Schlegel's (1977b:8–9) definition of gender equality pinpoints equality or inequality in any one area or even "high status" or "low status" overall based on a qualitative assessment of all of the spheres of a particular culture. I applied this methodology to traditional Yup'ik Eskimo culture as an experiment and found that equalities and inequalities between men and women were evident in various social spheres, though the genders were more equal than not. The method even reveals how little we know about certain aspects of some social spheres (Ackerman 1990).

The methodology used in this work may also be used comparatively to define the similarities and differences between neighboring groups, a problem that Regina Oboler addresses (1985:305). Oboler wants to ascertain not high or low status but how similar neighboring cultures compare in gender status.

Divale and Harris (1976:525) believe that a cultural preference for male over female children is widespread among preindustrial societies. This is not true in Colville Reservation culture, past or present. Women make such a large and necessary contribution to the culture that this is not a surprising point.

The observance of girls' puberty within a particular society indicates high female status (Whyte 1978:86). This is certainly true in the Plateau area, where puberty isolation is an extremely significant event in a female's life.

Avoidance taboos (mostly menstrual) often have been solely ascribed to women cross-culturally and are claimed to denote gender inequality (Divale and Harris 1976:525). Among the Colville Reservation people taboos were applied to men and women in a more or less balanced manner (see chapter 4). Even the ritual cleansing performed by men before hunting and fishing was balanced by the ritual cleansing performed by women before they began gathering. Thus, a perfect balance of prohibitions was present for both genders, and gender inequality cannot possibly be ascribed to the observances of taboos when both genders observe them. Nowhere else in the world to my knowledge do both men and women undergo ritual cleansing before undertaking their economic tasks, but it is possible and even likely that similar customs are practiced elsewhere and simply have not been recognized and recorded.

Although menstrual taboos have been viewed by some as an indication of low female status (e.g., Divale and Harris 1976:525), others see them differently. Buckley and Gottlieb (1988:14) argue that the meaning of menstruation differs from one culture to the next. Powers (1980:56–57) notes that first menstruation among the California Indians gives a girl supernatural power, while the Papago view menstruants as being endowed with religious power that is so different from men's that they must be separated. Walter Williams (1986:243) states that menstruation is seen as a "powerful spiritual essence" among the Plains tribes. He compares menstrual blood to the blood of a wounded man. Both kinds of blood would disrupt any venture that depended on spiritual power, like a hunt or warfare, requiring the separation of such people from others until the blood stops flowing. Menstruation, then, is not evidence of inferiority in many societies, particularly those in North America, and the Plateau peoples may be counted among them.

Jane Collier and Michelle Rosaldo (1981:276) state that "gathering never achieves the ritual acclaim earned by hunting." This is contradicted by the existence of the First Foods Ceremonies that honored gathering on the Colville Reservation in the past and present, just as the First Salmon

Ceremony honored fishing. The esteem accorded to the gathering activity on the reservation was further indicated by the ceremonies glorifying the future role of little girls when they dug their first roots or gathered their first berries. Rosaldo (1980:411) says that "in no report are we informed of women celebrated for their gathering skill." On the Colville Indian Reservation we now have such a report.

Friedl (1975:19) notes that in some foraging societies men manufacture women's tools, thereby curtailing female independence. This did not occur in Plateau societies. Colville women made their own digging sticks, baskets, and other tools in the traditional culture. They traded goods for horses or received horses as gifts from their consanguineal kin, which they owned exclusively. During the farming period, women hired blacksmiths to make their digging sticks of metal, paying for the service out of their own income. They had enough income to buy cattle, horses, and cars outright or received them as gifts from their kin. Thus, in the past women were self-reliant economically since they could independently acquire the tools that were necessary to make a living.

Divale and Harris (1976:524) concede that female shamans occur, but they believe that they do so in fewer numbers than men and are "less prominent." On the Colville Reservation the number of female shamans is equal to male shamans in a number of tribes; but whether they are equal in number or not, they are just as "prominent" or capable.

Judith Brown (1985:5) states that women do not often become shamans until they are older, since practicing as a healer interferes with motherhood. While this observation appears to be correct for a number of cultures, it is not true in the Plateau area. Women become shamans when they are young (in their twenties), if at all. Potential shamans learn the identity of their guardian spirits soon after puberty. One contemporary Southern Okanogan female shaman began to practice her profession in earnest when she was in her early twenties and started to be sought out for her curing ability. She was already a mother at the time. The social structure of Plateau culture permits this. Members of the extended family look after children while the female shaman goes into trance and otherwise pursues her profession.

Women are not devalued when they reach menopause in Colville society. Their age is an advantage, not a limitation, because they exercise influence over younger people within the extended household and even outside it. Nor does age bring great privileges except for respect, which is shared equally with male age-mates. Unlike women in other cultures (Brown 1985:3–4), Colville women do not have to wait for advanced age to obtain access to authority and autonomy.

The introduction of a money economy along with farming has often resulted in the reduction of female status in other cultures (Bossen 1975:593). It is interesting that this has not happened on the Colville Reservation. One explanation for this situation may lie in the fact that the Colville Indians were not exploited for their labor as in many colonial situations, though they were exploited through the loss of their land and resources. Most significantly, gender inequality did not develop because both genders chose to perform the new Euro-American work separately and/or equally, as described above. Choosing is perhaps the wrong concept here, however: they merely extended their cultural norms to new situations.

The custom of men and women eating separately in the traditional Colville culture may be similar to the aboriginal Iroquois practice, described by Brown (1970:157–58). Brown notes that among the Iroquois men and women ate separately, worked separately, and socialized only with members of their own gender. Colville men and women of the traditional culture ate separately and apparently traveled and worked apart from their spouses for at least part of the year. If the taboos in sexual relations before gathering and other economic activities were as general as my data suggest, I would speculate that sexual bonding may have had relatively few opportunities to take effect on married couples. Thus, opportunities for intimacy of any kind occurring between a married couple may have been restricted to certain times of the year. They certainly spent the winters together within the extended family; but intimate relations, sexual and otherwise, may have been somewhat diluted with so many people about. If there is any truth to my speculation, the impressive autonomy practiced by spouses today and in the past in all social spheres becomes readily comprehensible.

Colville Reservation culture may be sliding into gender inequality in a few areas. Women are prevented from participating in parts of the political sphere by some cultural changes. Women with young children, who have a right to compete for tribal council seats, are structurally unprepared to do so, since the extended family they depended on for child care in the past is no longer as dependable an institution today. If some women decide to wait until their children are grown to run for office, their highly valued grandmother role in raising their grandchild would seem to be threatened. In abstaining from the grandmother role, a woman loses the opportunity not only to influence her grandchildren but also to influence her great-great-grandchildren (her grandchildren's grandchildren) through family traditions. In the one case I observed, however, this did not happen. One female council member had a very strong influence on her grandchildren, though perhaps not on a daily basis. In the past, having young children in the household was not a check on a woman's movements and activities at any age.

Another factor that threatens gender equality is that women with young children are sometimes not able to support them well after a divorce. This presents a possibility that women along with children could evolve into a lower status, although I think that the people of the reservation, left to themselves and with control over their own resources, would prevent women from sliding into abject poverty and low status. Their ideology of gender equality would motivate them to rectify the situation if possible. If Colville women already occupied a low status or were on the verge of it, however, they might slip into poverty and low status unremarked until after the fact, like Euro-American women. One reason why lower female status might be a possibility among the Colville people is that the extended family could become more attenuated and resources even scarcer, but I believe that the ideology of gender equality within the culture would prevent this situation from developing. Women are not merely equal on the Colville Reservation; they are a necessary and structural part of society. They are so integrated into the everyday mechanism of life that to make them unequal would make the society unworkable. This description of Colville culture is not so much a feminist interpretation of a culture, describing the roles of women, as a description of the culture as its participants see it.

SPECULATIONS AND CONCLUSIONS

It is difficult for Euro-Americans to accept the proposition that a situation may be "separate, but equal," considering their failures with that premise in race relations. Diane Bell (1987:124) notes that "different but equal" is a dangerous platform for white feminists. Dangerous or not, however, different cultures live by different rules. "Separate but equal" works very well elsewhere, including the Plateau and other parts of North America where complementary roles are the rule (Klein and Ackerman 1995). Separate and different does not have to mean unequal or inferior.

Though this is speculative, I believe that gender differences in the Plateau are less important than they are among Euro-Americans. I found few overt symbols of gender among the Colville people, though, admittedly, this may be due to culture change. Gender differences do not seem to be a key to the definition of an individual as much as they are among Euro-Americans. Of course, Colville men and women are expected to behave in certain ways generally, but so much room for individualism exists in the culture that what might seem like deviations to Euro-Americans, like berdaches and spiritual talents pertaining to the work of the other gender, were not tolerated so much as considered nonissues. This attitude may explain why the Indians copied their white neighbors' farming methods but not their gender role models. I have the impression that the Colville people think of each other as the "other sex" rather than the "opposite sex." When I was trying to clarify a statement made by a consultant by trying to lead her into saying "men and women," she repeatedly insisted on saying "all the people" and became a bit impatient when I persisted in my questioning. The phrase "all the people" includes both genders in Colville society. The phrase did not always mean that in Euro-American society. The ready crossover of gender-typed tasks today suggests that men and women in early reservation times thought of themselves as truly complementary in their roles, not opposite.

This line of speculation is supported by the mild amusement and lack of indignation that elders express when a woman hunts or a man digs roots today. It seems that the Colville people take the "breakdown" of traditional gender roles less seriously than Euro-Americans do: witness their reluctance to accept female bank presidents, national vice-presidents, female priests, househusbands, and male nurses. It seems likely that gender-typed work is more sacred to Euro-Americans than to the Colville people. Colville roles are complementary; Euro-American roles are opposite. The Colville define people as individuals first then as a particular gender. Euro-Americans tend to see a particular gender first and individuals second.

It is unlikely that the Colville Indian Reservation is unique in its tradition of gender equality. Strong indications abound that gender equality was once a common phenomenon worldwide, which has been destroyed or weakened by colonialism and the market economy (Bossen 1975). The evidence indicates that the aboriginal Montagnais-Naskapi (Leacock 1978), aboriginal Iroquois (Brown 1970), Machiguenga (Johnson and Johnson 1975), Tlingit (Klein 1980), !Kung (Draper 1975), Washo (Friedl 1975), and peoples of parts of New Guinea (Lepowsky 1993), many parts of Africa (Boserup 1970; Lebeuf 1963), and most of North America (Klein and Ackerman 1995) have been or still are characterized by gender equality. Further, gender equality has survived in some contemporary industrial contexts, as among the modern Tlingit (Klein 1980:102, 105–6) and the Paiute (Knack 1995), indicating that the Plateau is not unique in retaining gender equality under capitalism.

The fact that gender equality does exist, not only among foragers but among participants in an industrial society, is an important theoretical point. Laurel Bossen (1975:599) states that high female status is destroyed by modernization, and Leacock (1978:255) does not think that gender equality is possible except on a hunting and gathering level. Reiter (1975), however, notes that early European capitalism inherited a social system in which gender inequality already existed, bringing into question the necessary association of gender inequality and capitalism. The case of the Colville Reservation shows that equality between men and women may flourish at any level of socioeconomic integration. Contemporary gender equality on the Colville Reservation suggests that it may be present in other unlikely or unexpected places, since modern economic conditions do not appear to be incompatible with gender equality after all. Where the Colville Reservation people have the authority and power to direct their society, they have adapted modern economic conditions to fit their ideology of gender equality.

References Cited

Ackerman, Lillian A.

1971 Marital Instability and Juvenile Delinquency among the Nez Perces. *American Anthropologist* 73(3):595–603.

1978–95 Field Notes on Colville, Nez Perce, and Coeur d'Alene Indian Reservations.

1982 Sexual Equality in the Plateau Culture Area. Ph.D. dissertation, Department of Anthropology, Washington State University, Pullman, Washington.

1987 The Effect of Missionary Ideals on Family Structure and Women's Roles in Plateau Indian Culture. *Idaho Yesterdays* 31(1–2):64–73.

1990 Gender Status in Yup'ik Society. *Etudes/Inuit/Studies* 14(1–2):209–21.

1994 Nonunilinear Descent Groups in the Plateau Culture Area. *American Ethnologist* 21(2):286–309.

Albers, Patricia C.

1985 Autonomy and Dependency in the Lives of Dakota Women: A Study in Historical Change. *Review of Radical Political Economics* 17(3):109–34.

1989 From Illusion to Illumination: Anthropological Studies of American Indian Women. In *Gender and Anthropology*, ed. Sandra Morgen, pp. 132–70. Washington, D.C.: American Anthropological Association.

Allison, Mrs. S. S.

1992 Account of the Similkameen Indians. *Journal of the Royal Anthropological Institute of Great Britain and Ireland* 21:305–18.

254   REFERENCES CITED
```

Alvord, Benjamin (Major)
    1857  Report Concerning the Indians in the Territories of Oregon and Washington. H. R. Ex. Doc. 75 (Serial 906), 34th Congress, 3rd Session, pp. 10–22. Washington, D.C.: Government Printing Office.

Amoss, Pamela T.
    1990  The Indian Shaker Church: The Northwest Coast. In *The Handbook of North American Indians,* ed. Wayne Suttles, vol. 7:633–39. Washington, D.C.: Smithsonian Institution.

Anastasio, Angelo
    1972  The Southern Plateau: An Ecological Analysis of Intergroup Relations. *Northwest Anthropological Research Notes* 6(2):109–229.

Angelino, Henry, and Charles L. Shedd
    1955  A Note on Berdache. *American Anthropologist* 57(1):121–25.

Appell, Laura W. R.
    1988  Menstruation among the Rungus of Borneo: An Unmarked Category. In *Blood Magic: The Anthropology of Menstruation,* ed. Thomas Buckley and Alma Gottlieb, pp. 94–115. Berkeley: University of California Press.

Atkinson, Jane Monnig
    1982  Anthropology: Review Essay. *Signs: Journal of Women in Culture and Society* 8(2):236–58.

Bacdayan, Albert S.
    1977  Mechanistic Cooperation and Sexual Equality among the Western Bontoc. In *Sexual Stratification: A Cross-Cultural View,* ed. Alice Schlegel, pp. 270–91. New York: Columbia University Press.

Bancroft, Hubert Howe
    1883  *The Native Races.* Vol. 1. San Francisco: A. L. Bancroft and Company, Publishers.

Bell, Diane
    1987  The Politics of Separation. In *Dealing with Inequality: Analysing Gender Relations in Melanesia and Beyond,* ed. Marilyn Strathern, pp. 112–29. Cambridge: Cambridge University Press.

Berik, Gunseli
    1996  Understanding the Gender System in Rural Turkey: Fieldwork Dilemmas of Conformity and Intervention. In *Feminist Dilemmas in Fieldwork,* ed. Diane L. Wolf, pp. 56–71. Boulder, Colo.: Westview Press.

Bilharz, Joy
    1995  First Among Equals? The Changing Status of Seneca Women. In *Women and Power in Native North America,* ed. Laura F. Klein and Lillian A. Ackerman, pp. 101–12. Norman: University of Oklahoma Press.
```

Binford, Lewis R.
 1980 Willow Smoke and Dogs' Tails: Hunter-Gatherer Settlement Systems and Archaeological Site Formation. *American Antiquity* 45(1): 4–20.
Bloodworth, Jessie A.
 1959 *Human Resources of the Colville Confederated Tribes.* Washington, D.C.: Government Printing Office.
Boserup, Ester
 1970 *Woman's Role in Economic Development.* New York: St. Martin's Press.
Bossen, Laurel
 1975 Women in Modernizing Societies. *American Ethnologist* 2:587–601.
Boyd, Robert Thomas
 1985 The Introduction of Infectious Diseases among the Indians of the Pacific Northwest, 1774–1874. Ph.D. dissertation, Department of Anthropology, University of Washington, Seattle.
 1994 The Pacific Northwest Measles Epidemic of 1847–1848. *Oregon Historical Quarterly* 95(1):6–47.
Brod, Rodney L., and Mary Jean Brod
 1981 *Educational Needs of the Colville Confederated Tribes.* LPS and Associates. Missoula: Printing Department, University of Montana.
Brown, Judith K.
 1970 Economic Organization and the Position of Women among the Iroquois. *Ethnohistory* 17:151–67.
 1985 Introduction. In *Her Prime: A New View of Middle-Aged Women,* ed. Judith K. Brown and Virginia Kerns, pp. 1–11. S. Hadley, Mass.: Bergin and Garvey Publishers.
Buckley, Thomas, and Alma Gottlieb
 1988 *Blood Magic: The Anthropology of Menstruation.* Berkeley: University of California Press.
Burns, Robert Ignatius, S.J.
 1966 *The Jesuits and the Indian Wars of the Northwest.* Moscow: University of Idaho Press.
Business Council Records, Confederated Tribes of the Colville Indian Reservation
 n.d. Cage 206, Manuscripts, Archives, and Special Collections, Holland Library, Washington State University, Pullman, Washington.
Callender, Charles
 1978a The Great Lakes–Riverine Sociopolitical Organization. In *The Handbook of North American Indians,* ed. Bruce G. Trigger, vol. 15, pp. 610–21. Washington, D.C.: Smithsonian Institution.
 1978b The Miami. In *The Handbook of North American Indians,* ed. Bruce G. Trigger, vol. 15, pp. 681–89. Washington, D.C.: Smithsonian Institution.

1978c The Sauk. In *The Handbook of North American Indians*, ed. Bruce G. Trigger, vol. 15, pp. 648–55. Washington, D.C.: Smithsonian Institution.

1978d The Shawnee. In *The Handbook of North American Indians*, ed. Bruce G. Trigger, vol. 15, pp. 622–35. Washington, D.C.: Smithsonian Institution.

Callender, Charles, Richard K. Pope, and Susan M. Pope
1978 The Kickapoo. In *The Handbook of North American Indians*, ed. Bruce G. Trigger, vol. 15, pp. 656–67. Washington, D.C.: Smithsonian Institution.

Chatters, James C., and David L Pokotylo
1998 Prehistory: Introduction. In *The Handbook of North American Indians*, ed. Deward E. Walker, Jr., vol. 12, pp. 73–80. Washington, D.C.: Smithsonian Institution.

Chittenden, Hiram Martin
1905 *Life, Letters and Travels of Father Pierre-Jean DeSmet, S.J., 1801–1873.* 4 vols. New York: Francis P. Harper.

Chodorow, Nancy
1974 Family Structure and Feminine Personality. In *Woman, Culture and Society*, ed. Michelle Zimbalist Rosaldo and Louise Lamphere, pp. 43–66. Stanford, Calif.: Stanford University Press.

Clignet, Remi, and Joyce A. Sween
1981 For a Revisionist Theory of Human Polygyny. *Signs: Journal of Women in Culture and Society* 6(3):445–68.

Cline, Walter
1938 Religion and World View. In *The Sinkaietk or Southern Okanagon of Washington*, ed. Leslie Spier, pp. 131–82. Menasha, Wis.: George Banta Publishing Company.

Collier, Jane F., and Michelle Z. Rosaldo
1981 Politics and Gender in Simple Societies. In *Sexual Meanings: The Cultural Construction of Gender and Sexuality*, ed. Sherry B. Ortner and Harriet Whitehead, pp. 275–329. Cambridge: Cambridge University Press.

Colville Confederated Tribes
1972 The Year of the Coyote: Centennial Celebration July 2, 1972. Nespelem, Wash.: Colville Confederated Tribes.
1979 Colville Confederated Tribal Health Plan. Nespelem, Washington.
n.d. Consider the Colville Indian Reservation! Booklet prepared by reservation to attract industry. In tribal offices at Nespelem, Washington.

Colville Indian Agency
1888–93 Reports of Agents in Washington Territory—Colville Agency. Reports to the Commissioner of Indian Affairs in Washington, D.C. Washington, D.C.: Government Printing Office.

n.d.   Cage 2014, Manuscripts, Archives, and Special Collections, Washington State University Libraries, Washington State University.

Cook, S. F.
1972   The Epidemic of 1830–1833 in California and Oregon. In *The Emergent Native Americans*, ed. Deward E. Walker, Jr., pp. 172–92. Boston: Little, Brown and Company.

Cucchiari, Salvatore
1981   The Gender Revolution and the Transition from Bisexual Horde to Patrilocal Band: The Origins of Gender Hierarchy. In *Sexual Meanings: The Cultural Construction of Gender and Sexuality*, ed. Sherry B. Ortner and Harriet Whitehead, pp. 31–79. Cambridge: Cambridge University Press.

Daugherty, Richard D.
1956   *Early Man in the Columbia Intermontane Province.* Anthropological Papers No. 24. Department of Anthropology, University of Utah.

Debo, Angie
1970   *A History of the Indians of the United States.* Norman: University of Oklahoma Press.

di Leonardo, Micaela
1991   Introduction: Gender, Culture, and Political Economy. In *Gender at the Crossroads of Knowledge*, ed. Micaela di Leonardo, pp. 1–48. Berkeley: University of California Press.

Diomedi, Alexander, S.J.
1978   *Sketches of Indian Life in the Pacific Northwest.* Fairfield, Wash.: Ye Galleon Press. Originally written in 1879.

Divale, William Tulio, and Marvin Harris
1976   Population, Warfare, and the Male Supremacist Complex. *American Anthropologist* 78(3):521–38.

Dobyns, Henry F.
1983   *Their Number Become Thinned: Native American Population Dynamics in Eastern North America.* Knoxville: University of Tennessee Press.

Draper, Patricia
1975   !Kung Women: Contrasts in Sexual Egalitarianism in Foraging and Sedentary Contexts. In *Toward an Anthropology of Women*, ed. Rayna R. Reiter, pp. 77–109. New York and London: Monthly Review Press.

Drury, Clifford Merrill
1936   *Henry Harmon Spalding.* Caldwell, Idaho: Caxton Printers, Ltd.
1958   *The Diaries and Letters of Henry H. Spalding and Asa Bowen Smith Relating to the Nez Perce Mission, 1838–1842.* Glendale, Calif.: Arthur H. Clark Company.

Duley, Margot I., and Mary I. Edwards
1986   *The Cross-Cultural Study of Women.* New York: Feminist Press.

Etienne, Mona, and Eleanor Leacock
1980 Introduction. In *Women and Colonization: Anthropological Perspectives*, ed. Mona Etienne and Eleanor Leacock, pp. 1–24. New York: Praeger Publishers.

Fenton, William N.
1978 Northern Iroquoian Culture Patterns. In *The Handbook of North American Indians*, ed. Bruce G. Trigger, vol. 15, pp. 296–321. Washington, D.C.: Smithsonian Institution.

Fletcher, Alice C.
1892 The Nez Perce Country. *Proceedings of the American Association for the Advancement of Science* 40:357.

Friedl, Ernestine
1975 *Women and Men: An Anthropologist's View*. New York: Holt, Rinehart and Winston.

Gidley, M.
1979 *With One Sky above Us*. New York: G. P. Putnam's Sons.

Gough, Stan, ed.
1990 *A Cultural Resources Overview, Sampling Survey, and Management Plan, Colville Indian Reservation, Okanogan and Ferry Counties, Washington*. Eastern Washington University Reports in Archaeology and Historical Services. Cheney: Eastern Washington University.

Gould, Robert
1976 Measuring Masculinity by the Size of a Paycheck. In *The Forty-nine Percent Majority*, ed. Deborah S. David and Robert Brannon, pp. 113–18. Reading, Mass.: Addison-Wesley Publishing Company.

Green, Rayna
1992 *Women in American Indian Society*. New York: Chelsea House Publishers.

Gregor, Thomas
1977 *The Mehinaku*. Chicago: University of Chicago Press.

Griswold, Gillett
1954 Aboriginal Patterns of Trade between the Columbia Basin and the Northern Plains. M.A. thesis, Montana State University.

Guemple, Lee
1995 Gender in Inuit Society. In *Women and Power in Native North America*, ed. Laura F. Klein and Lillian A. Ackerman, pp. 17–27. Norman: University of Oklahoma Press.

Gunther, Erna
1949 The Shaker Religion of the Northwest. In *Indians of the Urban Northwest*, ed. M. W. Smith, pp. 37–76. Columbia University Contributions to Anthropology 35. New York: Columbia University Press.

Hayden, Brian, ed.
1992 A Complex Culture of the British Columbia Plateau: Traditional *Stl'atl'imx* Resource Use. Vancouver: UBC Press.

Hoebel, E. Adamson
  1966 *Anthropology: The Study of Man.* 3rd ed. New York: McGraw-Hill Book
        Company.
Hoffer, Carol P.
  1974 Madam Yoko: Ruler of the Kpa Mende Confederacy. In *Woman, Cul-
        ture and Society,* ed. Michelle Zimbalist Rosaldo and Louise Lam-
        phere, pp. 173–87. Stanford, Calif.: Stanford University Press.
Hudson, Douglas, and C. Roderick Wilson
  1986 The Plateau—A Regional Overview. In *Native Peoples: the Canadian
        Experience,* ed. R. Bruce Morrison and C. Roderick Wilson, pp.
        436–44. Toronto: McClelland and Stewart.
Hunn, Eugene S.
  1981 On the Relative Contribution of Men and Women to Subsistence
        among Hunter-Gatherers of the Columbia Plateau: A Comparison
        with *Ethnographic Atlas* Summaries. *Journal of Ethnobiology* 1(1):124–34.
  1990 *Nch'i-wana "The Big River": Mid-Columbia Indians and Their Land.*
        Seattle: University of Washington Press.
Jilek, Wolfgang G.
  1974 *Salish Indian Mental Health and Culture Change: Psychohygienic and Ther-
        apeutic Aspects of the Guardian Spirit Ceremonial.* Toronto: Holt, Rine-
        hart and Winston of Canada, Ltd.
Johnson, Orna R., and Allen Johnson
  1975 Male/Female Relations and the Organization of Work in a Machi-
        guenga Community. *American Ethnologist* 2:634–48.
Joset, Joseph, S.J.
  n.d.   The Joset Papers. The Colville Mission. MSS. Folder M, XXI, XV.
         Oregon Province Archives, Crosby Library, Gonzaga University,
         Spokane, Washington.
Kehoe, Alice B.
  1995 Blackfoot Persons. In *Women and Power in Native North America,* ed.
        Laura F. Klein and Lillian A. Ackerman, pp. 113–25. Norman: Uni-
        versity of Oklahoma Press.
Kennedy, Dorothy I. D., and Randy Bouchard
  1992 Stl'atl'imx (Fraser River Lillooet) Fishing. In *A Complex Culture of the
        British Columbia Plateau: Traditional* Stl'atl'imx *Resource Use,* ed. Brian
        Hayden, pp. 266–354. Vancouver: University of British Columbia Press.
Klein, Laura F.
  1976 "She's One of Us, You Know": The Public Life of Tlingit Women: Tra-
        ditional, Historical, and Contemporary Perspectives. *Western Cana-
        dian Journal of Anthropology* 6(3):164–83.
  1980 Contending with Colonization: Tlingit Men and Women in Change.
        In *Women and Colonization: Anthropological Perspectives,* ed. Mona Eti-
        enne and Eleanor Leacock, pp. 88–108. New York: Praeger.

260   REFERENCES CITED

Klein, Laura F., and Lillian A. Ackerman, eds.

  1995 *Women and Power in Native North America.* Norman: University of Oklahoma Press.

Knack, Martha

  1986 Newspaper Accounts of Indian Women in Southern Nevada Mining Towns. 1870–1900. *Journal of California and Great Basin Anthropology* 8(1):83–98.

  1995 The Dynamics of Southern Paiute Women's Roles. In *Women and Power in Native North America,* ed. Laura F. Klein and Lillian A. Ackerman, pp. 146–58. Norman: University of Oklahoma Press.

Kroeber, Alfred L.

  1947 *Cultural and Natural Areas of Native North America.* Berkeley: University of California Press.

Lamphere, Louise

  1977 Review: Anthropology. *Signs: Journal of Women in Culture and Society* 2(3):612–27.

Leacock, Eleanor

  1971 Introduction. In *North American Indians in Historical Perspective,* ed. Eleanor B. Leacock and Nancy O. Lurie, pp. 3–28. New York: Random House.

  1978 Women's Status in Egalitarian Society: Implications for Social Evolution. *Current Anthropology* 19(2):247–75.

Leacock, Eleanor, and Nancy O. Lurie, eds.

  1971 *North American Indians in Historical Perspective.* New York: Random House.

Lebeuf, Annie M. D.

  1963 The Role of Women in the Political Organization of African Societies. In *Women of Tropical Africa,* ed. Denise Paulme, pp. 93–119. Berkeley and Los Angeles: University of California Press.

Lee, Richard Borshay

  1979 *The !Kung San: Men, Women, and Work in a Foraging Society.* Cambridge: Cambridge University Press.

Leibowitz, Lila

  1978 *Females, Males, Families: A Biosocial Approach.* North Scituate, Mass.: Duxbury Press.

Lepowsky, Maria

  1990 Gender in an Egalitarian Society: A Case Study from the Coral Sea. In *Beyond the Second Sex: New Directions in the Anthropology of Gender,* ed. Peggy Reeves Sanday and Ruth Gallagher Goodenough, pp. 169–223. Philadelphia: University of Pennsylvania Press.

  1993 *Fruit of the Motherland: Gender in an Egalitarian Society.* New York: Columbia University Press.

Louie, Martin, Sr.
  1991 Tales of Coyote: Eastern Washington Traditions. In *A Time of Gathering: Native Heritage in Washington State*, ed. Robin K. Wright, pp. 164–69. Seattle: University of Washington Press.

Lurie, Nancy Oestreich
  1971 The Contemporary American Indian Scene. In *North American Indians in Historical Perspective*, ed. Eleanor B. Leacock and Nancy O. Lurie, pp. 418–80. New York: Random House.

Malinowski, Bronislaw
  1929 *The Sexual Live of Savages in North-Western Melanesia*. New York: Readers League of America.

Mandelbaum, May
  1938 The Individual Life Cycle. In *The Sinkaietk or Southern Okanagon of Washington*, ed. Leslie Spier, pp. 103–29. Menasha, Wis.: George Banta Publishing Company.

Marsh, Harry Webb
  1918–66 Papers. University of Idaho Archives, MG23, Item 42. Moscow, Idaho.

Marshall, Alan G.
  1977 Nez Perce Social Groups: An Ecological Interpretation. Ph.D. dissertation, Department of Anthropology, Washington State University, Pullman, Washington.

Maxwell, Jean Alice
  1987 The Circle of Sharing among Colville and Spokane Indians. Ph.D. dissertation, Department of Anthropology, University of Michigan, Ann Arbor.

Maynard, Eileen
  1979 Changing Sex-Roles and Family Structure among the Oglala Sioux. In *Sex Roles in Changing Cultures*, ed. Ann McElroy and Carolyn Matthiasson, vol. 1, pp. 11–19. Occasional Papers in Anthropology. Buffalo: State University of New York.

McElroy, Ann
  1979 The Negotiation of Sex-Role Identity in Eastern Arctic Culture Change. In *Sex Roles in Changing Cultures*, ed. Ann McElroy and Carolyn Matthiasson, vol. 1, pp. 49–60. Occasional Papers in Anthropology. Buffalo: State University of New York.

McKee, Charlotte Ruth Karr
  n.d. Mary Richardson Walker, Her Book. 2 vols. Typescript in Holland Library of Washington State University, Pullman, Washington.

McKeown, Martha Ferguson
  1956 *Linda's Indian Home*. Portland, Ore.: Binfords and Mort.

Meillassoux, Claude
  1981 *Maidens, Meal and Money*. Cambridge: Cambridge University Press.

Miller, Jay
  1990 Introduction, In *Mourning Dove: A Salishan Autobiography*, ed. Jay
        Miller, pp. xi–xxxix. Lincoln: University of Nebraska Press.
Moore, Henrietta L.
  1988 *Feminism and Anthropology.* Cambridge: Polity Press.
  1994 *A Passion for Difference: Essays in Anthropology and Gender.* Blooming-
        ton: Indiana University Press.
Morgen, Sandra
  1989 Gender and Anthropology: Introductory Essay. In *Gender and Anthro-
        pology*, ed. Sandra Morgen, pp. 1–20. Washington, D.C.: American
        Anthropological Association.
Mourning Dove
  1990 *Mourning Dove: A Salishan Autobiography.* Ed. Jay Miller. Lincoln: Uni-
        versity of Nebraska Press.
National Archives of the United States, Washington, D.C.
  n.d.   Regarding Colville Indian Agency. File Names: Special Cases, Boxes
         61–70, Tribal Lands. Boxes 308–13.
Newman, George H.
  1897 *Report of Colville Agency.* Annual Reports of the Department of the
        Interior, 55th Congress, 2nd session, Document 5. Washington, D.C.:
        Government Printing Office.
Oboler, Regina Smith
  1985 *Women, Power, and Economic Change: The Nandi of Kenya.* Stanford,
        Calif.: Stanford University Press.
Odyssey Productions
  1978 *Lucy Covington: Native American Indian.* Chicago: for Britannia Ency-
        clopedia Educational Corporation.
Ormsby, Margaret A.
  1976 *A Pioneer Gentlewoman in British Columbia: The Recollections of Susan
        Allison.* Vancouver: University of British Columbia Press.
Ortner, Sherry B.
  1974 Is Female to Male as Nature Is to Culture? In *Woman, Culture and
        Society*, ed. Michelle Zimbalist Rosaldo and Louise Lamphere, pp.
        67–87. Stanford, Calif.: Stanford University Press.
  1984 Theory in Anthropology since the Sixties. *Society for Comparative Study
        of Society and History* 26:126–66.
  1995 Resistance and the Problem of Ethnographic Refusal. *Society for Com-
        parative Study of Society and History* 37:173–93.
Ortner, Sherry B., and Harriet Whitehead
  1981 Introduction: Accounting for Sexual Meanings. In *Sexual Meanings:
        The Cultural Construction of Gender and Sexuality*, ed. Sherry B. Ortner
        and Harriet Whitehead, pp. 1–27. Cambridge: Cambridge Univer-
        sity Press.

Parker, Samuel
1844 *Journal of an Exploring Tour beyond the Rocky Mountains.* Ithaca, N.Y.: Andrus, Woodruff, and Gauntlett.

Peaslee, Enos B.
n.d. Letters. Regarding court case in Chelan County. Archives and Manuscripts, Suzzalo Library, University of Washington, Seattle, Washington.

Planning Support Group, Bureau of Indian Affairs
1974 *Demographic Statistical Data Report for Selected Counties Having Significant Indian Population: Portland Area.* Report No. 237, vol. 3. Washington, D.C.

Point, Nicholas, S.J.
1967 *Wilderness Kingdom: Indian Life in the Rocky Mountains, 1840–1847.* New York: Holt, Rinehart and Winston.

Pokotylo, David L., and Donald Mitchell
1998 Prehistory of the Northern Plateau. In *The Handbook of North American Indians,* ed. Deward E. Walker, Jr., vol. 12, pp. 81–102. Washington, D.C.: Smithsonian Institution.

Post, Richard H.
1938 The Subsistence Quest. In *The Sinkaietk or Southern Okanagon of Washington,* ed. Leslie Spier, pp. 9–34. Menasha, Wis.: George Banta Publishing Company.

Powers, Marla N.
1980 Menstruation and Reproduction: An Oglala Case. *Signs: Journal of Women in Culture and Society* 6(1):54–65.
1986 *Oglala Women: Myth, Ritual, and Reality.* Chicago: University of Chicago Press.

Raufer, Sister Maria Ilma
1966 *Black Robes and Indians on the Last Frontier.* Milwaukee: Bruce Publishing Company.

Ray, Verne F.
1932 *The Sanpoil and Nespelem.* University of Washington Publications in Anthropology, vol. 5. Seattle: University of Washington Press.
1936 The Kolaskin Cult: A Prophet Movement of 1870 in Northeastern Washington. *American Anthropologist* 38:67–75.
1939 *Cultural Relations in the Plateau of Northwestern America.* Los Angeles: Publication of the Frederick Webb Hodge Anniversary Publication Fund, Southwest Museum.
1960 The Columbia Indian Confederacy. In *Culture in History,* ed. Stanley Diamond, pp. 771–89. New York: Columbia University Press.
1975 Final Report Colville Interpretive Theme. Vol. 2. In Tribal History office on the Colville Reservation.

Ray, Verne F., et al.
    1938 Tribal Distribution in Eastern Oregon and Adjacent Territories.
          American Anthropologist 40:384–415.
Reichwein, Jeffrey C.
    1988 *Native American Response to Euro-American Contact in the Columbia
          Plateau of Northwestern North America, 1840–1914: An Anthropological
          Interpretation Based on Written and Pictorial Ethnohistorical Data.* New
          York: Garland Publishing.
Reiter, Rayna Rapp
    1975 The Search for Origins: Unraveling the Threads of Gender Hier-
          archy. *Critique of Anthropology* 3(9–10):5–24.
Roe, JoAnn
    1992 *The Columbia River: A Historical Travel Guide.* Golden, Colo.: Fulcrum
          Publishing.
Rogers, Katherine M.
    1973 The Troublesome Helpmate: A History of Misogyny in Literature.
          In *Women from the Greeks to the French Revolution,* ed. Susan Groag Bell,
          pp. 84–89. Stanford, Calif.: Stanford University Press.
Romanoff, Steven
    1992 The Cultural Ecology of Hunting and Potlatches among the Lillooet
          Indians. In *A Complex Culture of the British Columbia Plateau: Traditional
          Stl'atl'imx Resource Use,* ed. Brian Hayden, pp. 470–505. Vancouver:
          University of British Columbia Press.
Rooney, Daniel J., compiler
    1973 Preliminary Inventory of the Records of the BIA, Colville Indian
          Agency, including the Spokane Subagency, 1865–1952 (Record
          Group 75 at Federal Archives, Seattle).
Rosaldo, Michelle Zimbalist
    1974 Introduction. In *Woman, Culture and Society,* ed. Michelle Zimbalist
          Rosaldo and Louise Lamphere, pp. 1–42. Stanford, Calif.: Stanford
          University Press.
    1980 The Use and Abuse of Anthropology: Reflections on Feminism and
          Cross-Cultural Understanding. *Signs: Journal of Women in Culture and
          Society* 5(3):389–417.
Ross, Alexander
    1986 *Adventures of the First Settlers on the Oregon or Columbia River, 1810–1813.*
          Lincoln: University of Nebraska Press. Originally published in 1849
          by Smith, Elder and Co., 65, Cornhill, London.
Ross, John Alan
    1968 Political Conflict on the Colville Reservation. *Northwest Anthropolog-
          ical Research Notes* 2(1):29–91.
    1996 Traditional Spokan Indian Religious Beliefs and Explanations of
          Congenital Birth Defects. In Indians of the Columbia Plateau, *Pacific
          Northwest Forum,* 2nd series, 9(1–2):14–29.

Royce, Charles C.
1899 *Indian Land Cessions in the United States.* Bureau of American Ethnology, 18th Annual Report. Washington, D.C.: Government Printing Office.

Salwen, Bert
1978 Indians of New England and Long Island: Early Period. In *The Handbook of North American Indians,* ed. Bruce G. Trigger, vol. 15, pp. 160–76. Washington, D.C.: Smithsonian Institution.

Sanday, Peggy R.
1974 Female Status in the Public Domain. In *Woman, Culture and Society,* ed. Michelle Zimbalist Rosaldo and Louise Lamphere, pp. 189–206. Stanford, Calif.: Stanford University Press.
1990 Introduction. In *Beyond the Second Sex: New Directions in the Anthropology of Gender,* ed. Peggy Reeves Sanday and Ruth Gallagher Goodenough, pp. 1–19. Philadelphia: University of Pennsylvania Press.

Schaeffer, Claude E.
1965 The Kutenai Female Berdache: Courier, Guide, Prophetess, and Warrior. *Ethnohistory* 12:193–236.

Schlegel, Alice
1977a Male and Female in Hopi Thought and Action. In *Sexual Stratification: A Cross-Cultural View,* ed. Alice Schlegel, pp. 245–69. New York: Columbia University Press.
1977b Toward a Theory of Sexual Stratification. In *Sexual Stratification: A Cross-Cultural View,* ed. Alice Schlegel, pp. 1–40. New York: Columbia University Press.
1990 Gender Meanings: General and Specific. In *Beyond the Second Sex: New Directions in the Anthropology of Gender,* ed. Peggy Reeves Sanday and Ruth Gallagher Goodenough, pp. 23–41. Philadelphia: University of Pennsylvania Press.

Schuster, Helen Hersh
1975 Yakima Indian Traditionalism: A Study in Continuity and Change. Ph.D. dissertation, Department of Anthropology, University of Washington.

Schwendinger, Julia R., and Herman Schwendinger
1983 *Rape and Inequality.* Beverly Hills: Sage Publications.

Scott, Jerry M.
1992 A History of the Formation of the Colville Indian Reservation. M.A. thesis in History, Washington State University.

Service, Elman R.
1962 *Primitive Social Organization: An Evolutionary Perspective.* New York: Random House.

Sheehan, Glenn W.
1997 *In the Belly of the Whale: Trade and War in Eskimo Society.* Aurora. Alaska Anthropological Association Monograph Series 6. Anchorage: Alaska Anthropological Association.

Simms, John A.

    1878   Annual Report of the Commissioner of Indian Affairs to the Secretary of the Interior. August 8, 1878, report by John Simms on Fort Colville Indian Agency. Manuscripts, Archives, and Special Collections, Washington State University, Pullman, Washington.

    n.d.   Papers. Cage 213, 3 boxes. Manuscripts, Archives, and Special Collections, Washington State University, Pullman, Washington.

Smith, M. G.

    1960   *Government in Zazzau 1800–1950.* London: Oxford University Press.

    1974   Corporations and Society: The Social Anthropology of Collective Action. Chicago: Aldine Publishing Company.

Spier, Leslie

    1935   *The Prophet Dance of the Northwest and Its Derivatives: The Source of the Ghost Dance.* General Series in Anthropology, No. 1. Menasha, Wis.: George Banta Publishing Company.

Splawn, A. J.

    1917   *Ka-Mi-Akin: The Last Hero of the Yakimas.* Portland, Ore.: Kilham Stationery and Printing Company.

Spokesman Review

    n.d.   Daily newspaper published in Spokane, Washington.

Stern, Theodore

    1993   *Chiefs and Chief Traders: Indian Relations at Fort Nez Perces 1818–1855.* Corvallis: Oregon State University Press.

    1996   *Chiefs and Change in the Oregon Country: Indian Relations at Fort Nez Perces 1818–1855.* Vol. 2. Corvallis: Oregon State University Press.

Strathern, Marilyn

    1984   Domesticity and the Denigration of Women. In *Rethinking Women's Roles,* ed. Denise O'Brien and Sharon W. Tiffany, pp. 13–31. Berkeley: University of California Press.

    1988   *The Gender of the Gift: Problems with Women and Problems with Society in Melanesia.* Berkeley: University of California Press.

Strong, Mary E.

    1988   History Maker. *Nespelem Ruralite* 35(6):16–17.

Suttles, Wayne

    1987   Plateau Pacifism Reconsidered—Ethnography, Ethnology, and Ethnohistory. In *Coast Salish Essays,* pp. 282–86. Seattle: University of Washington Press.

Teit, James Alexander

    1900   *The Thompson Indians of British Columbia.* Jesup North Pacific Expedition, vol. 1, part 4. New York: American Museum of Natural History.

1906 *The Lillooet Indians.* Jesup North Pacific Expedition, vol. 2, part 5. New York: American Museum of Natural History.

1909 *The Shuswap.* Jesup North Pacific Expedition, vol. 2, part 7. New York: American Museum of Natural History.

1930 The Salishan Tribes of the Western Plateaus. In Bureau of American Ethnology, *45th Annual Report,* pp. 23–396. Washington, D.C.: Government Printing Office.

Thomas, Anthony E.

1970 *Albert Thomas Moore, PI. LU' YE. KIN: The Life History of a Nez Perce Indian.* American Anthropological Association Monograph. Washington, D.C.: American Anthropological Association.

Trafzer, Clifford E., and Richard D. Scheuerman

1986 *Renegade Tribe: The Palouse Indians and the Invasion of the Inland Pacific Northwest.* Pullman: Washington State University Press.

Tribal Tribune

n.d. Newspaper of the Colville Confederated Tribes, published in Nespelem, Washington.

Turner, Nancy, Randy Bouchard, and Dorothy I. D. Kennedy

1980 *Ethnobotany of the Okanagan-Colville Indians of British Columbia and Washington.* Occasional Papers of the British Columbia Provincial Museum No. 21. Victoria: British Columbia Provincial Museum.

Turney-High, Harry Holbert

1937 *The Flathead Indians of Montana.* American Anthropological Association Memoir 48. Menasha, Wis.: American Anthropological Association.

Tyhurst, Robert

1992 Traditional and Contemporary Land and Resource Use by Ts'-kw'aylaxw and Xaxli'p Bands. In *A Complex Culture of the British Columbia Plateau: Traditional* Stl'atl'imx *Resource Use,* ed. Brian Hayden, pp. 355–404. Vancouver: University of British Columbia Press.

United States Congress

1966 Colville Termination. Hearings before the Subcommittee on Interior and Insular Affairs. House of Representatives, vol. 3, part 22, January–October 1965. 89th Congress, 1st Session, on H.R. 5925 and S. 1413 and H.R. 6331. Serial No. 89-23. Washington, D.C.: Government Printing Office.

United States Federal Archives and Records Center, Seattle, Washington

n.d.a Colville Indian Agency—Allotment Records and Other Land Transactions.

n.d.b Colville Indian Agency, Miscellaneous Files. Letters, Census, Land Transactions. Boxes 69–149, 158, 363, etc.

n.d.c Letters to Superintendent of Indian Affairs in Washington, D.C., from Indian Agent, Colville Indian Agency.

University of Washington
- 1985 *Everything Change, Everything Change.* (Film: Recollections of Ida Nason, Plateau elder.) Sponsored by NEH and Washington Commission for the Humanities.

Vibert, Elizabeth
- 1995 "The Natives Were Strong to Live": Reinterpreting Early Nineteenth-Century Prophetic Movements in the Columbia Plateau. *Ethnohistory* 42(2):197–229.
- 1997 *Trader's Tales.* Norman: University of Oklahoma Press.

Walker, Deward E., Jr.
- 1968 *Conflict and Schism in Nez Perce Acculturation: A Study of Religion and Politics.* Pullman: Washington State University Press.

Walters, L. V. W.
- 1938 Social Structure. In *The Sinkaietk or Southern Okanagon of Washington*, ed. Leslie Spier, pp. 73–99. Menasha, Wis.: George Banta Publishing Company.
- n.d. Field Notes (copy in possession of L. Ackerman).

Webster, John McAdams.
- n.d. Papers, Cage 145. Manuscripts, Archives, and Special Collections, Washington State University, Pullman, Washington.

Whitehead, Harriet
- 1981 The Bow and the Burden Strap: A New Look at Institutionalized Homosexuality in Native North America. In *Sexual Meanings: The Cultural Construction of Gender and Sexuality*, ed. Sherry B. Ortner and Harriet Whitehead, pp. 80–115. Cambridge: Cambridge University Press.

Whyte, Martin King
- 1978 *The Status of Women in Preindustrial Societies.* Princeton, N.J.: Princeton University Press.

Wight, E. L., Mary Mitchell, and Marie Schmidt
- 1960 *Indian Reservations of Idaho, Oregon, and Washington.* Portland: United States Department of the Interior, Bureau of Indian Affairs.

Williams, Walter L.
- 1986 *The Spirit and the Flesh: Sexual Diversity in American Indian Culture.* Boston: Beacon Press.

Winans, W. P.
- n.d. Papers. Cage 147, 9 boxes. Manuscripts, Archives, and Special Collections, Holland Library, Washington State University, Pullman, Washington.

Wolf, Diane L.
- 1996 Situating Feminist Dilemmas in Fieldwork. In *Feminist Dilemmas in Fieldwork*, ed. Diane L. Wolf, pp. 1–55. Boulder, Colo.: Westview Press.

Wolf, Margery
  1974 Chinese Women: Old Skills in a New Context. In *Woman, Culture and Society*, ed. Michelle Zimbalist Rosaldo and Louise Lamphere, pp. 157–72. Stanford, Calif.: Stanford University Press.
Woods, Rufus
  n.d.   Papers. Archives and Manuscripts, Suzzalo Library, University of Washington, Seattle, Washington.

Index

Abortion, 100, 163

Abstinence, sexual, 163

Ackerman, Lillian A.: methodology used, 5, 22–27; research techniques of, 30–34

Adultery, 99–100, 142, 143

Alaska, trade goods from, 64

Alcohol: Indians plied by, 130, 131; Kolaskin vs., 143. *See also* Alcoholism; Drunkenness; Saloons

Alcoholism, 85, 100, 179, 213, 221

Allison, Susan, 20

Allotment Act. *See* Dawes Act

Allotments, to Indians, 135–39, 146, 148, 150, 152–53, 158, 166, 167; under dam water, 175; gender aspects of, 203–206. *See also* Dawes Act

Anderson, A. M., 137–38

Annual rounds, 36, 96, 130, 157. *See also* Fishing; Gathering; Hunting; Trade

Army, U.S.: Indian women in, 208 ; Plateau Indians vs., 16, 193. *See also* World War II

Artifacts, trade in, 47

Assemblies, tribal, 103, 105; chiefs and, 166, 167; female members of, 48, 110–11, 169; power of, 23–24. *See also* Colville Business Council

Assiniboine Indians, 112

Astor, John Jacob, 11

Athapascan (lang.), 9

Athletes, encouragement of reservation, 185

Authority: of chiefs, 23, 26, 48, 149, 167, 169; domestic, 26, 95–99, 159–61, 201–207; economic, 26, 69–87, 150–55, 184–89; force and, 24; parental, 92 (*see also* Marriage, parent-arranged); political, 26, 105–10, 166–69, 213–19; power and, 23–24, 68; religious, 26, 113–15, 171–72, 222–24; Schlegel on, 23; women and, 235–36, 243

Automobiles, 156–57, 206, 207, 247

Autonomy, 5; domestic, 26, 99–103, 161–64, 207–11; economic, 26, 87–89, 155–57, 189–91l; Indian respect for personal, 234; political, 26, 110–13, 169–70, 219–20; religious, 27, 115–17, 172–73, 224–27; Schlegel on, 23

Awls, trade for, 18

Bank accounts, 206–208, 235

Basketry, 19, 79, 87, 247